D0560609

The Catholic Church
and American Culture:
Why the Claims
of Dan Brown Strike a Chord

The Catholic Church and American Culture:

Why the Claims of Dan Brown Strike a Chord

By Eric Plumer

UNIVERSITY OF SCRANTON PRESS
Scranton and London

© 2009   University of Scranton Press
All rights reserved.

Library of Congress Cataloging-in-Publication Data

Plumer, Eric Antone.
  The Catholic Church and American culture : why the claims of The
Da Vinci code struck a chord / by Eric Plumer.
      p. cm.
  Includes bibliographical references (p.   ) and index.
  ISBN 978-1-58966-135-6 (pbk. : alk. paper)
  1. Catholic Church--United States--History--21st century. 2. Christi-
anity and culture--United States. 3. Brown, Dan, 1964- Da Vinci code.
I. Title.
                    BX1406.3.P58 2009
                    282'.73090511--dc22
                    2009003406

Distribution:
UNIVERSITY OF SCRANTON PRESS
Chicago Distribution Center
11030 S. Langley
Chicago, IL 60628

PRINTED IN THE UNITED STATES OF AMERICA

Contents

Introduction

Regardless of how you felt about Dan Brown's novel—whether you loved it or hated it, whether you bought copies for all your friends or boycotted the bookstores that sold it—*The Da Vinci Code* was an extraordinary cultural phenomenon. First published in the United States in March 2003, within three years it had been translated into forty-four languages and had sold more than sixty million copies worldwide, making it one of the top ten best-selling novels of all time. Although the film version, released in May 2006, proved a disappointment to a large number of critics and viewers, it still managed to become the second-highest grossing film of the year.

Beyond its staggering financial success, *The Da Vinci Code* inspired or provoked the writing of many other books. One category consisted of novels that imitated *The Da Vinci Code* by featuring masterpieces of art with hidden messages, complex plots involving the Knights Templar or the Holy Grail, or simply professors with too much time on their hands who decided to solve some ancient mystery once and for all. A second category was that of nonfiction books providing information on subjects readers of *The Da Vinci Code* were eager to learn more about. I remember how delighted *I* was to find so many of my questions answered in *The Complete Idiot's Guide to Mary Magdalene*—I felt as though it had been written just for me. Another enjoyable read was Dan Burstein's *Secrets of the Code*, a kind of one-volume encyclopedia on the novel, including excerpts from *Holy Blood, Holy Grail* and other sources used by Dan Brown.

But the vast majority of nonfiction books on *The Da Vinci Code* (there were nearly sixty in print three years after the novel came out) fell into a third category; they were written mainly to debunk the novel's religious claims by exposing the errors Dan Brown had made regarding the Bible and the history of the Church. Writing debunking books became such a popular pastime that some authors indulged in "double dipping," publishing two in a row. Personally, I didn't think there was all that much debunking to be done, since most of the novel's religious claims were contained in just two of its one hundred and six chapters. In fact, it became clear to me after reading just a few debunking books that the same evidence and the same arguments were being used over and over again. Yet I continued to read these books until, somewhere around the twentieth, my mind went numb from sheer boredom, something that rarely happens to me (although it appears to happen regularly to my students—about as often as I lecture to them, in fact).

But why did I take the trouble to read these twenty or more debunking books, if they overlapped so much? The reason is that I was obsessed with a question that I kept hoping one of these books would address. Unfortunately, most of the books I read never even raised the question, or if they did, dealt with it in a way that left me dissatisfied. The question is this: If the religious claims of *The Da Vinci Code* are so riddled with errors, why have those claims struck a chord with so many millions of readers? Could it be that these readers feel that even if Dan Brown missed the bull's-eye a thousand times, and often by a very wide margin, he was still aiming in the right direction?

Let me give you an example. On pages 124–26 of *The Da Vinci Code*[1] the hero, Robert Langdon, muses about the Church's "deceitful and violent history." (In the novel "the Church" always means "the Catholic Church.") He recalls that "during three hundred years of witch hunts, the Church burned at the stake an astounding five *million* women." In what is undoubtedly the most comprehensive and well researched debunking book I have read, the authors criticize this claim by highlighting its errors: "Many of those deaths did not involve burning. Witches were hanged, strangled, and beheaded as well." The authors also contend that the number of witches killed was far fewer than Dan Brown claims, with "the best current estimate" being "30,000 to 50,000 . . . certainly a significant number, but not comparable to the Holocaust or Stalin's purges."[2] Thus we are assured that the Church authorities responsible for the witch hunts were not nearly as murderous as Hitler or Stalin. This may be the best example of damning with faint praise I have ever read.

Defenders of the Church have every right to expose and correct the errors in *The Da Vinci Code*. But even after this has been done, we are still left with the stubborn fact that the witch hunts continued for centuries, with official approval from Church leaders (Protestant as well as Catholic). Moreover, if one reads the passage in its context, it is clear that the character, Robert Langdon, is not looking at the witch hunts as an isolated phenomenon but rather as evidence of a deep-seated fear and hatred of women running through much of the history of the Church. He sees further evidence of the devaluation of women today in the Catholic Church's ban on women priests (125). He believes the Church's attitude is part of a general devaluation of women in modern culture that has created a sense of "'life out of balance'—an unstable situation marked by testosterone-fueled wars, a plethora of misogynistic societies, and a growing disrespect for Mother Earth" (126). It is this sense of the devaluation of women and its disastrous consequences—and the part the Church has played in creating this situation—that strikes a chord with many readers. If defenders of the Church do not confront this issue fully and openly, their arguments about details may appear as little more than special pleading and will leave those with suspicions about the Church unconvinced.

I do not, however, want to give the impression that these defenders of Christianity are only out to win an argument. The vast majority are also attempting to impart knowledge of the Bible and Church history which readers are unlikely to have unless they hold a graduate degree in theology. These authors are thus performing a very valuable service, and I think most readers can benefit from studying at least one of their books. The point of *my* book, however, is to suggest that after all the errors involving facts and the interpretation of facts have been highlighted and corrected, large questions remain, and these questions are vitally important to many. That at least is the lesson I have drawn from discussions about *The Da Vinci Code* with countless people over the past several years. To explain what I mean, I think it will be helpful to tell the story of the origin of this book.

How this book came to be written

I might not even have read *The Da Vinci Code* had it not been for separate visits from two of my students, Katie German and Jenna Brown, within days of each other in January 2005. They came to me, their theology professor, with serious questions about the novel's claims about Jesus, and I realized that if I was going to answer their questions responsibly I would have to read the novel. Jenna also told me that she knew many students who would be eager to hear a talk on *The Da Vinci Code*, so after I read it carefully, I put together a PowerPoint presentation, "*The Da Vinci Code*: Fact or Fiction?"

The subject (not the speaker) drew standing-room-only crowds at my University, other universities, and in many other venues. Before each presentation I asked the audience to fill out a questionnaire and express their initial responses to the religious claims of the novel. I was frankly amazed to learn how many women were thrilled by Dan Brown's claim that Jesus and Mary Magdalene had been married and sexually intimate. To them it made Jesus seem "more human." One young Christian woman, recently married, told me her husband was the love of her life, and nothing could be more wonderful than the thought that Jesus could fully understand *from his own experience* the power and the beauty of the love she shared with her husband.

Another feeling many women spoke of was the sense of affirmation, even empowerment, that Dan Brown's portrayal of Mary Magdalene had given them. This was a perspective that I, being your typical clueless guy, had not adequately appreciated until I heard it expressed with such clarity and conviction. But women's feelings of neglect and mistreatment by the Church were not the only ones Brown had tapped. There were many others, for men as well as women. I also wanted to explore related issues Dan Brown had not mentioned which had contributed to the conflict between Americans and the official teaching of the Catholic Church. Eventually ten issues would crystallize into the ten chapters of this book. These were among the key issues that had made millions of Americans respond to the novel's negative portrayal of the Church with satisfaction and delight.

It was not until a year after I began planning my book that I finally found two men who were wrestling with the same questions that I was—pastor and author Brian McLaren and Episcopal Bishop Paul V. Marshall. They had expressed their views just as the film version of *The Da Vinci Code* was about to be released. In an interview in *Sojourners*, Brian McLaren was asked, "What do you think the popularity of *The Da Vinci Code* reveals about pop culture attitudes toward Christianity and the Church?" This is part of his reply:

> I think a lot of people have read the book, not just as a popular page turner but also as an experience in shared frustration with status-quo, male-dominated, power-oriented, cover-up-prone organized Christian religion. We need to ask ourselves why the vision of Jesus hinted at in Dan Brown's book is more interesting, attractive, and intriguing to these people than the standard vision of Jesus they hear about in the church. . . . Is it possible that, even though Brown's fictional version misleads in many ways, it at least serves to open up the possibility that the church's conventional version of Jesus may not do him justice?

He goes on to say, "I think that the whole issue of male domination is huge and that Brown's suggestion that the real Jesus was not as misogynist [sic] or anti-woman as the Christian religion often has been is very attractive."[3]

Bishop Marshall's comments in an article he had written struck a similar note:

> Pointing out the endless "errors" of the *Code* misses the point and misuses this godsend of publicity for the Church. The real question is: why is the book, and presumably the movie, such a hit? As I travel the 14 counties in my diocese, I have heard two themes from Brown's fans. The first is that the *Code* resonates with the belief that religious institutions have occasionally been dishonest, manipulative, and very, very rich with no accountability. There is no major religion without blood on its hands, as anyone except the unlearned or the most defensive zealots will admit. The second and even more common response is from those women who feel themselves to have gotten a very dirty deal from the Big Three "religions of the book," and it is certainly hard to disagree.[4]

Some of the points these two men made were confirmed later that year in survey results published by the Scripps Howard News Service. One of the survey questions was this: "Do you think Church leaders, and especially the Catholic Church, would withhold important information about Jesus?" Forty percent of respondents said yes.

In their remarks, both Brian McLaren and Paul Marshall went on to suggest that the defenders of the Christian faith, in their zeal to refute the claims of *The Da Vinci Code*, were in danger of missing the opportunity that the novel had opened up for real dialogue about Jesus and his message. We know what aficionados of *The Da Vinci Code* can learn from the defenders of the faith about the Bible and Church history. In fact, any one of the fifty-odd debunking books by pastors, teachers, and scholars will tell us. But is there anything that those pastors, teachers, and scholars can learn—for example, about how their ongoing preaching and teaching and scholarship are coming across?

At the very least, shouldn't the aficionados be given a hearing? This sounds commonsensical, but some believe it is wholly mistaken. In one Catholic diocese I know of, the bishop and clergy were hoping that if discussion could be avoided, *The Da Vinci Code* phenomenon would simply go away. The Vatican itself was silent for two years until Cardinal Tarcisio Bertone, one of the most high-ranking officials in the Catholic Church, spoke out urging Catholics not to read *The Da Vinci Code* and asking Catholic booksellers not to carry it. Many American Catholics were happy to comply, but other Americans, including many Catholics, were either outraged at what they saw as an attempt at censorship or amused at the thought that millions who were not planning to read the novel would now do so simply because it was forbidden.

I will argue in this book that such sharply contrasting views are a sign of the culture wars that have been polarizing America for decades—and which have their counterparts in many other countries. I have taken this idea from James Davison Hunter's *Culture Wars* (1991), focusing particularly on one of the underlying issues emphasized there: Where is moral authority to be found?

Is the ultimate moral authority to be found in traditional, institutional Christianity (for the purposes of this book, the official teaching of the Catholic Church), or is it to be found in each individual's own conscience? One's answer to this question is likely to correlate, however imperfectly, with one's allegiance in the culture wars. Of course, this formulation of the question is oversimplified, but at least it provides one clear lens for looking at the variety of subjects covered in this book. Readers can then go on to obtain other more sophisticated lenses, some of which may be found in the bibliography.

How to read this book

This book is intended primarily for people like the hundreds I gave my PowerPoint presentation to—undergraduate students and general readers. For this reason I have gone out of my way to include information simply because it is interesting. For example, in discussing Thomas Jefferson in connection with the religious ideas in *The Da Vinci Code*, I also mention the very sophisticated decoding device that he invented. Such details might have fallen at the stroke of an editor's axe had this been a scholarly work in the strictest sense.

Another reason why I want to be clear that this is not a work for scholars is that I lack expertise in most of the subjects I write about. But I have worked diligently to compensate for my lack, and I feel confident that undergraduate students and educated readers will not be wasting their time. Although not a scholarly work in the technical sense, the book includes a bibliography and endnotes for people wishing to know my sources.

The book covers a variety of relevant topics, but it was never intended to be comprehensive, let alone exhaustive. Many topics have been omitted, such as the ways in which our thinking is shaped by consumerism, relativism, postmodernism, and the media. I myself have at least half a book of relevant material left on my computer which I did not have the opportunity to whip up into publishable form. Of course, I regret that I did not have the time to refine my work the way Leonardo did when he worked on and off for twelve years just on Mona Lisa's lips. But for the purposes of this book what I have left undone is not a serious problem, because I never intended that this would be the last word on the subject of the Catholic Church and American culture, but rather a springboard for further reading and discussion.

Since the book is not comprehensive and also not very long, you might have thought I would want you to read it from beginning to end in order to become acquainted with at least the limited number of topics that I did manage to cover. That, however, is not the case. I would prefer that you think of this book's table of contents as a buffet table; take what you like and leave the rest.

For example, some people, especially Catholics who lived through the explosive period in which Pope Paul VI issued the encyclical *Humanae Vitae*, may be tired of reading about the controversy surrounding contraception. If so, by all means skip Chapter 3. But for those unfamiliar with the story, and I believe they are the majority, that chapter is of crucial importance. (There are some judicious commentators, such as the Catholic priest and sociologist Andrew Greeley, who regard the rejection by most American Catholics of the Church's ban on contraception as having, for all practical purposes, marked the end of their acceptance of the Church's authority in matters of sexual morality.)

Other readers may choose to read or omit other chapters according to taste. My own goddaughter, for instance, who is pursuing a Ph.D. in the Department of Earth and Planetary Science at one of America's leading universities, might be well advised to forgo the short chapter in which I discuss Copernicus, Galileo, and Newton (Chapter 7).

Each chapter in this book is capable of standing on its own. But there are figures and ideas, such as Thomas Jefferson and the idea of religious freedom, which appear in more than one chapter, so I would encourage readers to consult the index for further references. Other historical figures could easily have appeared in a different chapter. Sigmund Freud, whose work is discussed in the chapter on psychology, would have fit perfectly in the chapter on anti-Catholicism. Evidence includes the following exchange that took place between Freud and a visitor in the 1930s. Finding that Freud looked sullen and gloomy, the visitor asked him why. "It's because I've been thinking about my mortal enemy," Freud said. "Oh, you mean the Nazi Party?" his visitor asked. "No," Freud said, "the Roman Catholic Church!"

Readers will find that, apart from Chapter 9, I do not examine in detail the explicit religious claims of *The Da Vinci Code*, since that has already been done many times. But I have often used a specific quotation from *The Da Vinci Code* to lead into the topic of a chapter.

My goal in writing this book

What has been my goal, my hope, my dream in writing this book? In all candor, I hope that every person who bought Dan Brown's novel will also buy this book as a kind of companion piece, to rest upon the mantel above the fireplace alongside *The Da Vinci Code*. If sixty million of you help me realize my dream, then perhaps I can at last buy that luxury villa in the Bahamas, with a butler, masseuse, personal trainer, and *cordon bleu* chef, to live the life of indolence and ease that I was meant to live, but which has so far eluded me.

Friends, however, tell me I might want to have a "Plan B." So here it is. I would like to encourage genuine discussion and dialogue. As I have said, the furor over *The Da Vinci Code* in this country is a sign of the American culture wars. In the halls of government in Washington, these wars have escalated to the point where public officials (with a few notable exceptions) appear to make little attempt to listen to any political views other than their own party's. As a teacher and as an American citizen, I think this degree of partisanship is extremely counterproductive.

Readers might look at my table of contents and conclude that my book is itself highly partisan. Admittedly, it focuses on criticisms that have been leveled against the Catholic Church. There is even one chapter, already mentioned, that concentrates on anti-Catholicism. But if you read it, I hope you will agree that I am not attempting to promote anti-Catholicism. Throughout this book I have tried my best to treat each subject with fairness, objectivity, and impartiality.

I must acknowledge that I do not provide *complete* answers to all the criticisms leveled against the Catholic Church, but I have made every effort to provide at least a summary statement of official Catholic responses. More than that would have required another book, and in any case there are already plenty of them in print.

Regarding the specific points made in *The Da Vinci Code*, I would particularly recommend *The Da Vinci Hoax* by Carl E. Olson and Sandra Miesel, which comes with a ringing endorsement from Cardinal Francis George, Archbishop of Chicago, who has gone so far as to call it "the definitive debunking."

And here I would like to take the opportunity to mention the wonderful influence Catholic priests have had in my own life. Though they are too numerous for me to list them all, I would like to name two, no longer living, whose wisdom and kindness I will always be grateful for: from my years at the University of Notre Dame, Father John Gerber, C.S.C., and from my years at Oxford University, Father Edward Yarnold, S.J. May they rest in peace.

There is one final thought I would like to add to this Introduction. Since questions about Jesus and women have been at the center of so much of the controversy over *The Da Vinci Code*, it may be helpful to recall a story about Jesus and a woman which appears in the Gospels of Matthew and Mark. At least *I* found it helpful when a Jesuit priest, Father J-Glenn Murray, offered his reflections on it in a lecture he gave a few years ago.

In Mark's Gospel we are told that Jesus went into a house to get away momentarily from the crowd's unceasing demands for him to minister to them. But a Gentile woman discovered where he was and begged him to come and heal her daughter. Matthew tells us that Jesus replied, "I was sent only to the lost sheep of the house of Israel." But she persisted, firm in her belief that Jesus could help her too, even though she was not a Jew. Jesus was won over by the fervor of her belief and granted her request.

To appreciate this story we need to realize how shocking it was at the time for a Jewish teacher like Jesus to speak even with a Jewish woman, let alone with one who was not Jewish. (Even a devout Jewish woman would have been thought to lack the capacity to understand the wise sayings of a Jewish teacher; only men had that capacity.) But Jesus decided to engage in conversation with this woman and ended up actually learning from her. And what he learned from her was not something trivial; it had to do with the very nature of the mission his Father had given him.

The woman helped him to realize that even if his mission was first and foremost to the Jews, that did not mean it was limited to them.

I think there is a lesson here for anyone who wants it. Are we honestly willing to listen, to enter fully into conversation, and perhaps to learn from someone we thought had nothing to teach us? That is the kind of openness to dialogue this book has been written to promote.

A Special Note
on *Angels & Demons*

As I write this, the release of the film version of Dan Brown's *Angels & Demons* is still two months away, but already the same kind of controversy that surrounded *The Da Vinci Code* has begun to flare. At the center of the controversy are claims made in *Angels & Demons* about the conflict between the Catholic Church and modern science, and in fact that conflict forms the great underlying theme of the novel.

In the popular imagination the supreme symbol of this conflict is Galileo, and the story of Galileo's trial and condemnation by the Catholic Church is highlighted in the novel. Today, on dozens of websites, defenders of the Catholic Church charge Dan Brown with having deliberately distorted the facts about the Galileo case in order to defame the Catholic Church. One point in particular surfaces again and again in these defenses, in response to the claim in *Angels & Demons* that in the course of his trial Galileo was tortured. Defenders of the Church insist that Galileo was never tortured, and they are right.

And yet to leave it at that is surely misleading. Church officials threatened Galileo with torture, and Galileo knew that this was no empty threat. Though his mind was as brilliant as it had ever been, Galileo was old and sick, and by the end of the trial his spirit had been crushed. He repudiated everything he had ever written in support of Copernicus's theory that the earth revolves around the sun. Galileo's books were then placed on the Church's official list of "Forbidden Books." Galileo himself was placed under house arrest, where he remained for the rest of his life. Thus, although it is true that he was not subjected to torture in the technical sense of the term, his suffering was very great.

To defend the Catholic Church on the grounds that it did not torture Galileo is like defending the Church's execution of witches on the grounds I referred to in the Introduction. Among other things, that defense included criticism of Dan Brown (actually his protagonist Robert Langdon) for implying that women convicted of witchcraft were invariably burned at the stake, when in fact "many of those deaths did not involve burning. Witches were hanged, strangled, and beheaded as well."

But the most troubling aspect of the defense of the Church with regard to Galileo—that he was not tortured—is that it totally misses the point Pope John Paul II went out of his way to emphasize in 1979, when he stated plainly the need for public recognition of and repentance for the wrong that had been done to Galileo and for the immense suffering he had been forced to endure.

On the other side of the controversy, many websites applaud some of the wilder statements made in *Angels & Demons* about the Catholic Church's opposition to modern science, as for example that its opposition is absolute and unwavering. But as Pope John Paul II stated in 1992, and as eminent historians of science agree, this is a myth which has unfairly tarnished the reputation of the Catholic Church, which has been one of the great supporters of modern science.

In Chapter 7 of this book ("The Rise of Modern Science as a Challenge to the Catholic Church"), I have attempted to present the alleged conflict between science and the Catholic Church in a more balanced perspective. Although I do not make direct reference to *Angels & Demons,* I have dealt with the trial of Galileo as it is now understood in light of the most recent scholarship, which indicates that there were misperceptions and mistakes not only by Church officials but also by Galileo himself. In other words, the Galileo case is complex, and the first step toward unraveling it is to acknowledge that the popular understanding of it is deeply flawed.

What I have attempted to do in my discussion of Galileo is the same thing I have attempted to do in Chapter 7 as a whole and indeed in my book as a whole: to suggest that much of the conflict needs to be seen in a broader, more balanced, and more nuanced perspective. There is currently much misunderstanding of both sides, which poses a formidable barrier to any positive dialogue. My book is intended to begin to dismantle that barrier. This is not to say that there are no disagreements at the level of fundamental beliefs. There are, and they must not be trivialized. But those disagreements lie far beyond the scope of this book, which is simply to clear away some of the popular misunderstandings so that dialogue and discussion may begin.

Chapter 1

People and Events in the
History of Anti-Catholicism

Nobody could deny the enormous good the modern Church
did in today's troubled world, and yet the Church had a deceitful and violent history.

The Da Vinci Code, 124–25

Why did the claims of *The Da Vinci Code* strike a chord with
tens of millions of readers? One answer that must be taken seriously is that of Carl Olson and Sandra Miesel, coauthors of what
Cardinal Francis George of Chicago has called "the definitive
debunking" of *The Da Vinci Code*.[1] They argue that Dan Brown
portrayed the Catholic Church as "a violent, misogynist [*sic*] institution run by murderers and liars" (their words) because he
was catering to widespread feelings of anti-Catholicism. "Brown
has drawn upon the old stereotype of the Catholic Church as a
blood-soaked, evil institution, an image that has sold well in the
United States for decades, even centuries."[2]

Olson and Miesel's view is shared at the Vatican, where some
of the highest officials in the Church have expressed outrage.
Here is what Archbishop Angelo Amato had to say: "[If] such
lies and errors had been directed at the Koran or the Holocaust,
they would have justly provoked a world uprising."[3] Another of
the Church's leading lights, Cardinal Francis Arinze, whom
many thought would be elected Pope after John Paul II died,

1

stated publicly that Dan Brown was guilty of blasphemy and libel against the Catholic Church and should be prosecuted wherever laws against blasphemy and libel exist. Cardinal Arinze's clarion call did not fall upon deaf ears. On June 19, 2007, the state prosecutor of Civitavecchia, Italy, announced plans to bring criminal charges against the makers of the film version of *The Da Vinci Code* if they ever set foot in Italy again. This means that Dan Brown and Ron Howard, if convicted, could face fines and up to three years in prison.

Of course, many readers say that all the furor is unwarranted. After all, *The Da Vinci Code* is just a novel. Moreover, the character in the novel who has the most to say against the Church is the arch villain, Sir Leigh Teabing, and the very fact that he *is* the arch villain should be a clue that what he says is not to be trusted. I certainly respect this point of view, but I have chosen to take another. I view *The Da Vinci Code* as a vehicle for religious ideas that stirred intense feelings in many readers. Among the most intense were feelings of hostility toward the Catholic Church.

In this chapter we will investigate some of the sources of these feelings by looking at a range of people and events from the history of anti-Catholicism. These people and events are intended to provide vivid illustrations of anti-Catholic attitudes, along with their causes and even some attempted cures. It is important to note that this chapter does not supply a continuous history of anti-Catholicism, but merely a sampling of evidence indicating that anti-Catholicism has been a recurrent theme in modern European and American history right up to our own time. This sampling will show what an abundance of kindling wood there was, both outside the Catholic Church and within it, just waiting to be set aflame by an author like Dan Brown.

Background to the Protestant Reformation

If anti-Catholicism is defined simply as opposition to the Catholic Church, no greater anti-Catholicism has been displayed in modern times than that which drove the Protestant Reformation of the sixteenth century and split the Catholic Church in two. It is customary to date the beginning of the Reformation to 1517, when Martin Luther posted his famous Ninety-Five Theses against indulgences, but in fact serious calls for the Church to reform itself had been made for centuries by such outstanding spiritual leaders as St. Bernard of Clairvaux (1090–1153) and St. Catherine of Sienna (1347–1380).

There is irony in the fact that St. Bernard's very words against Church corruption were still regarded as relevant and applicable in 1500. One of the central targets of criticism in the centuries leading up to the Reformation was the immorality of the clergy. Nor was the need for reform voiced only by individuals. In this same period there were eleven ecumenical councils, representing the entire Catholic Church, and in each of them the need for reform was recognized as a matter of importance and urgency. Yet each council in turn was forced to acknowledge the failure of the previous council to implement effective reforms.

The corrupt clerical practices which gave most offense were the taking of mistresses and the buying and selling of Church offices. The latter was called "simony" after Simon Magus, who tried to buy spiritual power from the Apostles and was sharply rebuked for it by St. Peter. Critics also remembered Jesus' condemnation of the moneylenders in the Temple for having made his Father's house a den of thieves. It was for simony that Dante, the greatest poet of the Middle Ages, portrayed three popes suffering eternal torment in hell in Canto XIX of his *Inferno*. And in the same Canto, the Church of the time is portrayed as the Whore of Babylon referred to in the Book of Revelation.[4]

To sustain the lavish lifestyle of the papal court, the faithful were drained of enormous sums of money. The pope's ownership of land in France and Italy, known as the Papal States, led to the establishment of his own military to protect and defend it. It also led to the Church's involvement in political intrigue throughout Europe.

Lorenzo Valla

"The Pope himself makes war on peaceable people, and sows discord among states and princes."[5] These are the words of Lorenzo Valla (1407–1457), an Italian scholar, priest, and opponent of the temporal power of the papacy. In 1440, he issued a brilliant study of the *Donation of Constantine*, a famous document in which the Emperor Constantine the Great supposedly granted the Pope supreme spiritual and temporal authority over the entire Empire in AD 313. Valla was able to point to telltale signs in the wording of the document that demonstrated it was forged—with the clear intention of bolstering the power of the papacy—centuries after the reign of Constantine. To hammer home his point, Valla included a tirade against the Pope's temporal power. Like a dragon roused from slumber, the Inquisition sent forth a fiery summons, demanding that Valla appear before their tribunal and answer charges. In a rare show of prudence, Valla entreated his royal patron King Alfonso I of Naples for protection and fled from Rome to safety.

Though it was now in tatters, the *Donation of Constantine* proved difficult for popes to abandon. Indeed, the extent to which it continued to be cherished was shown early in the next century when Raphael was commissioned to decorate the papal state rooms with frescos glorifying the *Donation*.

Later on, as the Protestant Reformation unfolded, Martin Luther came to see Valla's work as further evidence that the papacy was not just an institution that had been corrupted by a few bad men, but an institution that was corrupt in principle.

Before we get to Luther, however, it will be helpful to look at some of the popes who reigned in his lifetime, for they displayed the symptoms which led Luther to make a diagnosis and prescribe a cure.

Some Notorious Renaissance Popes

In the year Martin Luther was born (1483), the Pope was Sixtus IV (r. 1471–1484). Of his many outstanding qualities, that which most impressed the cardinals who elected him was his generosity in giving bribes, and indeed it was why they elected him. Although Sixtus was a Franciscan priest, he never felt the urge—as St. Francis had—to lead a life of poverty. His coronation as Pope provides an illustration of his personal attitude toward wealth. His tiara alone cost 100,000 gold ducats—more than a third of the papacy's annual revenues at the time. (But there is one expenditure made by Sixtus that few would hold against him: his commissioning of the Vatican chapel that bears his name, the Sistine Chapel.)

Another aspect of his papacy that rubbed some people the wrong way was his habitual use of his office for the benefit and enrichment of his family. Here is but one example: his favorite nephew, Pietro Riario, was first made a cardinal, then the Patriarch of Constantinople, and finally the Archbishop of Florence—titles which he held simultaneously. And he had attained all three titles, and the money that went with them, by the remarkable age of twenty-six. Whatever time was left after Sixtus had enriched his family and himself, he devoted entirely to the neglect of his duties.[6]

Sixtus was succeeded by Innocent VIII (r. 1484–1492). Prior to being elected, he had made a solemn vow not to place more than one member of his family in high office. Once he became Pope, however, he realized that the power of the papacy was the greatest power on earth and so could not be bound even by an oath. Many of his relatives thanked God for granting Innocent such insight. Innocent's family included three illegitimate children, whom he was not ashamed to acknowledge or to shower with honors and riches. Innocent is also remembered as the Pope who ordered the Inquisition to ferret out witches (see Chapter 9).

Innocent was succeeded by Alexander VI (r. 1492–1503), who achieved what might have seemed the impossible goal of bringing the papacy even further into disrepute. He had gained the papacy largely by bribing cardinals to vote for him. At the time, people liked to say of him, "Alexander is ready to sell the keys, the altars, and even Christ himself. And he has the right to do so, since he bought them." Like his predecessor, he openly acknowledged his illegitimate children. At the time he was elected, he already had eight—by at least three different women. After his election, he appears to have bridled his desires; as Pope, he had only one more illegitimate child.

All these children reaped benefits from their father. We can take time to mention only one—his favorite, Cesare Borgia. Although his father made him an archbishop and a cardinal before the age of twenty, he felt unsuited to ecclesiastical life, and his subsequent history bears out his judgment. Because Cesare preferred a military career, his father placed him at the head of the papal armies, where his fierce single-mindedness and his utter lack of scruples enabled him to recapture papal territories that had rebelled against the Pope and to rule them with an iron hand. Cesare has the dubious honor of being the model for Machiavelli's *The Prince*.

The next Pope of note was Julius II (r. 1503–1513), who took the name of Julius not in honor of any saint but in honor of Julius Caesar. A fierce warlord by nature, Julius refurbished the papal guard and led it successfully into war against both French and German armies in order to recapture papal lands. When any town resisted his authority, he ordered its walls to be blown up and then, dressed in splendid silver armor, led his troops into the breach. His ferocity as a warrior earned him the nickname "Julius the Terrible." It would be wrong, however, to think of his reign as all blood and gore, because he was also in touch with his sensitive side, as shown in his patronage of artists and architects, including Leonardo, Michelangelo, and Raphael.

Julius was succeeded by Leo X (r. 1513–1521), whose ecclesiastical career had been meteoric, outshining even that of Pietro Riario. A cleric at the age of seven and a cardinal at the age of thirteen, he was thirty-seven when elected Pope. After his election, one of his central goals was to raise funds for the rebuilding of St. Peter's Basilica in Rome, and one of his means of doing so was the sale of indulgences—which provoked Martin Luther. Leo is also remembered for other things, perhaps the most notable being his menagerie, which included lions, leopards, monkeys, bears, and parrots. But his favorite, which became the favorite of the Roman people as well, was a young Indian elephant named Hanno, which he received as a gift from the King of Portugal.[7]

Martin Luther

At this point readers may well be wondering: What on earth does Hanno the Elephant have to do with the Protestant Reformation? There is an answer. *Really.*

When Martin Luther launched his attack on the papacy, he said that instead of attending to urgent religious matters, the Pope was whiling away his time watching his elephant play in the papal gardens. Of course, Hanno's cavortings were not the main or even the immediate cause of the Reformation. The immediate cause was the selling of indulgences.

An indulgence, in simple terms, is a remission granted by the Church of the punishment still due to sins after they have been forgiven. But the full doctrine of indulgences was often misunderstood or even deliberately misinterpreted, as shown in an illustration given by the Chancellor of Oxford University in 1450: "Sinners say nowadays 'I care not how many or what evils I do in God's sight; for I can easily and quickly get plenary remission of all guilt and penalty by an absolution and indulgence granted me by the pope, whose written grant I have bought for [four or six pennies], or have won as a [prize] for a game of tennis.'"[8]

In 1517, Martin Luther, who was then a Catholic monk, priest, and professor of theology at Wittenberg University, posted his famous Ninety-five Theses against indulgences. In his eyes, the Church had become an essentially secular institution standing in the way of the individual's spiritual relationship with God. Luther insisted that all that mattered was faith in God's free gift of salvation. No amount of good deeds, let alone money, could buy salvation. (The Church did not teach this, but it had allowed this popular perception to flourish.)

When Luther was unable to get the Church to reform itself from within, he separated from it and denounced it. The source of the corruption rampant in the Church, Luther ultimately decided, was not any particular pope, but the papacy as an institution. The papacy was the Antichrist referred to in the New Testament, leading people away from the simplicity of the true Gospel by force and fraud. This identification of the papacy with the Antichrist became a central theme of the Reformation.

Ever since, the authority of the pope has been the central target of Protestantism's criticism of the Catholic Church, though few today would go so far as the Rev. Ian Paisley of Northern Ireland did in 1988—when he went to a meeting of the European Parliament being addressed by Pope John Paul II and unfurled a banner denouncing the Pope as the Antichrist.[9] Nevertheless, to the extent that the people of the United States are Protestant, they share at least an implicit rejection of papal claims to God-given authority.

Voltaire

After Martin Luther, perhaps no single individual did more to undermine the reputation of the Catholic Church than François-Marie Arouet (1694–1778), better known as Voltaire, the French poet, playwright, novelist, essayist, historian, philosopher, and popularizer of science, who became the most famous writer of the eighteenth century in the Western world.[10] To understand how and why he became so hostile to the Catholic Church and to institutional Christianity in general it will be useful to recall a few historical developments that took place between Luther's time and Voltaire's.

First and foremost, the Reformation sparked religious war fare. Luther's revolt against the Catholic Church depended upon the military might of German princes to prevent it from being crushed, and Luther also called upon the German princes to put down Protestant rebels of whom he disapproved. Among these early opponents was the radical Reformer Thomas Münzer, who turned against Luther after deciding that his revolt had not gone far enough. Münzer advocated the overthrow of *all* ungodly authority, civil as well as religious, and stirred up an armed revolt of the German peasants. Luther condemned the Peasants' Revolt, and it was crushed. As he later said, "I smote the peasants; all their blood is on my head. The Lord God ordered it."

For more than a century after Luther's death in 1546, Western Europe suffered the ravages of religious warfare, culminating in the horrors of the Thirty Years' War (1618–1648). One incident that would haunt Voltaire from the moment he first read about it was the St. Bartholomew's Day Massacre. Beginning in Paris on August 24, 1572, over several days the massacre of

Protestants by Catholics spread throughout France. By the time it was over, Catholics had butchered as many as thirty thousand Protestants—men, women, and children.[11]

The seemingly endless religious conflict, in which combatants on both sides claimed to have sole possession of absolute truth, left many longing for a new way forward. It was clear that religion and politics were far too dangerous a mixture, and one solution, proposed by the English philosopher John Locke (1632–1704), was to relegate religion to the private sphere. There, different religious groups could disagree without their disagreement leading to upheaval in the state. Locke's idea would have influence not only in England but as far away as America, where the separation of Church and State became enshrined in the First Amendment to the U.S. Constitution.

But for many who felt that the churches, Protestant as well as Catholic, had proven unreliable, vital questions remained: Where was truth to be found? And once found, how could it be safeguarded and protected? In the scientific method of John Locke's friend, Isaac Newton, whose dazzling achievements marked the climax of the Scientific Revolution, an obvious model presented itself. Newton's scientific method had uncovered the rational order of the entire physical universe. Inspired by this achievement, many began to wonder: If Newton's method could be adapted and applied, was there any major problem, whether social or political, economic or ethical, that could not be solved, or at least alleviated? Here at last was an instrument for arriving at truth which transcended the narrow boundaries of nations and churches. Indeed, it was universal.

Voltaire happened to be in England in 1727, the year that Newton died, and witnessed his funeral at Westminster Abbey. (Voltaire was in England because he had been exiled there in 1726 for telling a joke at the expense of a powerful French nobleman.) Voltaire returned from England in 1729 determined to make the French see the magnitude of what reason had accomplished in Newton ("the greatest man who ever lived"), and to inspire them with thoughts of what it might accomplish in the future. He pointed to Newton as an incomparable example of a man "who sways our minds by the prevalence of reason and the native force of truth."[12]

A further dissolvent of Christian claims to absolute truth was brought to Europe by travelers returning from colonial and commercial ventures overseas. They spoke of people who lived lives of virtue and faith without the benefit of Christianity. Above all, there were reports of the great religious traditions of India and China. The question inevitably arose: Is there an essence of truth common to all religions and corresponding to the spiritual dimension of human nature—in other words, a "natural religion"—which could unite all human beings?

The answer was yes, there must be. If God's justice and mercy extended to all peoples, and not just Christians, then all people must have been offered the possibility of knowing God's will. Precisely what that natural religion consisted in would be found by the application of the scientific method—gathering a wealth of observation and experience from people all over the world and examining it in the light of reason. The conclusion that many reached was that this natural religion consisted in fundamental moral principles recognized by people everywhere.

Voltaire absorbed all these insights and values, which coalesced in the Enlightenment of the eighteenth century. Indeed, he personified the Enlightenment in France just as Thomas Jefferson personified it in the United States. (Jefferson was an avid reader of Voltaire.) Although the two men differed in striking ways (for example, Voltaire was irrepressibly witty, Jefferson solemn to the point of seeming humorless), they shared many of the same assumptions: a belief that the essence of religion was morality; a Deist faith in a Supreme Being and Creator of the universe; a detestation of religious dogma and of the fanaticism that had led to religious censorship, persecution, and war; and a belief in the sacredness of religious and intellectual freedom.

Voltaire thought that Christianity had deviated far from the path of Jesus. Was it Jesus who established the Inquisition with its links to state torture? Was it Jesus who ordered that those who disagreed with him be burned at the stake? Voltaire pointedly asked Catholics, "[Do you] want to maintain by executioners the religion of a God who died at the hands of executioners and preached only gentleness and patience?"

Voltaire became the century's most vocal champion of religious toleration. "Of all religions," he said, "the Christian is undoubtedly that which should instill the greatest toleration, although so far the Christians have been the most intolerant of all men."[13] He noted that Christians had been butchering one another since the Council of Nicaea. Yet toleration was a natural right, expressed by Jesus himself in the saying, "Do unto others as you would have them do unto you." How then, Voltaire asked, could one person say to another, "Believe that which I believe and you cannot believe, or you will die." If everyone adhered to such a policy, there would be universal war.[14]

Instead, he urged, we should all recognize one another as brothers and sisters: "Aren't we all children of the same Father and creatures of the same God?"[15] Voltaire maintained that each individual should be free to believe according to the truth as grasped by his or her reason, so long as this belief did not lead to the disruption of the social order. He was deeply impressed by the religious toleration that existed in England, which he had seen firsthand after being exiled there. The religious situation in France, by contrast, was far from tolerant.

In 1759, in the face of what it regarded as a smear campaign against the Catholic Church by Voltaire and others, the state issued an edict making it a capital offense to criticize the Church.[16] For Voltaire, this was another illustration of how the Church, which enjoyed immense power, privilege, and wealth, had joined forces with the state to block social reform and the progress of civilization. His attitude toward this combined force of repression was expressed in his slogan, "*Écrasez l'infâme!*" ("Crush the infamous thing!"). His verdict on the different forms of Church-State relations that he had studied was that one religion leads to tyranny, two religions lead to religious war, but the English "have thirty, and they live happily and in peace."[17]

Voltaire's typical method in his campaign of reform was to hold up to ridicule what he perceived to be the gross injustices of Church and State. He made many enemies. Twice he was imprisoned in the infamous Bastille; innumerable times he was exiled from France; many of his writings were burned by the state executioner. Thirty-nine of his books were placed on the Church's Index of Forbidden Books, many to remain there until the Index was abolished in 1966. Among these was his *Philosophical Dictionary* (1764), which played a role in the following incident.

In Abbeville, a village in northern France, Capuchin monks were carrying the Eucharist in a solemn procession through the streets. As the monks passed by, a tipsy young man of twenty, the chevalier de La Barre, not only failed to show proper respect for the Eucharist by taking off his hat, he even sang bawdy songs. He was subsequently arrested. During his trial it came out that he was familiar with Voltaire's *Philosophical Dictionary* and also enjoyed reading stories about the wicked behavior that took place behind closed doors at convents. Although technically he had violated no law on the day of the procession, he was convicted of blasphemy. After officers had cut out his tongue and chopped off his hands, he was beheaded. His body was then publicly burned.

By the time Voltaire learned of the case, the chevalier was already dead, so he was not able to intervene. But he did denounce it immediately in writing as an egregious example of Catholic fanaticism leading to judicial murder, and it is recounted in the article he wrote on torture for the second edition of the *Philosophical Dictionary* (1769). Here is a brief excerpt from that article:

> When the chevalier de La Barre, the grandson of a lieutenant general of the army and a young man of much wit and great expectations, but with all the thoughtlessness of unbridled youth, was convicted of singing impious songs, and even of passing a procession of Capuchins without taking off his hat, the judges of Abbeville, people comparable to Roman senators, decreed not only that his tongue should be cut out, his hands cut off, and his body burned...; but they applied torture to him to find out exactly how many songs he had sung, how many processions he had seen pass, hat on his head.[18]

Although Voltaire does not mention the fact, the executioner also consigned to the flames La Barre's personal copy of Voltaire's *Philosophical Dictionary*. Voltaire's denunciation of the judicial murder of La Barre was one of many instances in which he literally risked his life to bring to public awareness an obscure victim of religious or political cruelty and injustice. In his zeal to condemn, Voltaire was often unfair to those he blamed, and it has frequently been pointed out that he shows very little appreciation of what must be regarded by any objective standards as the enormous positive contribution Christianity has made to Western civilization. Another frequent criticism of Voltaire is that some of the violence against the Church, the monarch, and the nobility that raged out of control during the French Revolution took its inspiration from his writings.

That having been said, Voltaire was revered by the American founding fathers. Here is one illustration: In 1778, the year of Voltaire's death, Benjamin Franklin came to Paris on behalf of the American Congress to secure an alliance between France and the new republic. While there, Franklin called on Voltaire, whom he had been reading for half a century, and whose works he had co-edited for an English edition sixteen years earlier. Before he left, Franklin asked Voltaire to bless his eight-year-old grandson, which he did in the name of God and Liberty.

Of Voltaire's lasting achievement, a distinguished recent biographer has this to say: "If we are able to take the principles (if not necessarily the reality) of freedom, tolerance and justice more or less for granted in modern Western society, it is because people like Voltaire proclaimed their value when the very expression of those views was neither free nor tolerated and was likely to result in unjust punishment."[19]

The Enlightenment, of which Voltaire was the supreme French representative, is often disparaged today, its vision of a world transformed by reason dismissed as a utopian dream, its failure to recognize the reality of human evil considered dangerously naïve. So it is worth reminding ourselves of its positive role in the history of civilization. In his introduction to an anthology of writings from the Age of Enlightenment, Sir Isaiah Berlin concluded, "The intellectual power, honesty, lucidity, courage, and disinterested love of the truth of the most gifted thinkers of the eighteenth century remain to this day without parallel. Their age is one of the best and most hopeful episodes in the life of mankind."[20]

Pope Pius IX

The reign of Pope Pius IX (r. 1846–1878), the longest in history, was and remains controversial. On the one hand, Pius IX did much to foster popular piety, especially devotion to the Blessed Virgin Mary. For that he won the hearts of many millions of Catholics. On the other hand, some of his teachings went so strongly against the current of the age that they provoked new waves of anti-Catholicism. Three of those teachings require closer examination.

The first teaching to consider is Pius's definition of the dogma of the Immaculate Conception (1854), which states that the Blessed Virgin Mary "was, from the first moment of her conception . . . preserved from all stain of original sin"—that is, preserved from that sinful nature which all other human beings (except for Jesus himself) inherit from Adam and Eve. The Pope declared this definition to be infallible (on the meaning of this term, see below). It then became necessary for all Catholics to believe this doctrine in order to be saved.

The first accusation made against the doctrine not only by Protestant but also by Eastern Orthodox critics was that it does not appear in the Bible and indeed is contradicted by the Bible where it says "all have sinned."[21] The second accusation was that if this teaching really expressed one of the foundational truths of Christianity, why was it not defined until 1,854 years after the birth of Christ? A third accusation was that the Pope was not only setting Mary apart from the rest of humanity by virtue of her Immaculate Conception, he was promoting her worship as a goddess, which is sheer idolatry.

There were, of course, Catholic answers to these accusations, though they can only be mentioned here. With regard to the first accusation, the Church felt that it had been guided by the Holy Spirit into fuller insight into the meaning of the Gospel declarations in St. Luke's Gospel that Mary was "full of grace" and "blessed . . . among women." Second, belief in the Immaculate Conception of Mary had been implicit in the Church's belief—traceable at least as far back as the third century—that Mary was "the Mother of God." If Mary was destined to be the Mother of God, it was only fitting that she should have been conceived without original sin in preparation for that unique role. Third, the Catholic Church never promoted the worship of Mary, only her veneration, and the two are absolutely distinct. Mary and the saints are worthy of veneration, but God alone is worthy of worship.

The Catholic distinction between veneration and worship was rejected, misunderstood, or most often simply unknown by Protestants. John Henry Newman, widely regarded today as the greatest Catholic theologian of the nineteenth century, acknowledged that some Catholic writers and even Cardinal Manning, the leading Catholic prelate in England, did not help the situation when they made extravagant claims about Mary which easily gave a false impression that Catholics worshipped her. This false impression is still prevalent in the twenty-first century. A recent scientific survey showed that four out of five non-Catholics in America believe that "instead of worshipping only God, Catholics also worship Mary."[22]

The second pronouncement by Pope Pius IX that offended Protestants and many others, including Catholics, was the encyclical *Quanta Cura*, to which was attached the *Syllabus of Errors* (1864), a list of the eighty principal errors of modern thought which were undermining the Catholic faith. To understand both documents, it is necessary to see them as being in part a reaction to an age of increasing secularization of thought and opinion and of tremendous social and political change. Popular movements for democracy were springing up and efforts were being made to sweep away ancient monarchies with which the Catholic Church had long been allied. A robust confidence that freedom and progress would grow hand in hand was spreading rapidly. Individual freedom was held as the highest value in human life. It was the age of liberal democracies.

Perhaps the most eloquent statement of the liberal ideal in the nineteenth century, at least in the English-speaking world, was that given by the British philosopher John Stuart Mill in his essay *On Liberty* (1859). His central thesis is expressed in these words: "The only purpose for which power can be rightfully exercised over any member of a civilized community . . . is to prevent harm to others. His own good, either physical or moral, is not a sufficient warrant. . . . The only part of the conduct of anyone, for which he is amenable to society, is that which concerns others. In the part which merely concerns himself, his independence is, of right, absolute."[23] Mill's essay articulated his idea of individual freedom so persuasively that it has since become, in the words of one distinguished historian, "the only moral principle that commands general assent in the western world."[24]

Let us examine what Mill specifically says about freedom of thought and expression. He believed that no society—indeed, no age—could claim to have the final truth in any matter. He saw history full of examples of one age after another that thought it had such a truth, only to have that "truth" thoroughly discredited in a later age. No opinion should be silenced, therefore, because it might well contain a part of the truth. "All silencing of discussion is an assumption of infallibility."

Even if a particular opinion were wholly false, Mill believed it should still be allowed to be heard so that its falsity can be demonstrated, since if an established truth is not defended, in time it will lose its vitality and meaning and become nothing more than empty words. The truth, Mill said, needs to be "fully, frequently, and fearlessly" discussed. "Both teachers and learners go to sleep at their post, as soon as there is no enemy in the field." Moreover, the active quest for the truth and the defense of it are necessary for the moral development of the individual. Merely following the dictates of others prevents one from becoming a fully mature human being.[25]

Not every form of liberalism went so far as Mill's, but for Pius IX all forms of liberalism were to be opposed because they threatened the authority of the Church. In his judgment, liberalism was the greatest of all the errors of the nineteenth century, and it was even poisoning the wells of the Church, where liberals were calling for the Church to separate itself from the State and its power. The Pope condemned the separation of Church and State, calling for the establishment of the Catholic religion everywhere. The Pope condemned freedom of religion, freedom of speech, freedom of the press, and freedom of conscience as forms of "insanity." As one recent commentator has remarked, "on a fair reading, [the *Syllabus*] condemned the core propositions of the American Bill of Rights."[26] It is not surprising, therefore, that Abraham Lincoln thought the document scandalous.[27]

The *Syllabus* concluded with a blunt rejection of "progress, liberalism, and modern civilization." *The Spectator* of London suggested that the Pope might just as well have condemned Newton's laws of motion,[28] and the *London Times* remarked that "There is scarcely a political system in Europe . . . that does not rest on principles which are here declared to be damnable errors."[29] And because those principles included ideas like freedom of conscience and equal justice under the law, the Pope's condemnation seemed not simply stupid but immoral as well.[30] The French Government was so appalled it actually banned the *Syllabus*. Along with cries of moral outrage, the anti-Catholic press in both England and America gloated over the fact that the

Church had revealed its true character as the enemy of culture and civilization, and as the last great bastion of ignorance, superstition, and tyranny.

If the *Syllabus* sent shock waves around the world, what followed went right to the top of the Richter scale. Partly to reinforce the condemnation of the errors listed in the *Syllabus*, partly to strengthen his own authority as head of the Catholic Church, in 1868 Pius IX convoked the first general council of the Church since the Council of Trent three centuries earlier. Now known as the First Vatican Council, it met from 1869 to 1870 and famously proclaimed the doctrine of papal infallibility. Throughout its history, the Church had believed that God would protect its essential teachings from error because the Gospels themselves said as much when Jesus promised to send his followers the Holy Spirit to guide them into all truth (John 16:13). But the Church had never defined precisely how this protection should be understood in the case of specific papal pronouncements.

Before the Council, some leading Catholics thought it was not the right time to define papal infallibility. The *Syllabus* had opened a gaping chasm between the Church and the world, and a proclamation of infallibility at this time might make that chasm unbridgeable by creating even more confusion and hostility. Newman thought the definition should be postponed indefinitely until careful study and devout prayer made the Church ready to formulate a wise and prudent document. The Catholic historian Lord Acton wrote to William Gladstone, the English Prime Minister: "We have to meet an organised conspiracy to establish a power which would be the most formidable enemy of liberty as well as of science throughout the world."[31] Doubts about the idea of defining papal infallibility had even been expressed to the Pope himself prior to the Council. But when the Archbishop of Bologna wondered whether the definition that

Pius was proposing was really consistent with Church tradition, the Pope burst out: "I am tradition! I am the Church!"

In the end, the Vatican Council voted for a definition of papal infallibility that was remarkably subtle. Unfortunately, its very subtlety led unsubtle minds to proclaim that it said more than it actually did, creating misunderstandings which have persisted until this day. Among the wildest is the notion that papal infallibility means that popes cannot sin. Another is that popes are omniscient and know all things, so that the Pope would be able to answer any question you could possibly ask him, from the intricacies of relativity theory to the reason why your car keeps stalling out.

In fact, papal infallibility is defined rather narrowly and refers to God's gift of immunity from error which the Pope enjoys when formally defining a doctrine of faith or morals which is binding on the whole Church. As it happened, the outbreak of the Franco-Prussian War made it necessary for the Council to be adjourned after only one session and without having clarified how the authority of the Pope stands in relation to the authority of the bishops and the authority of ecumenical councils. After all, wasn't it an ecumenical council, the Council of Nicaea, rather than the Pope, which defined the divinity of Christ? By focusing so much on the Pope, the definition gave the impression to some that the Catholic Church was a one-man show. We will return to the subject of infallibility at the end of this chapter.

Maria Monk

We turn now to one of the most notorious episodes in the history of anti-Catholicism in America—but first some background. From the beginning, the United States was overwhelmingly Protestant. The first census, taken in 1790, showed that only 25,000 Americans—1 percent of the population—were Catholic.[32] But especially because of the massive influx of German- and Irish-Catholic immigrants beginning in the 1820s, the Catholic population in the United States rose rapidly until, by 1850, the Roman Catholic Church was the largest single denomination in the country. With this extraordinary change in demographics there arose popular fear among Protestants that their national way of life was in danger and that America might fall under the control of the Catholic Church.

In response, a vast outpouring of anti-Catholic publications began to flood the market: "Between 1800 and 1860, American editors published at least 25 daily, weekly, or bimonthly newspapers and 13 monthly or quarterly magazines opposing Catholicism, while American publishing houses published more than 200 anti-Catholic books. The most titillating and popular of this literature presented accounts of priests and nuns who had abandoned their faith because of their experiences of torture, mental brutality, and even sexual offense."[33] The most famous of these accounts was Maria Monk's *Awful Disclosures of the Hôtel Dieu Convent* (1836), which was an overnight sensation and went on to become the best-selling American book of the first half of the nineteenth century.[34]

The author claimed that on the very night that she took her vows and became a nun, the full horror of what went on in the nunnery was revealed to her. She had previously been told that she must do whatever the priests told her to do; indeed, her very salvation depended on it, since only priests had the power to grant forgiveness of sins. On that night, she was led to a room where there were three priests, and in the course of the night she was forced to gratify all their lewd and lascivious desires. She would later be told by her superior that these priests lived solitary and laborious lives, and were forbidden to marry, so it was the nuns' task to gratify their natural desires.

She also found out what happened when nuns became pregnant. As soon as they gave birth, their babies were taken from them, baptized, and then killed, their lifeless bodies being thrown into a lime pit in the basement of the convent. Maria's superior assured her that this should not be viewed with horror, since these babies went straight to heaven. But later, when Maria herself became pregnant and gave birth, the thought of losing her child drove her to take the child and flee the convent.

Such were the *Awful Disclosures of the Hôtel Dieu Convent*. The book was soon discovered to be a fraud. Maria Monk had never been a nun, and her story had been written for her by a group of anti-Catholic propagandists. According to her own mother, the only connection Maria ever had with any Catholic institution was when her parents placed her in a Catholic asylum for wayward girls. Nevertheless, *Awful Disclosures* continued to sell, and lurid selections were published in anti-Catholic newspapers, *The American Protestant Vindicator* and *The Downfall of Babylon*, which enjoyed overnight success for doing so. It continued to be a bestseller into the twentieth century. In James Joyce's novel *Ulysses* (1922), when Leopold Bloom visits a pornographic bookstore in Dublin he is offered a copy of Maria Monk's book. What is even more striking is that when the Catholic John F. Kennedy ran for the presidency in 1960, references to the *Awful Disclosures* resurfaced as a warning of the dangers to America that Roman Catholicism posed.[35]

John F. Kennedy

Although American Catholics fought in World War II, anti-Catholicism persisted. At the very least, Catholics were still regarded as different, as "other," because they were associated with close-knit ethnic communities (Italians, Irish, Germans, etc.) and often went to Catholic schools. Their lives were typically centered on the Catholic parish and its activities. It was a world apart. The idea that a Catholic could ever become President seemed remote. Al Smith, Governor of New York, had run for the office on the Democratic ticket in 1928 but had been roundly defeated because (it was widely believed) he was a Catholic.

Thirty years later, one could still find no less a person than former President Harry Truman saying that "[Catholics] have a loyalty to a Church hierarchy that I don't believe in. . . . You don't want to have anyone in control of the government of the United States who has another loyalty, religious or otherwise."[36] Coming from the most well-known Democrat in the country, these words did not warm the heart of Senator John F. Kennedy as he prepared to announce that he would campaign to be the Democratic Party's presidential candidate in 1960.

Early in his campaign for the Democratic nomination, Kennedy visited West Virginia, a staunchly Democratic state. Months earlier, polls had shown him ahead of his leading rival by 40 percent, but suddenly he was behind by 20 percent. The only thing that had changed in the intervening months was that West Virginians had learned Kennedy was a Catholic. When he realized that religion was going to be the decisive, though unspoken, factor in the campaign, he decided to address it head on.

Speaking to a crowd in Morgantown, he asked them: "Did forty million Americans lose their right to run for the presidency on the day they were baptized as Catholics?" He went on to say: "Nobody asked me if I was a Catholic when I joined the United States Navy. Nobody asked my brother if he was a Catholic or a Protestant before he climbed into an American bomber plane to fly his last mission."

But Kennedy's most influential statement to the people of West Virginia was in a televised interview two days before the primary. On the question of religion, Kennedy said, "When any man stands on the steps of the Capitol and takes the oath of office of President, he is swearing to support the separation of Church and State; he puts one hand on the Bible and raises the other hand to God as he takes the oath. And if he breaks his oath, he is not only committing a crime against the Constitution, for which Congress can impeach him—and should impeach him—but he is committing a sin against God." The interview helped to turn the tide in his favor among the voters of West Virginia, and he won the Democratic primary there.[37]

Success in West Virginia did not, however, bring an end to religious opposition to Kennedy. Protestant ministers, most notably Norman Vincent Peale, spoke out publicly against him. Since the electorate was predominantly Protestant, it was clear to Kennedy that unless he could persuade Protestants that his political allegiance would not be to the Pope, his chances in the general election were nil. With this in mind, Kennedy arranged to address a convention of Protestant ministers in Houston. It was a tough crowd, and at least one question was based upon the repudiation of religious freedom in the *Syllabus of Errors*. But Kennedy was able to overcome much of the ministers' distrust by insisting that his religion was a private matter and that if elected his duty to uphold the Constitution would come before all others. He stated that if a conflict arose between his office and his religion, he would resign the presidency.

On November 8, 1960, Kennedy was elected President of the United States. Although the Catholic Church was the largest denomination in America, Protestants outnumbered Catholics two to one. Kennedy's election was taken to symbolize that Catholics were fully accepted as American citizens, capable of holding any position of trust up to the very highest. Fear of papal domination of the United States began to recede, even to appear ridiculous.

John Courtney Murray
and the Second Vatican Council

Before Kennedy gave his speech to the Protestant ministers in Houston, he had it checked by the American Jesuit theologian John Courtney Murray (1904–1967), who raised no objections. Murray was well-known as a Catholic theologian who was also an admirer of the doctrine of religious freedom championed by Thomas Jefferson and James Madison. Earlier that same year (1960), Murray had published a landmark book, *We Hold These Truths*, in which he argued that America's constitutionally guaranteed freedom of religion was highly compatible with Catholic doctrine.

Murray's story is in its own way almost as remarkable as Kennedy's. In the 1950s, Murray's writings on Church-State relations were regarded by Cardinal Ottaviani, head of the Vatican's Holy Office (now the Congregation for the Doctrine of the Faith), as radical and dangerous, and Murray was silenced. But he was so highly regarded in America that Cardinal Spellman of New York asked the Vatican for permission to bring him as an expert advisor to the Second Vatican Council (1962–65). When Cardinal Ottaviani said no, Cardinal Spellman replied that he would not come without Murray. The Vatican relented and Murray came in 1963.

At the Council, Murray became the chief architect of the momentous *Declaration on Religious Freedom* (*Dignitatis Humanae*) which the Council ratified in 1965. It did not get ratified, however, without passing through fierce resistance from a minority led by Cardinal Ottaviani. The minority thought it was impossible to affirm the principle of religious freedom after it had been clearly condemned by Popes for centuries, culminating in the condemnation by Pius IX. The *Syllabus of Errors* had called it a serious error to deny that the Catholic religion should be "the only religion of the state, all other forms of worship whatever being excluded."[38] The apparent harshness of this view had been eased in the nineteenth century by an interpretation according to which Pius was referring to the "ideal." But in the particular historical circumstances that exist in a pluralistic society such as the United States with its many religions, religious toleration was necessary for the time being.

The Vatican's *Declaration on Religious Freedom* states that its purpose is not to overturn past papal teaching but rather "to develop the doctrine of recent popes on the inviolable rights of the human person." It finds the roots of religious freedom in freedom of conscience. Religious freedom is inviolable because no individual's relation with God can be forced. Jesus never coerced anyone to believe in him. This *Declaration* marks the first time the Catholic Church officially accepted religious pluralism as a historical reality.

Among the implications of the *Declaration* for the United States was that the separation of Church and State was recognized as being the best safeguard of religious freedom, not only for the individual but for the Catholic Church itself. The State's role is to protect religious freedom, which had been severely threatened in the twentieth century by Communism and Fascism. The essential role of the State vis-à-vis the Church was not to establish one Church as the official religion but to guarantee the freedom of all religions from State interference. By so doing, the State safeguards the fundamental right to religious freedom, which is the cornerstone of all other human rights.

Murray interpreted earlier teaching on Church-State relations such as that of Pope Pius IX as appropriate in the context of earlier historical circumstances. At a time when governments were attempting to diminish the influence of the Catholic Church in many parts of Europe and were imposing heavy financial and other penalties on the Church, it was right for Pius to seek State support. But a century later, Catholics no longer needed this kind of paternalism. Education and a greater appreciation of the dignity of the human person called for a deeper concept of religious freedom. This was what the Second Vatican Council had given the world in its *Declaration on Religious Freedom*.

It is remarkable that this document was largely the work of a man who previously had been forbidden to write on the subject. Even more notable is that it had endorsed the ideals set forth nearly two centuries earlier by Thomas Jefferson and James Madison. The Church had thus accepted teaching from people who not only were outside its walls, but who had wholeheartedly opposed the idea of an established Church of any kind—Catholic or not.

Concluding Thoughts

One might have expected anti-Catholicism to begin to disappear in America, but its roots were deep, and in any case the 1960s brought changes to America and to the world that could hardly have been imagined a decade earlier. The Catholic Church itself overturned expectations with the promulgation in 1968, by Pope Paul VI, of the encyclical *Humanae Vitae*, whose absolute ban on artificial contraception caused an explosion of controversy within the Church and beyond. (See the next chapter.)

Far from persuading the faithful, the encyclical was widely rejected. Father Andrew Greeley, a sociologist and one of the most acute observers of the Catholic Church in America over the past half century, offers this reflection: "In the late 1960s and early 1970s, every age segment in Catholic America changed its convictions about the legitimacy of birth control, and, more ominously, about the *right* of the Church to lay down rules for sexual behavior. Authority was no longer centralized; it had become pluralistic. Similarly, acceptance of papal infallibility fell to 22 percent of Catholics in the United States."[39]

Professor Philip Jenkins offers an opinion which reflects many of these ideas and applies them directly to *The Da Vinci Code*: "I think anti-Catholicism is a contributory factor [to the novel's success], but the main reason for the book's popularity is deeper, a fundamental suspicion of traditional claims to authority, where they conflict with contemporary ideas and standards, especially over sex and gender."[40]

Chapter 2

The Controversy in the
Catholic Church over Contraception

One of the most important developments in the history of civilization was the growing power of twentieth-century science to control human fertility. So revolutionary was the discovery of new and more effective methods of birth control that the morality of these methods was and still is the subject of fierce debate. Even in the twenty-first century, the Bush administration cited moral grounds for its refusal to give funding to the United Nations for its family planning and maternal healthcare programs in the Third World.

In the twentieth century, nowhere was the debate over birth control taken more seriously than in the Catholic Church and at no time were the stakes higher than in 1968. That was the year Pope Paul VI issued his encyclical *Humanae Vitae* ("Of Human Life"), creating a firestorm of controversy that has still not been extinguished four decades later. The very public nature of the clash between the Pope and much of the rest of the Church, including entire assemblies of bishops in some countries, was unparalleled in modern times. Although the controversy was sparked by the Pope's absolute ban on artificial contraception, it soon spread to many other areas of Catholic sexual morality and raised fundamental questions about the Church's competence to teach in those areas.

In the end, the overwhelming majority of Catholics rejected *Humanae Vitae*'s teaching on artificial contraception, placing the dictates of their own conscience above the dictates of the Pope. The result was a widespread attitude toward the Vatican not only of uncompromising disagreement but in many cases of deep distrust as well. This is the story of how that attitude came about and how it influenced the readership of *The Da Vinci Code*.

The history of contraception has been traced as far back as 2700 BC in China. We know that the use of contraceptives was well established in Egypt by 2000 BC; we even have an ancient Egyptian illustration of a man wearing a condom. But it was not until some four thousand years later, in the 1800s, that contraception began to be understood scientifically. Before that, we find eminent medical authorities recommending methods such as this: immediately after intercourse, the woman should get up and hop backwards seven to nine times.[1] (Readers, please note that this method is no longer recommended.)

The 1800s also saw significant technological advances in contraception. In 1839, Charles Goodyear discovered how to make rubber more elastic and durable by the process of vulcanization, and soon he was applying his discovery to the manufacture of condoms and other contraceptive devices. By the 1870s, a wide variety of such devices were available in America. In addition to condoms, there were sponges, douching syringes, diaphragms, and cervical caps. In 1873, however, with the enactment of the Comstock Law, the United States became the first Western nation to criminalize birth control devices, labeling them "obscene material." The debate over the morality of birth control was well underway.[2] Still, in a nation in which, according to statistics, seven pregnancies were necessary to produce two children who would reach adulthood, that debate concerned relatively few Americans.

Another landmark year in the history of contraception is 1930. That was the year the Anglican Church became the first Christian denomination to give formal approval for the use of artificial contraception as a means of family planning. Although the approval was strictly limited to "those cases where there is . . . a clearly felt moral obligation to limit or avoid parenthood, and where there is a morally sound reason for avoiding complete abstinence,"[3] the leadership of the Catholic Church was scandalized.

In Rome, Father Arthur Vermeersch, the Catholic Church's most influential moral theologian, went so far as to say that the Anglican Church had demonstrated beyond a shadow of a doubt that it was not genuinely Christian. In the months that followed, Vermeersch helped to write the encyclical *Casti Connubii* ("Of Chaste Marriage") which Pope Pius XI issued on December 31, 1930. In it the Pope reaffirmed the Catholic Church's condemnation of artificial contraception in no uncertain terms, calling it "an offense against the law of God and of nature" because it totally defeats the primary purpose of sex within marriage—procreation.

Those who use artificial contraception, the Pope said, are guilty of "grave sin" and are doing something "intrinsically immoral," by which he meant that it is evil by its very nature and therefore forbidden in any and all circumstances. The term "intrinsically immoral" is not used lightly in Catholic moral teaching. Even killing another human being is not considered intrinsically immoral, since there are cases in which it can be morally acceptable, as when a soldier is fighting in a just war, or when an executioner is carrying out the death penalty.

The year 1930 was also notable in the history of contraception because that was when medical researchers announced that they could accurately determine the interval of infertility during a woman's menstrual cycle. This opened up the possibility for couples to have sex and yet avoid pregnancy without relying on contraceptive devices. When this infertile period, which alternates rhythmically with the fertile period, was used for the purpose of avoiding pregnancy, the practice came to be called "the rhythm method."

Pope Pius XI's successor, Pope Pius XII, emphatically reaffirmed the teaching of *Casti Connubii*, as expected, but he also made the momentous decision, in 1951, to approve the use of the rhythm method as a natural means of birth control. What made it natural and therefore morally acceptable was the fact that during intercourse the natural path of the man's sperm to the woman's egg was not blocked, as was the case, for example, when a condom or a diaphragm was used. The intention of avoiding conception and pregnancy was not considered wrong in itself, so long as the decision was based on legitimate reasons, such as the likelihood that another pregnancy would endanger the woman's health or push the family into poverty.

Nevertheless, many Catholics were surprised to hear this, since they were under the impression that the intention to avoid conception and pregnancy in marriage was always wrong. What would have surprised them even more, had they been aware of it, was that the Pope's approval of the rhythm method directly contradicted St. Augustine—perhaps the single most influential theologian in the history of the Catholic Church—who, more than fifteen centuries earlier, had flatly stated that any man who used this method was treating his wife as a whore.[4]

At the same time that Pius XII was giving his approval to the rhythm method, drug companies were testing contraceptive pills, which worked by preventing ovulation. One of these, the progesterone pill, also helped to relieve medical problems such as an irregular menstrual cycle or extreme bleeding during menstruation. Some priest-theologians, without bothering to consult women, stated that these medical problems were not severe enough to justify the use of such a morally questionable remedy as the pill. Nevertheless, in 1958 the Pope permitted the use of the pill for menstrual problems, though he insisted that it must never be used for birth control.

Meanwhile, most Protestant Churches had followed the lead of the Anglican Church and accepted the morality of artificial contraception. In 1959, the World Council of Churches went so far as to say that there was "no moral difference" between the use of the rhythm method and the use of artificial contraceptives. Surveys in America showed that most families were using some form of birth control, usually condoms, at a total estimated cost of $200 million per year.[5] One survey showed that by 1955 more than 80 percent of Catholic wives were using birth control and half of those were using methods that the Church condemned.[6] As for the rhythm method, it was regarded in Catholic circles as so unreliable that it was popularly called "Vatican roulette."

The U.S. Food and Drug Administration did not approve the use of the pill for birth control until 1960, but in 1957 it did approve its use for the relief of menstrual problems. As soon as that happened, an extraordinary number of married women suddenly began to complain of "menstrual problems" and requested prescriptions for the pill, which most doctors were only too willing to give them. After the FDA finally approved the pill for birth control, a Catholic doctor published an article in *Good Housekeeping* magazine in which he tried to encourage more women to use it.

The Catholic doctor was John Rock, the head of obstetrics and gynecology at Harvard Medical School and one of the co-developers of the pill. (A pioneer in the development of in vitro fertilization, he is also remembered as the first person to fertilize a human egg in a test tube—in 1944.) Two years after his article appeared in *Good Housekeeping*, Dr. Rock gained further publicity for his views when he published a book, *The Time Has Come: A Catholic Doctor's Proposal to End the Battle over Birth Control.*

Nature itself, he said, produced days of infertility each month. But women's cycles were often irregular. The pill simply stabilized and extended the natural period of infertility, making it far more dependable as a method of birth control than the rhythm method had proven to be. With the pill, a couple who had decided they needed to postpone having a child for at least a year could achieve that goal more reliably. Moreover, the pill did not obstruct the act of sexual intercourse in the way that condoms did. Although Church officials refused to accept Dr. Rock's arguments, a few distinguished priest-theologians were intrigued and were unwilling to dismiss them. Meanwhile, the pill was gaining greater acceptance in society as a whole and by 1966 six million American women were using it.

In the same year that Dr. Rock published his book, the Dutch bishops decided to drop their opposition to the pill as a method of birth control. The subject was not only on the minds of Church leaders, it was also on the minds of national leaders and members of international bodies such as the United Nations. The paramount concern was the rapid growth of the world's population—in 1600 it had been half a billion; by 1830 it had risen to one billion; by 1930, two billion; and by 1960 it had reached three billion. The population explosion was particularly menacing to the world's poorest nations, for whom famine and starvation were ever-present dangers. It was high time to deliberate on what could be done.

In light of these considerations, Pope John XXIII decided to reexamine the Catholic Church's absolute ban on artificial contraception, and in 1963 he appointed an advisory commission, later known as the Birth Control Commission, which consisted of three priests and three laymen (two medical doctors and an economist). Although John died before the Commission could meet for the first time, his successor Pope Paul VI called for the work of the Commission to proceed.

The Birth Control Commission met five times between 1963 and 1966. Each time, new members were added. For the second meeting in 1964, Pope Paul added five priest-theologians and two lay professors of sociology. One of the newly appointed theologians was Father Bernard Häring, perhaps the most well-known Catholic moral theologian in the world. He was one of those theologians who essentially agreed with Dr. Rock that it was wrong to lump the pill together with contraceptives that placed a physical barrier between the sperm and the egg. Father Häring's most important contribution, however, was an argument that met strong resistance at first but over the years managed to persuade the majority of the Commission.

Häring began with the assumption, already clearly stated in *Casti Connubii*, that sex within marriage serves two purposes, the *unitive* and the *procreative*. The unitive purpose is to nourish and strengthen the bond of love between husband and wife; the procreative purpose is to have children and share the couple's love with them. The crux of Father Häring's argument was his interpretation of the way the procreative purpose of marriage could be fulfilled. What mattered, he said, was not whether each and every act of intercourse was open to new life, but whether "the marriage in its totality" was. In other words, a couple who warmly welcomed children into the world and raised them in a loving manner should not be condemned merely because they sometimes used contraceptives.

Another notable contributor, whose impact was felt immediately, was John Noonan of the University of Notre Dame, who came to the fourth meeting of the Commission in 1965. He was not a member of the Commission but was invited to speak as an expert on the history of the Church's teaching on contraception through the ages. (His massive book *Contraception* was published in 1966 and is still regarded as a standard work in the field.)

In his two-hour presentation to the Commission, he showed that Catholic understandings of marriage and sexuality, far from being constant and unchanging, had varied significantly in different periods of the Church's history. For example, early Christian writers normally said sex was justified only for the sake of procreation. Later writers made exceptions, as in the case of sterile wives, who were permitted to have sex with their husbands even though procreation was not possible. Later still, Pius XII approved the use of the infertile days of the month as a means of avoiding conception. Many members of the Commission concluded from Noonan's talk that the next logical step would be for the Church to affirm that not every act of sexual intercourse needed to be open to procreation.

The fourth meeting of the Commission was also noteworthy for including three married couples. (Oddly, upon their arrival they were told husbands had to sleep in separate quarters from their wives.) One of the couples, Patrick and Patty Crowley of Chicago, headed the Christian Family Movement, made up of more than 125,000 sincere and committed Catholic couples worldwide. They had been specially honored for their work by Pius XII in 1957. In order to help the Commission, the Crowleys surveyed a significant part of the membership, asking them to share their personal experience of using the rhythm method.

The Crowleys were shocked by what they found. Most respondents were deeply dissatisfied with the rhythm method and considered it excessively burdensome and extremely unreliable.

One husband, who had been married for thirteen years and had fathered six children, wrote this:

> Rhythm destroys the meaning of the sex act: it turns it from a spontaneous expression of spiritual and physical love into a mere bodily sexual relief; it makes me obsessed with sex throughout the month; it seriously endangers my chastity; it has a notable effect upon my disposition toward my wife and children; it makes necessary my complete avoidance of all affection toward my wife for three weeks at a time. I have watched a magnificent spiritual and physical union dissipate and, due to rhythm, turn into a tense and mutually damaging relationship. Rhythm seems to be immoral and deeply unnatural. It seems to me diabolical.[7]

His wife, writing independently of her husband, had this to say:

> I find myself sullen and resentful of my husband when the time for sexual relations finally arrives. I resent his necessarily guarded affection during the month and I find I cannot respond suddenly. I find, also, that my subconscious dreams and unguarded thoughts are inevitably sexual and time consuming. All this in spite of a great intellectual and emotional companionship and a generally beautiful marriage and home life.

Most of the Commission members were deeply moved by these personal testimonies, which were confirmed by the results of research conducted by John Cavanagh, one of the medical doctors on the Commission. In particular, he highlighted a survey of 2,300 women showing that the days of fertility, which of course had to be avoided when using the rhythm method, were also the days when a woman's sexual desire was at its peak. With the evidence of so many witnesses, there was a growing feeling in the Commission that the Church should relax its ban on artificial contraception for those couples for whom the rhythm method had obviously failed.

This was the feeling when the Commission came together for its fifth and final meeting in 1966. But it was not shared by everyone. Father Marcellino Zalba from Spain was horrified at the idea of a change in the Church's teaching and exclaimed, "What then with the millions we have sent to hell, if these norms were not valid?" To this, Patty Crowley replied, "Father Zalba, do you really believe God has carried out all your orders?"

Another member of the minority opposed to any change was the American John Ford—a Jesuit priest, like Father Zalba. He took a decidedly minimalist view of the importance of sexual intercourse in marriage, insisting that "conjugal love is above all spiritual . . . and requires no specific carnal gesture." To illustrate his point, he offered the parallel case of the loving relationship between a father and his daughter. Obviously, he said, they are able to love each other "without the necessity of carnal gestures." However well intended, the comparison backfired. Even those who felt that Father Ford—a celibate priest—could hardly be expected to understand the relationship of a husband to his wife or a father to his daughter still felt he should have understood the recent statement of the Second Vatican Council that married love is "uniquely expressed and perfected through the marital act."[8]

Another argument presented by Ford was taken much more seriously, however. If the Church were to allow artificial contraception, he said, it would in effect be saying that in 1930 the Holy Spirit had been with the Anglican Church rather than with the Catholic Church—which was unthinkable. Furthermore, the Church would have to admit that for nearly two thousand years it had been wrong in a matter that had required enormous personal sacrifice on the part of married couples. The result would be that its authority in all areas of sexual morality would be questioned. Finally, he said, to allow artificial contraception would be to change what is by nature a generous act of bringing new life into the world into a selfish act of mere sexual gratification.

But for many, the most memorable statement from the 1966 meeting of the Commission was the one made by Colette Potvin. She and her husband Laurent were one of the three couples on the Commission. Laurent was an internist who had also established a clinic in Ottawa to advise couples on the use of the rhythm method. In the course of their seventeen-year marriage, Colette had given birth to five children, suffered three miscarriages, and had undergone a hysterectomy. No one could deny that she and her husband had fought the good fight under the banner of the Church.

Colette felt it was important for the Commission, which was more than 90 percent male, to understand "the true woman, how she thinks, how she reacts, how she suffers, how she lives." She thought there was a danger in focusing so much on the "biological integrity of the act," as it was referred to, that other aspects would be neglected. So she summoned up all her courage and spoke frankly about what sexual intercourse meant to her: "The conjugal orgasm is the result of a very strong physical attraction and a spiritual bonding which joins bodies and spirits in a union on all levels: physical, intellectual, and moral, and it carries with it a whole gamut of wonderful, sensual pleasures. The day after such a communion with her spouse, the woman is more serene. . . . She is more patient with her children, more loving toward everyone."

She went on to acknowledge that the rhythm method can have a positive value so long as it does not hinder the couple's serenity and intimacy, but if it does, it raises serious questions:

Must we sacrifice the psychological benefits of marital relations in order to preserve the biological integrity of an act? Is that a human way to act? Is it Christian? More than any other testimony, Colette Potvin's touched the hearts of Commission members and especially its celibate priests.

After the Commission had deliberated for nearly three months, it was time to vote. The result was 52 to 4 in favor of advising Pope Paul to end the ban on artificial contraception. It was an astonishing outcome. All of these people had originally been chosen by the Vatican for their devotion and fidelity to the Church, and almost all of them had strongly supported the Church's traditional teaching on contraception at the time of their appointment. Nobody had arrived wearing a T-shirt that said, "Sex, drugs, & rock 'n' roll!"

The final view of the majority, as expressed in the report they sent to the Pope, was that the morality of sexual intercourse should be viewed in the light of what was beneficial for the marriage as a whole. If a couple used artificial contraception because they were in danger of not being able to care for the family if it got any larger, they would still be fulfilling the procreative purpose of marriage in raising the children they already had in the only loving way possible in the circumstances. If, by contrast, they brought more children into the world when they knew they could not care for them adequately, they would be acting irresponsibly and not fulfilling the procreative purpose of marriage. The report concluded by saying that the Church's absolute ban on artificial contraception "could not be sustained by reasoned argument."

It is important to be clear about the majority's position, which can easily be misunderstood. They still believed that avoiding contraceptives was the ideal; all they were recommending was that the Church allow *exceptions* to the ideal. As they saw it, their recommendation called for an alteration, not a reversal, of the Church's traditional teaching.

The vote of the majority in favor of altering the Church's teaching still had to be reviewed by a committee of cardinals and bishops, who would then have the final vote on how to advise Pope Paul VI. On the question of whether contraception was intrinsically evil, the committee voted nine to three that it was not, with three abstaining. On the question of whether allowing contraception would be in line with the tradition and teachings of the Church, the committee voted nine to five that it would be, with one abstaining.

When the Commission broke up after its final meeting in June, 1966, the majority of its members firmly believed that its deliberations had been guided by the Holy Spirit and that the Pope would authorize lifting the absolute ban on artificial contraception. Moreover, they were confident that their views were in harmony with those of the Second Vatican Council (1962–1965). The Council, as the whole world knew, had been summoned by the late Pope John XXIII for the purpose of *aggiornamento*—a thorough updating and renewal within the Church, and a new openness on the part of the Church to dialogue with the world.

When the Commission's majority opinion was leaked to the press in 1967, the American public was not scandalized, as Father John Ford had predicted, but filled with hope. Like the majority of the Commission, most Catholics thought the signs of the times had underscored the need for such a change and that the Church would recognize that need and respond decisively.

The Commission had submitted two reports, one expressing the majority opinion and the other expressing the dissenting opinion of the minority. For two whole years Pope Paul VI agonized over what to do with these conflicting reports. On the one hand, he worried that if he sided with the majority, then people would expect the Church to change its teaching whenever scientists announced a new discovery, as if science were the ultimate arbiter of truth. Worse still, he feared that the Church's teaching authority would be shattered, since *Casti Connubii* would be viewed as having been mistaken in a matter of the highest importance for all Catholic couples. On the other hand, if he sided with the minority, then in the minds of Catholic couples the Church's relevance and credibility in the modern world would be called into question.

On July 29, 1968, Pope Paul finally issued his encyclical *Humanae Vitae* ("Of Human Life"). In light of contemporary events, his timing could hardly have been worse—1968 was the year the world was turned upside down. Americans, still stunned by President Kennedy's assassination in 1963, now had to cope, within the space of two months, with the assassinations of two of their most admired leaders, Bobby Kennedy and Martin Luther King, Jr. After Dr. King's assassination, riots erupted in more than a hundred U.S. cities. In Vietnam, U.S. troops were on the defensive, and the Vietnam War appeared likely to become the first war the country ever lost.

In the Communist world, the government of Czechoslovakia attempted to introduce liberal reforms—the "Prague Spring"—only to be ruthlessly crushed by the military might of the Soviet Union. At the same time, students throughout Europe and America were rioting; in Paris the rioting included workers and reached such a pitch that it threatened to topple the government. Among the billion-plus population of Communist China, the destructive and socially disruptive Cultural Revolution was in its second year. Everywhere there were signs of hatred for established authority in whatever form. Such was the mood when the Pope issued an encyclical that he hoped would be received calmly and dispassionately as a simple statement of self-evident truth.

The Pope began the encyclical by acknowledging that the majority of the Commission had urged change in the Church's teaching. However, he said, after further consultation and prayer he had reached a different conclusion. By his papal authority, therefore, he was reaffirming the Church's absolute prohibition of artificial contraception. He declared that between the two purposes of the sexual act, the unitive and the procreative, there is an "inseparable connection, willed by God and which man may not break on his own initiative."[9] For this reason "each and every marriage act must remain open to the transmission of life."

To block the transmission of life is a direct contradiction of the will of God. Even if the goal of the couple is unquestionably good, by using artificial contraception they are doing evil in order to attain it, and a good end can never justify an evil means. The rhythm method, by contrast, because it simply adheres to a woman's naturally occurring periods of infertility, does not block the transmission of life. It follows that there is "an essential difference" between using the infertility produced by natural processes and using the infertility produced by artificial contraception, even though "in both cases the husband and wife agree in positively willing to avoid children." Paul stated his belief that his argument would be clear and cogent to ordinary men and women of good will.

Unfortunately, it was precisely clarity and cogency that many found lacking. Pope Paul had explicitly rejected the principle of totality. This meant that even if a couple had demonstrated their openness to the transmission of life by bringing a dozen children into the world, they still had no right to use contraceptives to prevent additional children from being conceived. Critics of the Pope felt that contraception ought to be permissible in such cases.

Other critics went so far as to say that the encyclical appeared to contradict itself. On the one hand it said that the unitive and procreative purposes are willed by God to be inseparable and must be present in every act of intercourse; yet on the other hand it said that the use of the rhythm method is lawful. But when the couple used the rhythm method successfully, these critics asked, wasn't the procreative purpose thwarted?

The question of logical inconsistency was not the first question to be raised, however. It was the question of the way the Pope had made his decision. Historian Patrick Allitt has captured the prevailing mood in America: "What made *Humanae Vitae* so galling to many American Catholics was the fact that it seemed to contradict the spirit of Vatican II. Was not the Church now "the People of God" rather than an autocracy? Was it not supposed to draw on its members' experience and expertise? If so, who could possibly have less experience in sexual matters than a celibate clergy, and who could have more expertise than married Catholics?"[10]

On the day the encyclical was announced at a Vatican press conference, the Pope's spokesperson emphasized that it was not to be taken as an infallible statement. In fact, he said, it was "up to theologians to debate and expand all moral aspects involved." This prompted some Catholic theologians to question the Pope's teaching publicly on the very next day. Father Charles Curran, a young professor at the Catholic University of America, led a group of eleven theologians who produced a statement disagreeing with *Humanae Vitae* and then called a press conference to announce it. In the conclusion to their statement they said that "spouses may responsibly decide according to their conscience that artificial contraception in some circumstances is permissible and indeed necessary to preserve and foster the value and sacredness of marriage."

This statement was eventually signed by six hundred other Catholic theologians and scholars in the United States. A similar statement was issued in Europe—with a similarly impressive list of endorsements. A firestorm had broken out. On August 7, the headline of the *National Catholic Reporter* ran, "Paul Issues Contraceptive Ban: Debate Flares on His Authority." Cardinal Patrick O'Boyle, the Archbishop of Washington D.C., demanded that dissenting priests of his archdiocese recant. He later suspended several of them from active ministry.

The Pope wanted all national bishops' conferences to issue statements in support of the encyclical, but many of the statements fell far short of the level of support he had expected. Some national bishops' conferences (the Canadian, Austrian, English, German, and Belgian), while respectful of the Pope's teaching, stated that individuals retained the right to follow their own informed consciences. The strongest statement of dissent came from the Dutch bishops: "The assembly considers that the encyclical's total rejection of contraceptive methods is not convincing on the basis of the arguments put forward."

The fact that *any* bishops' conference would give less than wholehearted backing to his encyclical sent the Pope reeling. But the situation among priests and nuns was even worse. Most of them silently rejected the Pope's teaching; many decided to leave their ministries. And the rejection by the laity was simply overwhelming. The Pope was filled with dark foreboding: "Through some crack in the temple of God," he said, "the smoke of Satan has entered." And Father Häring wrote at the time, "No papal teaching document has ever caused such an earthquake in the Church as the encyclical *Humanae Vitae*."[11]

For fear its aftershocks in America would split that Church in two, the Vatican urged Cardinal O'Boyle to reinstate the priests he had suspended from active ministry, and to do so without requiring them to recant. In hindsight, conservative Catholic scholars have seen "the Washington Case" as typical of the

Vatican's capitulation to the dissenters at that time. What most American Catholics took away from the spectacle of dissenting priests and nuns was that they too had a perfect right to question and even resist the Pope's teaching if they felt strongly about it. The result, says Catholic scholar George Weigel, was the birth of the "culture of dissent" and "cafeteria Catholicism"—take what you like and leave the rest—that have since come to plague the Catholic Church in America.[12]

But it would be wrong to think American priests found it easy to dissent. Many who believed in the morality of artificial contraception, and at the same time wanted to be loyal to the Pope, felt their consciences being torn in two. Before *Humanae Vitae*, they had joined their parishioners in eager anticipation of a change in the Church's teaching. When the encyclical was issued, however, many were simply dismayed. Significant numbers chose to leave the active priesthood and marry. Many who stayed felt that *Humanae Vitae* was wrong. A major survey conducted five years after the encyclical was issued showed that a staggering 42 percent of American priests thought the Pope had abused his authority and an additional 18 percent thought he had used his authority inappropriately.[13]

Those priests who believed that *Humanae Vitae* was wrong often felt inhibited from speaking out to their parishioners on the sexual revolution that was shaking society. Even those who thought the encyclical was right often refrained from speaking on it, for fear of the anger they might stir up among their parishioners. Their silence on this matter, combined with the steep decline in the number of parish priests, meant that priests were often becoming more and more distant from their parishioners. Their guidance in matters of marriage, family life, and sexuality became less sought after. A wall had gone up in the night, catching both priests and parishioners by surprise, but once it had gone up few had any idea how to dismantle it.

In 1972, Yves Congar, a French Dominican priest and one of the most influential Catholic theologians of the twentieth century, wondered aloud whether *Humanae Vitae* might be a case of a Church doctrine that is "not received" (not accepted) by the Church as a whole and therefore of doubtful validity. The distinguished American theologian Avery Dulles, who was later made a cardinal by Pope John Paul II, has noted that there have been a number of cases in Church history where the "non-reception" of a papal teaching by the Church as a whole resulted in that teaching being overturned.[14] In 1993, Bishop Christopher Butler of England thought the dissent among the faithful regarding the Church's teaching on contraception was so strong and so widespread that it did indeed invalidate the teaching.

In reaction to the widespread revolt against the teaching of *Humanae Vitae*, in 1975 the Vatican issued a *Declaration on Certain Questions Concerning Sexual Ethics* in which it strongly reaffirmed the teaching of *Humanae Vitae* and emphasized that unless the person's responsibility was significantly diminished, *all* violations of sexual morality should be regarded as mortal sins worthy of eternal damnation. Thus if a boy masturbates he does something that is not only "unnatural" but sufficiently evil to rupture his relationship with God. (It is worth noting that in Catholic teaching, sexual sins are the *only* sins that are always serious; there are no sexual sins that are slight.)

In 1978, two of the most powerful influences on Pope Paul VI at the time he was writing *Humanae Vitae*, Americans John Ford and Germain Grisez, wrote a joint article claiming that the teaching of *Humanae Vitae* was infallible, not because the Pope had declared *Humanae Vitae* to be such (he had not), but because its teaching had been taught universally and unanimously by Catholic bishops from the earliest days of the Church.[15] Thus *Humanae Vitae* was simply reaffirming a teaching which was already infallible.

Others called for further reflection. Cardinal Basil Hume of England stated that those who experience the sacrament of marriage are an authentic source for theology and that the Church as a whole can learn from them. It is only right, therefore, that they should be listened to.

When Karol Wojtyla became Pope John Paul II in 1979, he knew that for most Catholics around the world, *Humanae Vitae* had failed to make the Church's teaching on sexuality and birth control convincing. He decided to make it one of his chief pastoral goals to do just that, and part of his strategy was to place the teaching on birth control more clearly within the broad context of the Church's overall teaching on marriage and the family. His first book, *Love and Responsibility* (1960) was devoted to these matters, and he had been an important advisor to Pope Paul VI on the composition of *Humanae Vitae*. So in 1979, the first year of his pontificate, Pope John Paul II began a long series of talks later published as *The Theology of the Body*—which has since been widely praised for its insights into the theology of marriage.

John Paul explained that contraception denies the meaning of the sexual act, both as the way by which new life comes into being and as the way the couple expresses their total self-giving to each other in love. Contraception, he said, prevents such self-giving[16] and is really a kind of holding back. The Pope's prolific writings and talks on the sacredness of marriage and sexuality are regarded by many as making the Church's teaching on these subjects thoroughly convincing, especially at a time when sexual problems such as teenage pregnancy and HIV/AIDS seem out of control.

But John Paul's deep insights were not enough to persuade everyone, especially those who disagreed with the Church's teaching that each and every act of intercourse must be open to procreation and that artificial contraception was intrinsically evil. Lisa Sowle Cahill, a moral theologian at Boston College, has questioned John Paul's assertion that the use of contraception prevents—indeed, contradicts the very idea of—total self-giving. "I am confident," she said, "that most Catholic couples would be incredulous at the proposition that the use of artificial birth control necessarily makes their sexual intimacy selfish, dishonest and unfaithful."

In his prolific writings and speeches, John Paul alternated gentle persuasion with stern warnings that the use of contraception directly opposes the will of God, even if one's conscience says otherwise. In his 1988 encyclical *The Splendor of Truth*, he named those acts which are intrinsically evil, and contraception appears on the same list as genocide. In other words, wrote Charles R. Morris in *American Catholic*, "The vast majority of Catholic married couples . . . stand on the wrong side of the abyss with Hitler and Pol Pot."

In another statement made at that time, John Paul declared, "The Church's teaching on contraception does not belong to the category of matter open to free discussion among theologians."[17] But to most educated people of the free world, the idea of open discussion being off-limits was so countercultural as to be almost unintelligible.

So important did the Pope regard this teaching that he even made it a litmus test for appointing new bishops around the world. As Father Avery Dulles observed, priests who dissented from the absolute ban on artificial contraception were considered unfit to be bishops, whereas some of those appointed, while faithful to the ban, have proven to be of "debatable quality" in other respects. Yet even this attempt by the Pope to guarantee that the bishops would speak with one voice on this matter did not win over the rest of the Church.

"The more the hierarchy insists on adherence to *Humanae Vitae*," Dulles said, "the more alienated do the majority of the faithful feel."[18] Indeed, surveys show that disobedience to the Church's teaching on birth control rose significantly after the promulgation of *Humanae Vitae*. The majority of American Catholic couples practice artificial contraception at a rate comparable to that of Christians whose churches thoroughly approve artificial contraception.

Recent surveys have suggested that as many as 93 percent of American Catholics believe that one can practice contraception and still be a good Catholic. More significantly, one major survey found that only 42 percent of American Catholics thought it was "very important" to accept the teaching authority of the Vatican. For a Church that more than any other emphasizes its teaching authority, this is a crisis of the first order.

In every country where serious research has been carried out, it is clear that the debate over artificial contraception is over. In fact, young Catholics today are often unaware that such a fierce debate ever occurred, let alone what the precise issues at stake were. A majority seem even to accept the general view of their peers that sex for recreational purposes is a good thing, even if they admit they will have to change their views when they decide to get married.

In light of this state of affairs and with the support of statistical research, sociologist and author Father Andrew Greeley has argued that, since *Humanae Vitae*, there has been a "catastrophic collapse of the old Catholic sexual ethic."[19] The tragedy is that much of the wisdom of the Christian tradition on the meaning of marriage and love has been forgotten at a time when

Western civilization needs to hear it more than it ever has in the past two thousand years.

Undoubtedly the Church's absolute ban on artificial contraception still has its supporters who, while relatively few in number, are clear and steadfast in their convictions. For them, Pope Paul VI was a modern-day prophet whose dire warnings have come true. As he predicted, the acceptance of contraceptives promoted a "contraceptive mentality," in which children are regarded as a burden to be avoided rather than a blessing to be joyously received. They note that the current birthrate of every western European nation is well below the level necessary to sustain its population. Historian Niall Ferguson has even spoken of the present trend as the greatest "sustained reduction in European population since the Black Death of the fourteenth century."[20]

Yet many Catholics who approve the use of contraceptives vehemently reject the suggestion that they must therefore have a contraceptive mentality. Nor do they regard Pope Paul VI as prophetic in his promulgation of *Humanae Vitae*. Rather, they see his encyclical as misguided and his argumentation as seriously flawed. To them, *Humanae Vitae* shows little understanding of the reality of marriage and sexuality as they have experienced it. Because of this, and the Vatican's repeated condemnations of contraception, feelings of alienation and resentment, suspicion and distrust, and in the end overwhelming sadness are still present when they consider the Church's teaching on marriage and sexuality, perhaps most of all when they consider that the Church they love has by its intransigence made itself into a cipher in the lives of so many.

The debate over contraception reappeared in the news briefly in April, 2006, when it was rumored that the Vatican, in view of the AIDS crisis in sub-Saharan Africa, was about to permit the use of condoms by married couples if one of them (usually the husband) had HIV/AIDS. But the Vatican quickly dispelled these rumors by saying that it was only considering this possibility in the abstract and not in any way preparing to act on it. In any case, the Vatican has repeatedly and categorically stated in recent years that the only way to prevent the spread of HIV/AIDS is by practicing abstinence, and that condoms actually promote the spread of HIV/AIDS.

Medical experts, however, strongly disagree and point to statistical evidence from countries such as Uganda and Thailand showing that condoms, when accompanied by education, dramatically reduce the spread of HIV/AIDS. Moreover, Dr. Marcella Alsan, after working in a Catholic hospital in Swaziland, concluded that abstinence is not a real option for women trying to avoid being infected by their husbands. If a woman refuses to have sex with her husband, she "risks ostracism, violence, and destitution for herself and her children." In such circumstances, she asks, "Isn't opposing the use of condoms tantamount to condemning countless women to death?"

And what will become of their children? In sub-Saharan Africa, there are already twelve million AIDS orphans desperately struggling for survival, many of them infected themselves. The media's portrayal of the disaster which has befallen these people, most of them the poorest of the world's poor, has left many appalled by the Church's unwillingness to allow the use of condoms in order to save lives.

The Church's ban on contraception has also been criticized by those who see the current growth in world population not only as unsustainable in terms of the fixed amount of resources on the planet, but as contributing directly to the looming ecological catastrophe. No matter how much we cut back on per-capita energy use in order to reduce our "carbon footprint," critics say, it will be useless if the population increases as it is projected to do. Many Catholics who hold this view believe that the Catholic Church will change its teaching on contraception, but they also fear that if it proceeds at the speed it did in rehabilitating Galileo, it will be too late, with a loss of human life possibly in the hundreds of millions worldwide.

Concluding Thoughts

On November 23, 2005, Patty Crowley died at her home in Chicago, at the age of 92. Looking back on her long life, Father Andrew Greeley, who knew her well, said, "In terms of lay activism, Patty was the most important woman of her time, and the Christian Family Movement was the most important movement of the Church [prior to the Second Vatican Council]." After her work for the Birth Control Commission ended in 1966, Patty continued to find ways to carry the Gospel message to all areas of life—visiting women in prison, working to provide public housing for the poor, and co-founding the largest private women's shelter in Chicago. All the while she remained an active member of her church, regularly bringing Communion to the homebound.

On the twenty-fifth anniversary of *Humanae Vitae* in 1993, she wrote an article in which she reflected on the encyclical and its aftermath: "I feel betrayed by the Church. The Pope continually states that birth control is evil, yet I know that couples must be practicing birth control. One never hears from the pulpit that birth control is intrinsically evil and should not be practiced. Is the Church hypocritical? . . . I long for a Church that is honest about its teachings, that admits its errors and faces the effects of rigidity with openness."

Such sentiments were not shared by everyone. Bishop Fabian Bruskewitz of Lincoln, Nebraska wrote an article in which he called Patty "a very old degenerate who roams about promoting sexual immorality." Patty laughed and kept that article in a scrapbook as a source of amusement for family and friends. But it shows how deep a chasm exists in the Church in the aftermath of *Humanae Vitae.*

The long-term effect for the majority of Catholics has been an unwillingness to take seriously the Church's teaching on a wide variety of aspects of sexual morality. As Pope Paul had feared, reaffirming the absolute ban on contraception resulted in a feeling among most Catholics that much of the Church's teaching on sexual morality is not only irrelevant but incredible as well. Cynics see the teaching not as an attempt on the part of the Vatican to preserve revealed truth against the onslaughts of a corrupt age, but rather as an attempt to retain its own power by controlling the minds and behavior of the faithful.

The idea that the Church will go to any lengths to attain precisely this type of control is, of course, a central theme of *The Da Vinci Code.* Dan Brown shows his ingenuity by taking an already existing suspicion among his readers and playing it for all it's worth. Church leaders have dismissed this suspicion as blind prejudice, which Catholic rebels have always used as an excuse for willful disobedience. Not only that, they say, but anti-Catholicism is a massive if often hidden feature of our cultural landscape, affecting not only a large segment within the Catholic Church but also a large segment of American society as a whole. In such an atmosphere, they say, it was inevitable that many readers and filmgoers would take pleasure in *The Da Vinci Code*'s dark portrayal of the Catholic hierarchy.

If a vague undercurrent of distrust for its hierarchy and a diminished respect for its authority were the only problems the Church had to face in the years following *Humanae Vitae,* its situation would be bad enough. But those problems would be nothing in comparison with the one that resulted from a news story that broke in January, 2002, and was still sending shockwaves around the world when *The Da Vinci Code* was published in March 2003—the scandalous story of child sexual abuse by priests of the Catholic Church.

Chapter 3

The Catholic Church
and the Sex Abuse Scandals

"Anyone who welcomes one child like this for my sake is welcoming me. But if anyone leads astray one of these little children who believe in me he would be better off thrown into the
depths of the sea with a millstone hung round his neck!"

(Matthew 18:6)[1]

The Da Vinci Code is based on the premise that for centuries the
Catholic Church has lied about Jesus. So important is this premise that without it the entire plot would collapse. The first great
lie of the Church, according to the novel, is that Jesus was divine.
We are told that up until the Council of Nicaea in 325, "Jesus was
viewed by His followers as a mortal prophet . . . a great and powerful man, but a *man* nonetheless. A mortal."[2] Admittedly, this
statement is made by the novel's arch villain, Sir Leigh Teabing,
but the same view is held by the hero, Robert Langdon.

Teabing explains to Sophie Neveu that the Emperor Constantine wanted the Council to establish the divinity of Jesus in order
to unify the Roman Empire under one official religion, that of the
Catholic Church, which would then be seen as the only way to
salvation. To further secure the position of the Catholic Church,
Constantine had all the ancient Gospels except Matthew, Mark,
Luke, and John "outlawed, gathered up, and burned."[3] In this

way, essential truths about Jesus in the Gnostic Gospels were suppressed, including the fact that Jesus was married to Mary Magdalene and intended his work to be carried on under her leadership, not Peter's. The upshot of all this, Teabing says, is that "almost everything our fathers taught us about Christ is *false*," and we are victims of "the greatest cover-up in human history."[4]

How many people are ready to believe that the Catholic Church would actually cover up the truth about Jesus? Some idea may be gained from a poll conducted in December, 2006, which found that an astonishing 40 percent of the American public thought it likely that religious leaders and especially the Catholic Church would withhold important information about Jesus.[5]

This leads us back to the fundamental question addressed in this book: Why would so many people be ready to believe the claims made about the Catholic Church in *The Da Vinci Code*? Debunkers of the novel[6] have said that it plays upon "the last acceptable prejudice in America"—anti-Catholicism. That such prejudice exists (and not only in America) is undeniable; that it intensifies the delight that many take in the novel and in the film is equally undeniable.

Several chapters in the book you are reading, especially Chapter 1, refer to anti-Catholicism and offer suggestions as to how it arose. In this chapter, however, I want to move beyond the question of sheer prejudice and ask whether there are substantial reasons why the portrayal of the Catholic Church as a suppressor of the truth would resonate with readers and filmgoers. In order to answer this question, I propose to examine one of the most shameful episodes in the entire history of the Catholic Church, the sexual abuse scandal of 2002.

The Scandal

Prior to 2002 there had been ominous rumblings, even prominent news stories, of the sexual abuse of children and teenagers by Catholic priests. But when the *Boston Globe*, one of America's leading newspapers, began publishing the results of its ongoing investigation in January 2002, there was a volcanic eruption which left the Catholic Church covered in soot and ash.

Owing to limitations of space, only one story of clergy sexual abuse can be told in detail here. I have chosen the story of Father John Geoghan because, of all the stories of clergy sexual abuse publicized in 2002, this was the first and in some respects (though not all) the most shocking, and therefore the one most likely to have influenced readers of *The Da Vinci Code*.

On January 6, 2002, the *Boston Globe* ran a front-page article with the headline: CHURCH ALLOWED ABUSE BY PRIEST FOR YEARS. The opening sentences revealed the priest's name and the nature of the charges against him: "Since the mid-1990s, more than 130 people have come forward with horrific childhood tales about how former priest John J. Geoghan allegedly fondled or raped them during a three-decade spree through a half-dozen Greater Boston parishes. Almost always, his victims were grammar-school boys. One was just four years old."

Over the next hundred days, the *Globe* published nearly three hundred stories of clergy sexual abuse in a series that would shock the nation and the world. As these stories were being read by Massachusetts Attorney General Thomas Reilly, the product of a devout Catholic upbringing, he reacted with the same horror that virtually every other reader felt: "I found myself yelling out loud, 'My God, this is about children!'" What ultimately horrified readers even more than the abuse itself was the evidence that it had been known and covered up for decades by the ecclesiastical superiors of these pedophile priests. In the case of Father

John Geoghan, many bishops, including two cardinal archbishops, had failed to protect children from a known pedophile and instead put them directly in harm's way.

These stories might have remained hidden forever in confidential files if not for the dogged refusal of the *Boston Globe* to capitulate in the face of a barrage of legal threats and obstacles put in their way by the Catholic Archdiocese of Boston. So certain was the Archdiocese of its power to thwart the investigation that it was taken totally by surprise when Judge Constance Sweeney, herself a Catholic, ordered all the documents to be unsealed.

Kevin Burke, a district attorney who worked closely with the Attorney General, was appalled by what he found: "[They] were the most stunning set of documents, when it comes to secondary responsibility, I have ever read. They showed that if someone had met their moral responsibility, let alone whether they had a legal responsibility, hundreds of people would not be suffering today."

When his Office issued its report in July 2003, the Attorney General called the sexual abuse scandal in the Archdiocese of Boston "the greatest tragedy to befall children *ever*" in the State of Massachusetts.[7] What follows is just one of the stories of clergy sexual abuse uncovered by the *Globe* and pursued by the Attorney General.

Born in 1934 or 1935, John Geoghan was ordained a priest in 1962 and assigned to Blessed Sacrament parish in Saugus, Massachusetts. Soon after his arrival, he began abusing boys, including four brothers aged 11, 10, 9, and 7, whom he molested over a period of two-and-a-half years. A quarter of a century later, Geoghan told a psychiatrist, "They [the brothers] were just happy to have a father figure, with their own father being so angry and distant from them."[8] His uncanny ability to recognize a boy's most vulnerable point, especially when it was a longing for a father figure, was probably rooted in his experience of losing his own father at the age of five. Instead of calling forth compassion, however, this recognition only inflamed his predatory nature and moved him to exploit the situation.

Father Geoghan's next assignment, at St. Bernard's parish in Concord, lasted only a few months, from September 1966 to April 1967. There is no indication in the archdiocesan records as to why his stay was so brief.

From St. Bernard's, Father Geoghan went to St. Paul's parish in Hingham. Before long, however, there were enough accusations of child molestation for him to be sent by the archdiocese for psychiatric treatment at the Seton Institute in Baltimore. After completing his treatment, he returned to St. Paul's.

While there, he managed to befriend Joanne Mueller, a single mother with four boys who lived in another parish twenty three miles away. She was delighted that he was willing to visit her sons and spend time with them, often taking them out for ice cream. In fact, he became so close to the family that he would even help the boys in and out of the bathtub at night and then read them bedtime stories. Joanne was deeply grateful for his kindness.

One night in 1973, Father Geoghan called Joanne to ask if he could come over and visit. She said yes. When she told her third son, then 7 or 8, he said he did not want the priest to visit. His mother was baffled by his response and pressed him about it. In the language of a child, he tried to tell her that Father Geoghan had fondled his penis. Stunned, she asked the boy again, and he told her again, but still she could not believe it. Then, according to his mother, "He literally threw himself on the floor and sobbed. He was hysterical."

Soon, the other three boys were also sobbing. She learned from the eldest that Father Geoghan had told the boys they were bound to secrecy, just as if they had gone to confession. (Father Geoghan had twisted the Catholic teaching about "the seal of confession," according to which priests, *not penitents*, are required to maintain absolute silence about anything a penitent may tell them in the sacrament of confession. Failure on the part of a priest to maintain silence carries a penalty of automatic excommunication.)

Joanne Mueller frantically bundled her children up and hastened to see Father Paul Miceli. As she later recalled, Father Miceli assured her that it would never happen again and that Father Geoghan would never be a priest again, and he asked her to keep quiet about what had happened. But decades later, in a court deposition, Father Miceli denied that the interview had ever taken place. He admitted that he had taken a phone call from a woman who said Father Geoghan was spending too much time with her children, but he denied there was ever any mention of sexual abuse. Father Miceli further admitted to having driven to see Geoghan in order to express the woman's concerns to him face to face, which seems inconsistent with his claim that the phone call was not all that serious. The Mueller family ultimately sued and won a settlement from the Catholic Church.

In 1974, Geoghan was reassigned to St. Andrew's parish in Jamaica Plain. In 1979, accusations against Geoghan reached Father Frank Delaney, the pastor, but he rejected them out of hand, saying that Geoghan was "an outstanding, dedicated priest who is doing superior work." Delaney blamed the accuser.

While at St. Andrew's, Father Geoghan befriended Maryetta Dussourd, a single mother who was struggling to raise not only her own three sons and one daughter but also her niece's four sons. One of the boys was just four years old. She longed for a priestly influence in her children's lives, and Father Geoghan, who supervised the altar boys and a local Boy Scout troop, seemed like the answer to her prayers. Soon, Father Geoghan was visiting Maryetta's apartment almost every evening, taking the boys out for ice cream and tucking them into bed at night.

This went on for two years. All the while, Geoghan was secretly molesting the seven boys in their bedrooms. When Maryetta discovered to her horror what had been going on, she reported it to another priest, Father Thomas, who confronted Geoghan. Much to his amazement, Geoghan denied nothing, so Thomas promptly notified Bishop Daily. Daily in turn immediately telephoned Geoghan and ordered him to leave the parish at once and go home. This took place in February 1980 and marked the end of Geoghan's time at St. Andrew's.

Several weeks later, Father Thomas went back to Maryetta and begged her not to go public with the story. Geoghan had only done this in the case of two families, he told her, and if she went public, all the years Geoghan had spent studying for the priesthood would be in vain. It seems never to have occurred to Father Thomas how much Maryetta and her children had suffered. As she later put it, "Everything you have taught your child about God and safety and trust—it is destroyed."[9]

Father Geoghan was placed on sick leave and ordered by Cardinal Medeiros, the Archbishop of Boston, to undergo counseling. After being on sick leave for a year, Geoghan was assigned to St. Brendan's in Dorchester, where the pastor had not been told anything about Geoghan's troubled past.

At this point, Geoghan's sexual abuse of children had gone on for nearly twenty years. Church officials knew they had a pedophile on their hands, but they chose to keep it hidden—with disastrous consequences for the children supposedly in their care. In light of this, it is only a slight exaggeration to say that there were already enough grounds to distrust Church leaders to fill a dozen *Da Vinci Code*s. But in fact we have scarcely passed the midpoint of Geoghan's career.

At his new assignment at St. Brendan's in Dorchester, Geoghan quickly began working with the seven-year-olds preparing for their First Holy Communion. He won their parents over and even persuaded some of them to allow their boys to go with him to his family's summer home on the Atlantic Ocean. There he molested the boys. By the summer of 1982, troubling rumors were circulating.

On July 24, Maryetta Dussourd[10] complained to Bishop Daily after one of her sons encountered his former abuser in an ice cream shop. Father Geoghan had been there with another boy. On August 16, her sister, Margaret Gallant, sent a long letter to Cardinal Medeiros expressing her deep concern that the Church was still allowing Geoghan to serve as a priest. Her concern was not only for the seven boys her sister was raising, but for any other boys Geoghan might come into contact with. From her letter, it appears that the Church had asked the family to keep silent about the matter and to bear in mind that a layperson in Father Geoghan's position would only be confined for a limited time.

She acknowledged the truth regarding a layperson in Geoghan's position but then protested, "He would also be *exposed*. Parents would know then not to allow children near this type [of] person. In this case, not only do they not know, but by virtue of his office he gains access quite easily, which compounds our responsibility! . . . Regardless of what he says, or the doctor who treated him, I do not believe he is cured; his actions strongly suggest that he is not, and there is no guarantee that persons with these obsessions are ever cured."

Toward the end of her letter, she expressed her sorrow: "My heart is broken over this whole mess—and to address my

Cardinal in this manner has taken its toll on me too." Yet her love for the Church remained, she said, even though the family had never received so much as an apology from the Church or any offer to provide counseling for the boys. If anyone ever fulfilled the biblical injunction to speak the truth in love,[11] it was Margaret Gallant in this letter.[12]

Although Margaret Gallant could not have known it, the two doctors who vouched for Geoghan's readiness to resume ministry were plainly unfit to do so. The first was Dr. Robert Mullins, to whom Geoghan was sent for psychotherapy. But Mullins was a family physician with no credentials in psychotherapy. Moreover, as a longtime friend of Geoghan and his family, he was not capable of giving a truly independent evaluation of Geoghan and should never have agreed to do so. In the end, Mullins chose to substitute a few friendly conversations with Geoghan for the serious psychotherapy that was called for, and soon accepted Geoghan's assurances that he was fit to resume his priestly duties.

The second doctor asked to evaluate Geoghan was John Brennan, a psychiatrist but not one with expertise in sexual disorders. Moreover, at the very time he was seeing Geoghan, he himself had been forced to pay $100,000 in a lawsuit brought by a female patient who claimed to have been molested by him. In the years that followed, these two doctors would see Geoghan at the request of Church officials whenever he was caught committing further offenses, and each time they would conclude their evaluation by stating that he was ready and able to resume his priestly ministry.

Let's return to the correspondence between Margaret Gallant and Cardinal Medeiros in the summer of 1982. While Margaret Gallant's letter was a passionate statement of her love for the Church and her desire to preserve its sanctity and holiness, the Cardinal's reply was brief and bland almost to the point of obscurity. He said he would look into the matter, but his insistence that "God forgives sins" hinted that Geoghan's ministry would not be brought to an end. It was not.

Six days after writing to Gallant, Medeiros wrote to Geoghan to announce the good news that he would receive a generous grant for a three-month sabbatical in Rome. "It is my hope," the Cardinal wrote, "that the three months will provide the opportunity for the kind of renewal of mind, body and spirit that will enable you to return to parish work refreshed and strengthened in the Lord." Yet no sooner had his sabbatical in Rome ended than Geoghan returned to St. Brendan's and resumed his abuse of young boys.

Cardinal Medeiros died in 1983, and Bishop Daily carried out administrative duties for the archdiocese until Bernard F. Law was appointed as archbishop in January 1984. That September, Margaret Gallant wrote another letter, this time to inform Law that despite Cardinal Medeiros's attempts to have Geoghan rehabilitated, he was once again taking boys out and not bringing them home until late at night. She expressed her genuine fear for "my fellow members in this Body of Christ who are left in the dark as to the danger their children are in, while I have knowledge of the truth."

Two weeks later, Law replied to Gallant. Although he did not mention it to her, he had been briefed by Bishop Daily about Geoghan's history of sexual abuse and specifically about Geoghan's repeated abuse of the seven boys being raised by Gallant's sister, Maryetta Dussourd. Yet Law's reply to Margaret Gallant showed no concern whatever for what had happened. Instead, he responded in a cold, perfunctory manner that "appropriate pastoral decisions will be made both for the priest and God's people." What Law actually did after replying to Gallant was to transfer Geoghan to yet another parish, St. Julia's in Weston, where he was promptly put in charge of three youth groups.

Alarmed by the news of Geoghan's transfer, Auxiliary Bishop John D'Arcy wrote to Law warning him of Geoghan's "history of homosexual involvement with young boys." He went on to say that "if something happens, the parishioners . . . will be convinced that the Archdiocese has no concern for their welfare and simply sends them priests with problems." In retrospect, this letter stands out as the one and only known instance of a clergyman protesting to Law about the reassignment of *any* pedophile priest in the Boston Archdiocese.

Nevertheless, within a week of this letter, Drs. Mullins and Brennan assured Law that Geoghan posed no risk whatever. In the end, Law did nothing, nor did D'Arcy pursue the matter further, since he himself was soon made Bishop of the Diocese of Fort Wayne-South Bend in Indiana.

In September 1984, a story of clergy sexual abuse made the national news. Gilbert Gauthé, Jr.,[13] a parish priest in Louisiana, had been indicted on thirty-four counts of sexual abuse involving nine boys, including one count of raping a child under the age of twelve. He eventually pled guilty to charges involving pedophilia with eleven boys and was sentenced to twenty years in prison.

In response to the Gauthé case, and with the strong support of Cardinal Law, a confidential report on clergy sexual abuse of minors was written for the United States Conference of Catholic Bishops. The report warned repeatedly and emphatically of the danger of the problem and described pedophilia as a "lifelong disease with NO HOPE AT THIS POINT IN TIME for cure" [capitals in the original]. A memo written at that time[14] by the papal ambassador to the United States, Archbishop Pio Laghi, shows that he particularly wanted Cardinal Law's backing of the report's recommendations and intended to discuss the matter with him. In 2002, however, Law said in a civil deposition that he could not remember having studied the report.

Meanwhile, in St. Julia's parish, Geoghan's appetite for boys was insatiable, so he began going to the Boys & Girls Club in the neighboring town of Waltham, where his pattern of abuse continued. But even the Boys & Girls Club was not enough. In 1986, Geoghan learned that the alcoholic father of a poverty-stricken family he had known at St. Andrew's parish in Jamaica Plain had committed suicide several years earlier, so he decided to visit the family at their apartment. After expressing his sorrow for their loss, he offered to take twelve-year-old Patrick McSorley, the youngest of the six children, out for ice cream. On the way home Geoghan pulled the car off to the side of the road and began masturbating both the boy and himself. The boy was traumatized, and when his mother asked him what was wrong, he was at a loss for words.

In time, he managed to bury the memory of what had happened, but he also developed chronic depression and alcoholism. It was not until thirteen years later, when he learned of a lawsuit against Geoghan, that he was able to recall the traumatic incident and link it to his depression. Patrick McSorley went on to become one of the strongest voices against clergy sexual abuse, inspiring many others to come forward with their own stories.

When he received a settlement from the archdiocese of nearly $200,000 in 2002, McSorley commented, "The money is not going to change my life. My heart is always going to be broken because of this. I mean, these are people my family once loved."[15] In June 2003, he tried to commit suicide by throwing himself into the Neponset River.[16] Finally, on February 23, 2004, at the age of 29, he died of a drug overdose, leaving behind a five-year-old son, Patrick McSorley, Jr.

His friend Alexa MacPherson, also a victim of clergy sexual abuse, offered her reflections: "Many of us try to forget the memories. His choice of action was to drink and to use drugs to try to escape the pains that he felt and the memories that he had." Alexa had brought him to hospitals and drug rehabilitation centers many times during the last year of his life, but all to no avail. "It's something that you never get over," she said. "Once it happens to you, it's with you for the rest of your life."[17]

But we must return to St. Julia's in the 1980s. In 1989, in the face of mounting allegations against Father Geoghan, Cardinal Law sent him to the St. Luke Institute, a Catholic psychiatric hospital in Maryland where he was diagnosed as a high-risk homosexual pedophile. Upon his return, Bishop Banks, one of Cardinal Law's auxiliaries, told Geoghan he could no longer serve as a priest and placed him on sick leave. Geoghan then spent three months at the Institute for Living, a secular psychiatric hospital in Hartford, Connecticut.

When Geoghan's treatment was completed, Bishop Banks, in a remarkable about-face, decided to press the Institute for Living for a more favorable prognosis that would enable Geoghan to be reassigned to parish work. The Institute obliged, and Banks allowed Geoghan to resume work at St. Julia's. Years later, when the Attorney General's report was released, Banks was singled out for covering up sexual abuse by Geoghan and many other priests. By that time, however, he was no longer working in the Boston Archdiocese, having been promoted to become Bishop of Green Bay, Wisconsin.[18]

After Geoghan returned to St. Julia's, his abuse of boys started up again. Among the incidents of abuse, his indecent assault of a ten-year-old boy in the pool at the Boys & Girls Club in Waltham in 1991 proved fateful. That was the crime for which he would be tried and convicted in 2002.

Meanwhile, in 1993, former priest James Porter made national news when he pleaded guilty to 41 counts of molesting some 28 children while serving in the Diocese of Fall River, Massachusetts, adjacent to the Archdiocese of Boston. Cardinal Law stated publicly that Porter's transgressions were the aberration of a single depraved individual and not a sign of structural problems within the Church. He insisted that the matter had been deliberately blown out of proportion by the anti-Catholic secular media, especially the *Boston Globe*. He also stated that he had instituted an aggressive new policy to deal with priests suspected of sexual abuse.

That aggressiveness was nowhere to be seen, however, when in 1993 Geoghan was removed from St. Julia's for the second time and reassigned to work at the Office for Senior Priests in Boston. There he continued to seek out and abuse minors in nearby Waltham. In December 1994, with further charges against Geoghan pouring in, Law put him on administrative leave with pay. Once again he was sent to the St. Luke Institute in Baltimore. After his treatment there was finished, he allegedly molested a boy from Weymouth in 1995. One of the incidents was said to have occurred at the baptism of the boy's sister.[19]

In July 1996, a woman from Waltham filed a lawsuit claiming that Geoghan had molested her three sons after she asked him to counsel and support the boys when their father abandoned them. It was the first time charges of child sexual abuse against Geoghan had been made public. As far as Cardinal Law was concerned, this was the last straw. On August 4, he placed Geoghan on sick leave. Geoghan was sent for therapy to the Southdown Institute in Ontario.

In October, Geoghan wrote to Law requesting permission to retire. On December 12, 1996, Law granted his request, adding, "Yours has been an effective life of ministry, sadly impaired by illness. On behalf of those you have served well, and in my own name, I would like to thank you. I understand yours is a painful situation. The Passion we share can indeed seem unbearable and unrelenting. We are our best selves when we respond in honesty and trust. God bless you, Jack."[20] In his reply to Law, Geoghan expressed his appreciation for the warmth of the Cardinal's letter. When Attorney General Thomas Reilly read the letter after the scandal broke in 2002, he noted bitterly, "The cardinal didn't send letters like that to the victims."[21]

In 1998, the Archdiocese announced that it had paid out as much as $10 million to settle a dozen lawsuits against Geoghan. With more accusations streaming in, John Geoghan was finally removed from the priesthood.

In June 2001, the investigative staff of the *Boston Globe* discovered that in November 1984, Law had assigned Geoghan to St. Julia's parish even though he knew that Geoghan was alleged to have abused seven boys. This is what launched their investigation. Some time after the Geoghan story broke in the *Globe* on January 6, 2002, the estimated number of his victims had to be revised upwards from 130 to 148—among them, 23 girls. Mitchell Garabedian, the attorney representing 86 victims, said that almost all of them came from poor families, and 90 percent of those families were being raised entirely by women.[22] In the eyes of the predator, they had been the perfect prey.

On January 18, 2002, nearly forty years after he began molesting children as a priest, Geoghan was convicted on one count of indecent child assault based on the incident at the Boys & Girls Club in 1991. He was sentenced to ten years in prison, the maximum punishment allowed under the law.

Geoghan's trial caused an avalanche of troubles to fall upon the Boston Archdiocese. In early February 2002, while the trial was still going on, Cardinal Law tried to reassure the public:

"There is no priest, or former priest, working in this archdiocese in any assignment whom we know to have been responsible
for sexual abuse." Yet within a week, eight priests were removed
from ministry in the Boston Archdiocese. In the days that followed, three more priests were removed. Of these eleven priests,
five were pastors.

Meanwhile, a seemingly endless flow of stories of past sexual
abuse by clergy was appearing in the *Globe*. In his Good Friday
Letter to the Faithful, Cardinal Law stated his belief that a betrayal of trust was at the heart of the crisis: "Priests should be
trustworthy beyond any shadow of a doubt. When some have broken that trust, all of us suffer the consequences." The troubling
implication of his remarks seemed to be that the bishops themselves bore no responsibility for what had happened. Shortly afterwards, a survey showed that nearly two-thirds of Boston's two
million Catholics were deeply dissatisfied with Law's handling of
the crisis and felt he should resign from office.

The investigation by the *Boston Globe* sparked similar investigations around the country. In the first few months of 2002,
more than 175 priests suspected of the sexual abuse of minors
either resigned or were relieved of their ministerial duties na-
tionwide. On April 15, as the crisis deepened, Pope John Paul II
summoned all thirteen American Cardinals to the Vatican.

Meanwhile, people everywhere were discussing what could
have caused the crisis in the first place. Many thought the
Church's requirement of priestly celibacy was a contributing factor. Cardinal Francis Stafford, president of the Vatican's Pontifical Council for the Laity, said that he expected the question of
mandatory celibacy to be discussed when the American Cardinals met in Rome. Whatever discussion there might have been,
however, was nipped in the bud by the Pope three days before
the meeting began when he said, "The value of celibacy as a

complete gift of self to the Lord and his Church must be carefully safeguarded."

When the Pope addressed the American Cardinals at the Vatican on April 23, he said that the crisis extended beyond the Church to society as a whole: "It is a deep-seated crisis of sexual morality, even of human relationships." In the discussions that followed, Vatican officials emphasized to the American Cardinals that disobedience to hierarchical authority in matters of morality was a major contributing factor to the scandal. Cardinal Stafford singled out the need to reinforce the Church's ban on contraception.[23] In light of the finding that most of the victims were teenage boys, some concluded that the problem was not actually pedophilia but homosexuality. As Cardinal Anthony Bevilacqua of Philadelphia later put it, "We feel that a person who is homosexually oriented is not a suitable candidate for the priesthood even if he has never committed any homosexual act."

The causes of clergy sexual abuse are not simple. One observer, A. W. Richard Sipe, a former priest and now psychotherapist, who has worked for many years with troubled priests—including Father Geoghan at the Seton Institute in 1968—had this to say: "It's a great question, why do priests act out sexually against minors, and the answer is far more complex than saying it's just a reflection of society in general. People don't like to deal with multifactored realities, but this is a multifactored reality. It's not just one thing. You have to understand that the priesthood is a powerful, enduring, beautiful, productive culture that has a very, very dark side."

When the meeting of the American Cardinals at the Vatican ended with a press conference, Cardinal Law was conspicuously absent. "[It] was rather late, you know," he told reporters afterwards. "I had other things to do."[24] At the press conference a joint statement by the Cardinals was read in which they proposed dismissing any priest "who has become notorious and is guilty of the serial, predatory, sexual abuse of minors."

Journalist Andrew Sullivan[25] drew the following conclusions: "Occasional or on-off child-abuse violations could perhaps be forgiven. And even serial abuse might be overlooked if it had not been 'predatory.' A simple question: How is an adult's exploitation of a minor ever anything but predatory?" Given the additional requirement that the priest be "notorious," it was not even clear whether someone like Geoghan, whose abuse was almost totally concealed, would have been dismissed any sooner.

After returning to America, Cardinal Law continued to stumble badly. In the case of another priest, Paul Shanley, who had been charged with raping a six-year-old boy, Law claimed that negligence on the part of the boy's parents—and indeed on the part of the boy himself—had contributed to the crime. Then, two weeks later, the Archdiocese decided to renege on its earlier promise to compensate eighty-six of Geoghan's victims, provoking their attorney, Mitchell Garabedian, to condemn Law as "a despicable human being."

In June, the U.S. Conference of Catholic Bishops managed to fare better. At its annual meeting in Dallas, which the media and the public were invited to observe, it instituted sweeping reforms. It published a Charter on the Protection of Children and Young People, set up an Office of Child and Youth Protection, and appointed an independent National Lay Review Board.[26] When the Review Board issued its report in 2004 on the causes of the sexual abuse crisis, with recommendations for the prevention of further abuse, Cardinal Law was among those mentioned by name for his failure to deal appropriately with abusing priests.

Back in Boston in 2002, a group called the Priests' Forum had come together to express their desire for changes in the Church. Their boldest move was to gather the signatures of fifty-eight priests on a petition calling for Cardinal Law's resignation on the grounds that he had failed them and the people as a spiritual leader.[27]

In December of 2002, the Pope reluctantly accepted Cardinal Law's resignation as Archbishop of Boston. In a public statement, the Cardinal offered his apologies for the "mistakes" he had made. His choice of the word *mistakes* outraged some critics, who felt that "egregious sins" would have been more appropriate. Some doubted whether he even recognized the gravity of the abuse that had taken place on his watch.

In July 2003, Massachusetts Attorney General Thomas Reilly issued his report on the sexual abuse crisis and the Church's handling of it. His words were words of moral condemnation for the failures of Church leaders: "For decades, cardinals, bishops, and others in positions of authority within the Archdiocese chose to protect the image and reputation of their institution, rather than the safety and well-being of children." He also criticized the Church for its ongoing failure to reform itself: "The Archdiocese has . . . not demonstrated a commitment to the protection of children that is proportionate to the harm that it has caused." He also rebuked the national Church for its failure to hold bishops accountable for protecting known pedophile priests.[28]

Not everyone appreciated the Attorney General's investigation. William Donohue, president of a watchdog group, the Catholic League for Religious and Civil Rights, said Reilly had wasted "a colossal amount of public funds," since in the end he decided to issue no indictments of Church leaders.[29]

It is true that no indictments were issued, but the fact of the matter is that—unlike teachers, doctors, social workers, and police officers—clergy were not required under Massachusetts law to report suspected child abuse. Their position had long been privileged. Regarding the question as to why Cardinal Law was not prosecuted as an accessory to the crimes committed by known pedophile priests under his authority, one reason given by the Attorney General was that, in transferring known sex abusers to new parishes, the Cardinal did not share the abusers' criminal intent. For the same reason, his dealings with these sex abusers could not be regarded as conspiracy in the strict, legal sense. But the Attorney General was mystified by the reaction of Church leaders to the sufferings of the victims, many of whom had been raped: "Where's the indignation? Where's the moral outrage?"

In view of the lack of clear remedies under the law, Massachusetts State Senator Marian Walsh introduced legislation that would make it a crime to move a known sex abuser from one job to another. A committed Catholic and former admirer of Cardinal Law, she had been stunned by the revelations in the *Globe*: "I never thought that a leading facilitator for child abuse would be the Church, where the Church would supply the victims and hide the perpetrators. I understand why pedophiles do what they do. I still can't understand, I still can't appreciate, how the Church could do this, how sophisticated and how diabolical this was. And how the cardinal could preside over it."

In retrospect, it was clear that Church officials consistently lied to victims and their families and strenuously resisted attempts by journalists and lawyers to investigate claims of abuse. To avoid disclosing the truth, the Archdiocese pursued every legal means available, including the services of some lawyers who did not hesitate to revictimize the victims. Ultimately, Church authorities yielded only because they were confronted by the superior power of the State of Massachusetts.

In May 2004, a year and a half after his resignation as Archbishop of Boston, Cardinal Law was appointed Pastor of St. Mary Major—one of four great basilicas in Rome, along with St. John

Lateran, St. Paul's Outside the Walls, and of course St. Peter's. His new position is one of immense dignity and honor. Cardinal Law also serves on seven of the nine congregations which are part of the Vatican bureaucracy that assists the Pope in the governance of the universal Church. One of the congregations he serves is the Congregation for Bishops, whose responsibilities include assisting bishops in the proper exercise of their pastoral functions. Another is the Congregation for the Clergy, which has responsibility for the assignment of clergy around the world. In light of all that had taken place in Boston, the fact that he should end up serving these two congregations in particular struck some observers as full of tragic irony.

After Pope John Paul II died in April 2005, Cardinal Law presided at the Mass in St. Peter's that marked the second day of mourning. Many felt his conspicuous presence and the memories it brought back of the sex abuse scandal detracted from the homage due to the Pope.

The story of Cardinal Law is a tragedy not unlike the classical tragedies in which a man of outstanding abilities is brought to ruin by one fatal flaw. Here was a man once thought likely to succeed Pope John Paul II and become the first American Pontiff. Here was a man who, as a young priest on his first assignment in Mississippi in the early 1960s, wrote passionately on behalf of the civil rights movement even after receiving death threats from racists. Yet here too was a man blind to the evil of clergy sexual abuse and to the suffering of its victims. Even after Law's resignation, many still wished that he would spend time listening to those victims. But with his departure for St. Mary Major, the possibility of dialogue and the healing that might have come from it all but disappeared.

This chapter has also been about one of the abusers, the one whose story launched the series on clergy sexual abuse in the

Boston Globe—Father John Geoghan. As mentioned earlier, he was convicted on one count of indecent child assault in January 2002, and was sentenced to ten years in prison. In the next few months, nearly two hundred people filed claims that they too had been abused by Father Geoghan. However, on August 23, 2003,[30] while in his prison cell, Geoghan was attacked and strangled to death by Joseph Druce, a fellow prisoner believed to have been a victim of child sexual abuse himself. Because Geoghan's conviction was being appealed at the time of his murder, both the conviction and the original indictment were declared null and void by the Massachusetts Court of Appeals.

Geoghan's case was extreme in the number of its victims, but it was by no means unique. The cases of Father Paul Shanley and Father Joseph Birmingham in the Boston Archdiocese, and Father James Porter in the neighboring Fall Rivers Diocese, are in certain respects even more appalling than Father Geoghan's.

In the aftermath of the *Globe*'s investigation of Geoghan, the Boston Archdiocese turned over to authorities the names of more than ninety priests alleged to have abused minors, and the *Globe*'s investigation led to similar investigations around the country. Among the findings[31] that emerged was that every single one of the 188 Catholic dioceses in the United States was facing or had faced claims of child sexual abuse.

The quest to uncover scandalous behavior in the Church—by June 2002 there had been more than twelve thousand stories[32] in the U.S. media—provoked a Cardinal from Honduras[33] to compare the media exposés to the persecution of the Church by Hitler and Stalin. At the other end of the spectrum, there were those who were deeply grateful for the investigative work that had been done.

Father Andrew Greeley voiced the appreciation of many when he wrote in the *Chicago Sun-Times*: "If the *Boston Globe* had not told the story of the Church's horrific failures in Boston, the abuse would have gone right on. There would have been no crisis, no demand from the laity that the Church cut out this cancer of irresponsibility, corruption, and sin, and no charter for the protection of children. The *Globe* did the Church an enormous favor."[34] In honor of the vast changes for the good that it had set in motion in Boston and beyond, the *Boston Globe* was awarded the 2003 Pulitzer Prize for Public Service Journalism.

In this chapter, I have focused on one of the darkest episodes in the two-thousand-year history of the Catholic Church. For this reason, it is only fair to state plainly that, based on my own experience, the overwhelming majority of priests and bishops follow Christ with deep devotion and lead lives of immense integrity and great service to others. And my personal experience is shared by countless others.

Having made that statement in all sincerity, I return to why *The Da Vinci Code*'s portrayal of the Catholic Church as a suppressor of the truth would have resonated with readers when it was published in early 2003. More than any other single cause, it was due to the sexual abuse scandal of 2002. Because of that, as the Pope himself said, "[A] dark shadow of suspicion is cast over all the other fine priests who perform their ministry with honesty and integrity."[35]

We have seen that Father Geoghan deliberately preyed upon the most vulnerable—usually little boys who needed a father figure in their lives. What those children experienced at his hands was a kind of death—the death of innocence, the death of trust, the death of hope. The same kind of death was experienced by the victims of many other predatory priests. Meanwhile, the number of priests, bishops, and cardinals who knew of this abuse and yet allowed it to continue is simply staggering. Across the world, people were asking themselves, "If for the sake of their own power, authority, and prestige, Church officials were willing to hide the truth that could have saved hundreds of innocent children and teenagers from having their lives shattered, what truth wouldn't they cover up?"

Post Script

On his visit to the United States in April 2008, Pope Benedict XVI met privately with a group of five victims of clergy abuse, all from the Boston area. The meeting had been requested by Cardinal Sean O'Malley, the Archbishop of Boston, who also presented the Pope with a notebook listing the names of a thousand victims of clergy abuse from the Boston Archdiocese, and asked that they be remembered in his prayers. After their meeting with the Pope, a number of them said that the conversation had been open and heartfelt on both sides, and had brought some genuine healing. One said, "I didn't end up saying anything [to Pope Benedict]. I got up to him and I burst into tears. But honestly, I don't think any words I could have said . . . my tears alone—it just spoke so much." Others spoke of their sense of the Pope's empathy and love, which gave them hope that he would take further action.

Chapter 4

The Controversy in the
Catholic Church over Homosexuality

> Da Vinci had always been an awkward subject for historians,
> especially in the Christian tradition. Despite the visionary's
> genius, he was a flamboyant homosexual and worshipper of
> Nature's divine order, both of which placed him in a perpetual
> state of sin against God.
>
> The Da Vinci Code, 45

Erotic love is a theme that runs through *The Da Vinci Code* like
an electric current. It first appears in the familiar form of "boy
meets girl, etc." when Robert Langdon and Sophie Neveu have
their fateful encounter in the Louvre. A romance between our
dashing hero and demure heroine is about to begin, even if it
must, for now, be confined to the hidden places of their hearts.
For most of the novel, there are no dewy eyes, no heartfelt sighs—
except of course our own. (I'm sure I'm not the only incurable
romantic who read the book!) Knowing that love conquers all,
we are not surprised at the end of the novel when Robert and Sophie arrange to spend a week together in Florence (not to study
Renaissance art).

Another form that eros takes in the novel—one that appeals
especially to those whose thoughts of love move more in the direction of the Playboy Mansion—is that of the orgiastic rites of

hieros gamos, the celebration of the sacred marriage between the god and goddess in which Jacques Saunière once took part at his château north of Paris, to young Sophie's lasting horror.[1]

But homosexuality, the subject of this chapter, is hardly mentioned in the novel. In fact, apart from the reflections of Robert Langdon quoted above, it is not explicitly referred to at all. Yet that single reference links it to the novel's repeated portrayal of the Catholic Church as a totalitarian regime of sexual repression, and it is that portrayal which resonated deeply with many readers of *The Da Vinci Code*. So I have chosen homosexuality as another topic in sexual morality, alongside contraception, to help explain why the claims of *The Da Vinci Code* struck a chord with so many readers.

Historical Background:
Homosexuality and Christian Society

Like abortion, homosexuality has provoked some of the fiercest fighting in the culture wars that have divided America in recent decades. But prior to the culture wars, the idea that homosexuals would ever campaign openly for equal rights under the law and an end to discrimination was unthinkable. For centuries they had sought to hide their sexuality for fear of the legal penalties they might suffer. Christian societies understood the biblical laws against homosexual behavior as binding on all citizens, whether Christian or not. Such behavior was not only a sin but a crime, and the governments of Christian nations punished it severely.

Although there may well have been earlier instances, the first incontrovertible evidence of the use of the death penalty against homosexuals by a Christian ruler is that of the Byzantine Emperor Justinian. From the outset of his reign in 527, he declared himself the enemy of all homosexual men and made their punishment castration—followed by death. Homosexuality, he insisted, required no less a punishment if the Empire was to avoid God's wrath in the form of famine, pestilence, and earthquake.

Justinian's influence as a lawmaker was so great that it was still felt in Christian countries more than twelve hundred years later. In eighteenth-century France, for example, sodomy (homosexual intercourse) was a capital offense, and those found guilty of it were burned at the stake. This did not change until the French Revolution, whose leaders viewed the sodomy laws as barbarous relics of the despised Catholic Church. But their repeal of the sodomy laws in 1791 did not indicate approval of homosexual behavior, only a belief that capital punishment was the wrong way to deal with it. A more civilized solution, they said, would be to eliminate its social causes, starting with boys-only schools.

In Elizabethan England, a statute which made sodomy a capital offense punishable by hanging had been in place since 1564, the year of Shakespeare's birth. It was not until nearly three centuries later, in 1861, that the penalty was reduced to imprisonment. The statute was finally abolished by Parliament in 1967, when homosexual activity was decriminalized altogether. Even so, for society at large, homosexuality continued to be "the love that dare not speak its name."

In the United States, the death penalty for sodomy was done away with state-by-state during the nineteenth century, though sodomy remained a crime. In 1961, the American Bar Association recommended that laws governing private sexual relations between consenting adults be dropped. In 1962, Illinois became the first state to do just that. In the 1960s and 1970s, most northern, western, and midwestern states did away with their sodomy laws. By the start of the new millennium, sixteen states still had sodomy laws, but in 2003, in the case of *Lawrence v. Texas*, the

United States Supreme Court declared all such laws unconstitutional.[2]

If we turn from legal history to the history of American psychiatry and psychology, we find that attitudes toward homosexuality changed dramatically in the twentieth century. In the first half of the century, homosexuality was regarded as a mental illness which might require hospitalization and even electroshock therapy. This was how it was viewed by the American Psychiatric Association in 1952 when it published its first *Diagnostic and Statistical Manual* (*DSM*), a systematic guide to the classification of psychological problems and disorders. But soon, scientific studies began to call this view into question. In 1973, a gradual process of redefining homosexuality began, and in 1987 the revised third edition of the *DSM* no longer referred to homosexuality as an illness at all. Today the American Psychiatric Association officially views homosexuality as a normal variation of human sexuality.

There is an interesting but little-known footnote to this development. One of the leading advocates for the removal of homosexuality from the *DSM* in 1973 was Robert Spitzer, M.D. Nearly three decades later, at the 2001 meeting of the American Psychiatric Association, Spitzer announced that he had stepped back from his earlier position. His studies had revealed that a significant percentage of homosexual persons had undergone genuine, long-lasting change through therapy and counseling and were now functioning well as heterosexuals. "Like most psychiatrists," he remarked, "I thought that homosexual behavior could be resisted—but no one could really change their sexual orientation. I now believe that's untrue—some people can and do change."[3]

By 2001, however, Spitzer was going against a powerful current that had been gaining strength for decades, not just among his colleagues, but among the public at large. As far back as 1948, Professor Alfred Kinsey had published a landmark study of the sexual behavior of the American male, based on lengthy interviews with over five thousand men. His book created a sensation. Not only was it a phenomenal bestseller, but its conclusions were widely publicized in the press as well. Kinsey even made the cover of *Time* magazine. Sexuality became a topic of open discussion in a way that it had never been before. Five years later Kinsey dropped another bombshell with his study of the sexual behavior of the American female. One of the many conclusions that both fascinated and astonished the public was that homosexuality was common in both sexes and among all social classes.

In the 1960s, the sexual revolution prompted many homosexuals to "come out of the closet" and announce their homosexuality. At the end of that decade, a movement for gay and lesbian rights was launched, inspired in part by the accomplishments of the feminist and civil rights movements. Demanding an end to the discrimination they had endured for so long, gays and lesbians insisted that they only wanted the rights guaranteed to all American citizens. Their cry for justice won the support, or at least the compassion, of many.

Others, however, were alarmed by what was taking place. They feared that if the gay and lesbian movement went as far as many activists wanted—to the point where gay and lesbian marriage was recognized in law—the institution of marriage as they knew it, and which they regarded as the indispensable foundation of society, would be fatally undermined. Marriage and raising a family, they said, are the common road to life's highest and most difficult achievement, and for that reason both must be vigorously protected. Allowing gay and lesbian marriage would be opening the floodgates to domestic and social chaos.

A further alarm was sounded in 1981, when the AIDS epidemic broke out. Medical authorities initially called it GRID, for Gay-Related Immune Deficiency, and the public thought of it as an exclusively gay disease. Stories in the media about individual victims of AIDS portrayed a gay lifestyle involving casual sex with hundreds of male partners, often in gay bathhouses. The public was appalled. The Rev. Jerry Falwell spoke for many evangelical Christians when he said that AIDS was the gay plague—a just punishment for behavior that was an abomination in the sight of God. But other Christians were shocked by Falwell's statement and the picture it conjured up of a God of fierce vengeance and savage cruelty.

Several years later, many of them felt there was a powerful lesson for Falwell in a story that made headlines across the nation. In 1991, Mel White, a ghost writer for Falwell and other prominent evangelicals, "came out" and told the story of his desperate attempts over nearly three decades to change his homosexual desires. Neither exorcisms nor electroshock therapy had been of any use. In despair, he even attempted suicide. But slowly he came to believe that God loved him unconditionally, just as he was, and this belief enabled him to accept his homosexuality as God-given. Later he established a committed relationship with another gay man, and the two of them became leaders in a Christian ministry reaching out to gays, lesbians, and others who feel rejected by their Churches.

Stories like Mel White's were not the only ones that were changing people's attitudes. The media were also reporting startling new scientific discoveries. The most dramatic was the announcement in 1993 that a team led by Dean Hamer of the National Institutes of Health had discovered a "gay gene." The story made front-page headlines in major newspapers around the world. As was to be expected with such an explosive topic, the discovery was sensationalized and oversimplified. Many assumed it would be Galileo and Darwin all over again, with science discrediting traditional Church teaching. Few in the public paid attention to or even heard Hamer's own cautionary remark that his team "hadn't actually isolated the 'gay gene,' only detected its presence, and the results would need to be replicated and confirmed" by other scientists.[4]

More important, even if the existence of a "gay gene" were to be confirmed (and, to date, it has not), this would not resolve the question of how much environmental factors such as family upbringing contribute to male homosexuality. There is, for example, the well-known hypothesis that homosexual orientation arises from a child's failure to identify with the parent of the same sex, so that a gay man longs to bond with another man because he never successfully bonded with his father. Most scientists, however, suspect that a combination of genetic, hormonal, psychological, and social factors are involved—in other words, that both nature and nurture play essential parts in the origins of homosexuality.

In the same year that the "gay gene" made headlines, the gay rights movement showed its strength when an estimated 750,000 people took part in a gay-rights march on Washington. Meanwhile, television shows from *Will & Grace* to MTV's *The Real World* made gay and lesbian people familiar to a wider audience than ever before.[5] Not only that, but as more and more individuals revealed that they were gay or lesbian to their families and friends, long-standing walls of hostility began to come down. To reject homosexuality in principle is one thing; to reject a person you know and love is quite another. And so, homosexual relationships gradually gained broader acceptance.

This is not to say that they gained general acceptance, however. In 1996, 56 percent of the American population still thought that homosexual acts were always wrong.[6] There were also vehement reactions against the trend toward acceptance, and by the mid-1990s, acts of violence against gays and lesbians had reached epidemic proportions. Studies showed that an overwhelming majority of gays and lesbians had been victimized, often with extreme brutality. A sampling of gays and lesbians in Pennsylvania, for example, found that 87 percent reported having been victims of violence.[7]

When such acts were reported in the news, the public was as shocked and disgusted as it had been when racist violence was televised during the civil rights movement in the 1960s. Opposition to gay and lesbian rights began to be associated with hatred and bigotry—and labeled "homophobia." The most notorious instance of homophobia was the savage murder of 21-year-old Matthew Shepard in 1998. In its aftermath, a wave of sympathy swept the nation, prompting President Clinton to call for such acts against homosexuals to be punishable at the federal level as hate crimes.

After the Bush Administration came to power in 2000, the most conspicuous aspect of the debate over gay and lesbian rights became the question of same-sex marriage. During the 1999 presidential campaign, Bush had responded to a question about same-sex marriage by saying, "Don't try to trap me in this states' issue." Once in office, however, it was clear that he was determined to oppose same-sex marriage by any means possible, including an amendment to the United States Constitution. But in 2006, a proposed amendment to define marriage exclusively as a union between a man and a woman was defeated in both houses of Congress.

Christian Attitudes toward Homosexuality

I have already mentioned the late Rev. Jerry Falwell. I mention him again here because he was one of the most influential voices in the fundamentalist movement and a leading figure in the American culture wars, which provide a necessary context for understanding the resonance of *The Da Vinci Code*.

The most notorious statement Falwell ever made came two days after the terrorist attacks of September 11, 2001 when he appeared on Pat Robertson's television show *The 700 Club*. Commenting on the attacks, Falwell said, "I really believe that the pagans, and the abortionists, and the feminists, and the gays and lesbians who are actively trying to make that an alternative lifestyle, the ACLU, People For the American Way—all of them who have tried to secularize America—I point the finger in their face and say, 'You helped this happen.'"[8] Pat Robertson totally agreed. But when their comments were picked up and broadcast by the secular media, they provoked such an uproar of indignation that both men publicly apologized. Nevertheless, their underlying belief that homosexuality and its public acceptance deserve to be severely punished by God is widely shared in America, most conspicuously by evangelicals and others who call themselves "biblical Christians." It represents one end of a spectrum of Christian attitudes toward homosexuality.

At the other end of the spectrum are two "liberal" views, which may be stated briefly before moving on to a more detailed discussion of the official teaching of the Catholic Church. The first of these views gives qualified acceptance to committed homosexual relationships, regarding them as less than the ideal of heterosexual marriage but better than being denied the possibility of an intimate and loving relationship entirely. The second view goes further and advocates the full acceptance of homosexual relationships. In this view, they are on the same level as heterosexual relationships and should be judged by the same criteria (fidelity, self-giving, and so on).

The General Synod of the United Church of Christ is an example of a mainline Protestant Church in America that has taken the second view. It should be noted, however, that these two views represent a very small minority of official church positions. In the United States, most Christian churches and denominations disapprove of homosexual acts, though they do not want to reject homosexual persons. This is the basic position of the Catholic Church, which we will look at next.

The Official Teaching of the Roman Catholic Church

Partly in response to the sexual revolution of the 1960s, partly in response to growing debate within the Church itself, the Vatican decided it must reaffirm and clarify its traditional teaching in a time of unprecedented moral confusion. In 1975, it issued a *Declaration on Certain Questions Concerning Sexual Ethics* which reinforced the Church's condemnation of contraception, masturbation, premarital sex, and homosexual activity. All were judged to be "intrinsically evil," meaning that they are always objectively and seriously immoral. The Declaration also included the first official recognition by the Church of homosexual orientation (as distinguished from homosexual acts) as a deep-seated "condition" not freely chosen by the individual.

In 1986, the Vatican issued another document, "Letter to the Bishops of the Catholic Church on the Pastoral Care of Homosexual Persons." After a brief introduction, the letter proceeded to correct a misunderstanding with regard to homosexual orientation. It stated that while homosexual orientation was not sinful, neither was it a good or even a neutral condition. Rather, it was a disorder. (The meaning of this term will be explained below.)

From there the letter went on to summarize the basis for its moral evaluation of homosexual acts, beginning with the evidence in the Bible. Although there are only a handful of relevant passages, the Church has always regarded them as unambiguous condemnations of homosexual activity.

The first Old Testament passage, Genesis 19:1–29, tells the story of how the city of Sodom was wiped off the face of the earth. Two angels in the form of men visited the city and met Lot, who welcomed them and took them into his home as his guests. But when the men of Sodom learned of this, they wanted to rape Lot's guests, so they went to him and demanded that he hand them over. Lot refused, and for his heroic resistance, he and his family were spared when God destroyed the city by raining down fire and brimstone. This passage is interpreted by the Church as the first explicit condemnation of homosexuality in the Bible. From it we get the term *sodomy*. The episode is recalled in the New Testament Letter of Jude when it refers to the destruction of Sodom for its sexual immorality.

The next relevant Old Testament passage occurs in the Book of Leviticus, which condemns male homosexual activity in these words: "If a man lies with a male as with a woman, both of them have committed an abomination; they shall be put to death."[9]

In the New Testament, the Letters of St. Paul contain three clear references to homosexual behavior. The weightiest of these is Romans 1:24–27, where St. Paul speaks of homosexual acts as being "against nature" and a sign of the participants' alienation from God. (This passage also contains the Bible's only mention of female homosexuality.) The phrase "against nature" is understood to mean that such acts are against God's purpose as discoverable in the design of nature.

This idea reappears and is developed in the Church's "natural law" tradition, whose most influential exponent was the great philosopher and theologian St. Thomas Aquinas (c. 1225–1274).

One sense of natural law, according to St. Thomas, is "what nature has taught all animals."[10] With regard to sexuality, what nature has taught all animals is that genital activity is for procreation. It follows that homosexual activity, since it cannot serve the purpose of procreation, is opposed to the natural order and is "disordered." These fundamental ideas are reflected in the *Catechism of the Catholic Church* when it states, "[T]radition has always declared that 'homosexual acts are intrinsically disordered.' They are contrary to the natural law. They close the sexual act to the gift of life."[11]

In addition to procreation, official Church teaching since the Second Vatican Council (1962–1965) has emphasized another primary purpose of sex within marriage: the expression of love. As was discussed in the earlier chapter on contraception, these two purposes are inseparable and must be present in every act of intercourse. Pope John Paul II spoke eloquently of intercourse as a sign and instrument of the complete self-giving of each spouse to the other. True love is also *life*-giving, and the love of husband and wife is designed by God to extend beyond the spouses to embrace the child who is the fruit of that love. Non-procreational love, whether contraceptive or homosexual, blocks the purpose of total self-giving and is ultimately selfish, reducing the partner to an object to be used for personal pleasure. This idea is reflected in the 1986 letter when it speaks of homosexual activity revealing "a disordered sexual inclination which is essentially self-indulgent."[12]

Although the Catholic Church teaches that homosexual acts are intrinsically evil, it also teaches that the degree of guilt attaching to them is often mitigated if they are done without full knowledge and consent. It may be the case, for example, that the individual simply does not know any better, or that the individual is addicted to homosexual activity and so is unfree. Finally, it must be kept in mind that the Church's rejection of homosexual activity is not intended to cast the slightest doubt on the God-given dignity of homosexual persons, who are created in the image of God.

These are a few of the main points included in the Catholic Church's teaching on the morality of homosexuality.

Criticism of the Official Church Teaching

Critics of the Church's official teaching, both inside and outside the Roman Catholic Church, have questioned each of these points. With regard to the Genesis story of the destruction of Sodom, critics pose this question: How can a story of attempted gang rape possibly be relevant to an assessment of the morality of homosexual acts between two consenting adults?

Second, critics have argued that the chief crime the biblical author was trying to emphasize was not homosexual rape but *inhospitality*; the men of Sodom violated the sacred laws of hospitality. It is hard for us today to imagine how the welcoming of strangers could be a sacred duty, especially in America where living in a gated community is regarded by many as part of the American dream. But a very different outlook prevailed in ancient Israel. In this desert region, hospitality was often a matter of life and death (think of your car breaking down in Death Valley), so it came to be understood as an obligation imposed by God.

That Lot was thinking of this obligation is implied in the reason he gave to the men of Sodom for not handing over his guests: ". . . for you know they have come under the shelter of my roof." So sacred was the duty of hospitality that Lot was even willing to offer the townsmen his own daughters rather than have his guests abused: "I have two daughters who have never had intercourse with men. Let me bring them out to you, and you may do to them as you please."[13] Critics are quick to point out that this willingness, so appalling to modern readers, completely undermines any attempt to use this story as a source of teaching about sexual morality.[14]

Critics have also questioned how the Church can uphold the prohibition against homosexuality found in the Book of Leviticus while disregarding other prohibitions listed there. They point out, for example, that although Leviticus forbids eating pork, the same Christians who oppose homosexuality are often the first in line at the supermarket when pork butts go on sale. A more thoughtful comment comes from the distinguished Jewish scholar Jacob Milgrom, who has argued that the prohibition against homosexual behavior applies to non-Jews *only* if they live within the boundaries of the Holy Land. Thus Christian homosexuals living in America or England, for example, would be exempt from this law.[15]

A further objection raised by some critics is that homosexuality is condemned because it is a practice of the pagans, who do not worship the God of Israel. Thus homosexuality is associated with idolatry. They argue that this is what Paul is thinking when he speaks out against homosexual acts in his Letter to the Romans. (It should be noted that these critics have found little support among New Testament scholars.)

Having looked at criticisms of the Catholic Church's use of Scripture, we turn now to criticisms of the Church's claim that same-sex activity is "against nature," or "unnatural." We have already mentioned scientific research suggesting that there is a genetic component involved in the origin and development of homosexual orientation. Other scientific research also points in the direction of biological factors. Recent studies have established that homosexual activity occurs in virtually all animal groups.[16] By 2007, it had been scientifically documented in more than 1,500 animal species,[17] including elephants, rhinoceroses, giraffes, zebras, lions, dolphins, whales, walruses, penguins, ostriches, tortoises, turtles, frogs, chipmunks, squirrels, and koala bears.[18] In addition to same-sex genital activity, scientists have observed long-term bonding, courtship behavior, and even the raising of offspring by two individuals of the same sex. As biologist James Weinrich has stated, homosexual behavior is no less natural than heterosexual behavior.[19]

Homosexual behavior among the great apes is particularly striking. Among bonobos (also known as pygmy chimpanzees), who share between 95 and 99 percent of our DNA and are, together with the more familiar "common chimpanzees," our closest biological relatives, same-sex behavior is not only natural but very frequent. The *most* frequent type observed in females is genital-to-genital rubbing, often to the point of orgasm. It has been observed that "partners gaze intensely into each other's eyes and maintain eye contact throughout the interaction."[20] Is this the equivalent of lesbian behavior? Without having access to the bonobo mind, we can only guess. But the very fact that while having sex they gaze into each other's eyes—once thought to be a uniquely human behavior—is haunting.

A further question that arises in the context of this discussion is whether such behavior can be called "disordered," as homosexual behavior is labeled in the teaching of the Catholic Church. It is hard to see how. In bonobo society, homosexual activity promotes peace and harmony by calming feelings of aggression that arise when, for example, two females are competing for the same food.

The question of the relevance of same-sex behavior among the great apes to our understanding of homosexuality in humans is bewildering in its complexity, and the debate over how to answer it is still in its early stages. But according to biologist Bruce Bagemihl, an authority on same-sex behavior in animals, there

is one conclusion that can be drawn: the prevalence of such behavior among the great apes and monkeys means that "homosexuality is part of our evolutionary heritage as primates."[21] It is
interesting to note that Bagemihl's work is so highly esteemed
that it was cited by the American Psychiatric Association in its
"friend of the court" brief to the U.S. Supreme Court in the 2003
case of *Lawrence v. Texas*, in which the Texas anti-sodomy laws
were struck down.[22]

We turn now to critical responses to a third point emphasized in official Catholic teaching—that homosexual acts are
essentially self-indulgent. Critics have countered that this is a
misleading stereotype, implying as it does that homosexuals use
their sexual partners as mere objects for their own sexual gratification.[23] These critics insist, first, that it is wrong to pass judgment on homosexual acts without considering them in the context of the overall relationship of which they are an expression.
Second, they claim that homosexual relationships can exemplify
the same loving qualities that are found in the best heterosexual
marriages.

Some gay men, for example, have stood by their partners as
they lay dying of AIDS, when those partners' own parents and
siblings had disowned them. Other homosexual couples have
made enormous sacrifices to adopt and raise orphaned children
in stable, loving families, and evidence suggests that homosexual couples are just as capable of providing healthy parenting
as heterosexual couples.[24] Finally, there are many homosexual
couples who testify to their experience of joy and love, faithful-
ness and self-sacrifice, forgiveness and peace. What can these
things be, they ask, but signs of God's blessing?

In the end, for many gays and lesbians it is a question of the
kind of God one believes in. They do not believe that God would
have created them homosexual at the deepest core of their being,

only to decree that they were forbidden to ever experience loving intimacy with another person. As they understand the Church's teaching, not only can't they fulfill their desire for loving intimacy, they must run from it in fear, since it is a desire that draws them toward evil. To them, despite the Church's claim otherwise, the Church's condemnation of homosexual activity amounts to a condemnation of them as persons, since sexuality is an essential aspect of personality. They feel that the Church has made them outcasts, and they ask, "Wasn't it precisely the outcasts whom Jesus reached out to and befriended? Is he not calling all of us to do the same today?" Such are some of the feelings that gays and lesbians have expressed.

Possible Responses to Critics

How might the Catholic Church respond? One way of answering this question would be to look at each criticism in turn and consider the responses that might be given. But this book is not intended to investigate the pros and cons of every point in exhaustive detail; other books do that. Here it must suffice to consider two fundamental responses that the Catholic Church would surely make. The first is a very general one used to assess the morality of any behavior. We must ask ourselves whether the reasons we give to justify our behavior are the ones that are actually driving us, or are we being driven by selfish motives so subtle yet so powerful that they have deceived us? A related question to be considered is this: Are we honestly willing to listen to what others might have to say, or are we fundamentally afraid that the truth might be too painful to bear?

The second response that the Church could make applies specifically to the question of homosexual conduct. While acknowledging that the various branches of knowledge, such as genetics and psychology, can contribute to our understanding of homosexuality, the Church believes it is bound to consider those contributions in the light of revelation, especially the words of Jesus as recorded in the Four Gospels. In answer to a question from the Pharisees concerning divorce, Jesus referred to God's will for marriage as revealed in the biblical story of creation: "Have you not read that the one who made them at the beginning 'made them male and female'?" and said, "For this reason a man shall leave his father and mother and be joined to his wife, and the two shall become one flesh."[25]

Although these words were given in answer to a question about divorce, they reflect an understanding of marriage which rules out homosexual acts. Moreover, this understanding carries the highest possible authority for Christians, being drawn from the very bedrock of the Old Testament—the "law of Moses"—and given its definitive interpretation by Jesus himself. By the power of the Holy Spirit, that interpretation has been faithfully preserved through the centuries in the Church's tradition so that it may be taught with certainty in our own time. Such is the basic belief of the Catholic Church that underlies its official statements.

Of course this teaching implies an enormous burden—indeed the Church speaks of it as a cross—that homosexuals are called to bear. But in being called to bear their cross, homosexual persons are no different from any other person who wants to follow Christ. And the strength to bear that cross is not expected to come from their own resources, but from the grace of God. As Jesus said, "For human beings this is impossible, but for God all things are possible."[26]

Concluding Comment

At the present time, the conflict between the official teaching of the Catholic Church on the one hand and the position of many gays and lesbians and their supporters on the other is at an impasse. It is another area where the moral authority of Catholic teaching is being seriously questioned, both outside the Church and within it, by people who wonder how many of the moral laws that the Catholic Church proclaims to be unalterable and eternal are really the decrees of men—and not of God. It is this attitude of questioning which permeates *The Da Vinci Code* and resonates with readers.

Chapter 5

Opus Dei and Conspiracy

Few things capture our attention like news of a conspiracy. For many of us, a day without a conspiracy is like a day without sunshine (or should I say, like a day without ominous clouds looming on the horizon). A fascination with dark, sinister plots is one of the defining characteristics of our age. Across America and much of the world today, one conspiracy theory looms larger than any other: the theory that the horrific events of September 11, 2001 were planned and executed not by al-Qaeda but by the U.S. Government to provide a pretext for invading oil-rich Iraq.

According to a survey conducted in August 2006, no less than a third of all Americans think it likely that federal officials launched the attacks of 9/11 or at least knew about them in advance.[1] Various official organizations have attempted to dispel these suspicions, but their arguments have been greeted with skepticism. After all, skeptics say, when most of the original justifications the White House gave for going to war with Iraq have proven to be false, is it so unreasonable to suspect that a government conspiracy lies behind the events of 9/11?

In *The Da Vinci Code*, Dan Brown plays upon our fascination with conspiracies like a virtuoso. First, there is the conspiracy of the Priory of Sion to guard the greatest secret in human history—the existence of the bloodline of Jesus and Mary Magdalene. Second, there is the conspiracy of Bishop Aringarosa and Silas, both of Opus Dei, and a mysterious "Teacher" to destroy

103

the Priory in order to ensure that its secret is never leaked to the world. And then there are those who have worked their way into the midst of these conspiracies: the arch villain, Sir Leigh Teabing, who intends to out-conspire the conspirators; and Robert Langdon and Sophie Neveu, who seek to carry out the final wishes of her grandfather, Jacques Saunière, who turns out to be the Grand Master of the Priory.

The skillful handling of such a complex plot is perhaps Dan Brown's greatest achievement in the novel. The plot is made even more intriguing by the reader's uncertainty over how much of it is based on fact and how much of it is pure fiction. The title page reads, "*The Da Vinci Code*: A Novel," but on page 1, we are presented with a number of arresting claims under the heading "Fact." Some of the book's debunkers have alleged that the confusion of fact and fiction in *The Da Vinci Code* is itself part of a conspiracy on the part of the author and publisher to mislead the reader.

There are specific reasons why both the Catholic Church and Opus Dei were under a cloud of suspicion almost everywhere when *The Da Vinci Code* was first published in March, 2003. In Chapter 3 we looked at the sexual abuse of children and teenagers by Catholic priests and the scandal that broke—in 2002—around that abuse. In this chapter, we will consider the scandal that tarnished the reputation of the Catholic movement and organization called Opus Dei.

In 2001, Opus Dei found itself entangled in one of the most electrifying news stories of the year. FBI agent Robert Hanssen, a long-time Opus Dei member, was arrested on charges of spying for the Russians on a scale unprecedented in American history. Not only that, but decades earlier he had confessed his espionage to an Opus Dei priest, who advised him to donate the money he had received from the Russians to the Church.

Before we examine the Robert Hanssen story in detail, however, it will be useful to look briefly at two conspiracy theories that have had worldwide impact and that reveal much about the culture of conspiracy in which we live.

The Deaths of Princess Di and JFK

In December 2006, an official British report found that the death of Princess Diana in Paris was wholly accidental. However final the report was intended to be, in the popular imagination it did little to quell the suspicion that behind her death was a conspiracy involving the British Royal Family or the House of Saud. We have seen this phenomenon before in the astonishing vitality of the conspiracy theories following President Kennedy's assassination, theories that are still thriving more than forty-five years after the event.

It was the crime of the century. President John F. Kennedy, the man who was widely held to embody the hope of a better future not only for America but for the entire free world, had been killed by a sniper in broad daylight while traveling in a motorcade through Dallas, Texas. When news of the assassination was broadcast that Friday afternoon, November 22, 1963, it was so unexpected and shocking as to be literally incomprehensible.

Within ninety minutes of the assassination, Dallas police arrested Lee Harvey Oswald, a known Communist sympathizer. Less than two days later, live on national television, Oswald himself was gunned down while being escorted out of the Dallas Police Station. Stunned, many Americans wondered if Oswald had been silenced to make certain that he never revealed he was part of a conspiracy. A week after the assassination, a Gallup poll found that only 29 percent of Americans believed that Oswald acted alone.[2]

In an effort to calm the nation, President Lyndon Johnson appointed a commission headed by Earl Warren, Chief Justice of the Supreme Court, to determine who was responsible for the assassination. In September 1964, the Warren Commission published its report, which was praised for demonstrating conclusively that Oswald alone was responsible. But in 1966, attorney Mark Lane published *Rush to Judgment*, a full-scale assault on the Warren Commission's methods and conclusions. A runaway bestseller, *Rush to Judgment* ignited a firestorm of controversy, kept blazing by thousands of other books, articles, and television programs.

In 1975, Abraham Zapruder's amateur film of President Kennedy's final moments was shown on national television. Previously, only selected frames from it had been seen when they were published as photographs. As Americans watched the film, they were shocked and horrified to see the President's head jerk violently backward after one of the shots, apparently showing that this shot had come from the "grassy knoll" in front of the limousine and not from the Texas School Book Depository where Oswald had been. The television broadcast of the Zapruder film caused such an outcry from the public that the U.S. House of Representatives set up a committee to reinvestigate the assassination.

One new piece of evidence brought the main conclusion of the Warren Report tumbling down. It came from acoustics experts who had investigated a tape recording of sounds picked up at the time of the assassination from the radio microphone of one of the motorcycle police officers in the President's motorcade. Using the latest scientific techniques, the acoustics experts claimed to have proven beyond all reasonable doubt that one of the shots had been fired from the grassy knoll.[3] In light of this new finding, the Committee concluded that Kennedy was probably assassinated as a result of a conspiracy involving a second gunman.[4]

By 1993, more than two thousand books had been written on the Kennedy assassination, most of them claiming it was a conspiracy.[5] But no number of books could compare with the impact made by Oliver Stone's blockbuster film, *JFK*.[6] Using what he called "dramatic license,"[7] Stone combined fact and fiction to create a compelling story that convinced a whole new generation that the Kennedy assassination was the work of conspirators operating at the highest levels of the U.S. government. Stone's method of interweaving hard fact and extravagant speculation would be paralleled by Dan Brown's method in *The Da Vinci Code*, with strikingly similar results. Despite attacks on its historical inaccuracies and distortions, *JKF* went on to win two Academy Awards and to be viewed by fifty million people in movie theaters.[8] Since then, it has been viewed by millions more on video and DVD.

Of course, Oliver Stone's film benefited from the deep distrust of the U.S. government that arose because of the Vietnam War, the Kent State Massacre, Watergate, and so on. Nor was this atmosphere of distrust limited to the government; it extended to virtually all institutions. In such an atmosphere, conspiracy theories are likely to cling to President Kennedy's assassination indefinitely, even though all-but-ironclad refutations of them are now available.[9] In 2003, the same year that *The Da Vinci Code* appeared, more than two-thirds of Americans believed that Lee Harvey Oswald did not act alone.[10]

Opus Dei

The Da Vinci Code portrays Opus Dei as a shadowy and sinister organization that provides a natural habitat for conspirators. There are many reasons why this portrayal resonated with readers, not the least of which is our instinctive distrust of clandestine organizations. But one reason stands out above all others—the revelation, coincident with his arrest, that Robert Hanssen, the most damaging spy in U.S. history, had been a loyal member of Opus Dei. The unwelcome publicity that Robert Hanssen brought Opus Dei is referred to early in *The Da Vinci Code*: "Of course the ultimate embarrassment had been the widely publicized trial of FBI spy Robert Hanssen, who, in addition to being a prominent member of Opus Dei, had turned out to be a sexual deviant, his trial uncovering evidence that he had rigged hidden video cameras in his own bedroom so his friends could watch him having sex with his wife. 'Hardly the pastime of a devout Catholic,' the judge had noted."[11]

What Dan Brown says here contains minor inaccuracies ("friends" should be "friend," for example), but what is striking to anyone who knows the facts is how restrained his words are. The truth is, a more sensational story could hardly be imagined.[12] Robert Hanssen worked for what has been called the world's most sophisticated counterespionage organization, the FBI. His task was to protect American security by tracking the activity of Russian agents. Yet he chose to risk all—his career, his family, his very life—to work as a double agent for Russia. Off and on for a period of twenty-two years, he spied for the Russians, selling more of his country's secrets than any other spy in American history—secrets stolen from the FBI, the CIA, the National Security Agency, and the White House.[13]

The government commission that later investigated this breach of security called the Hanssen case "possibly the worst intelligence disaster in U.S. history." What is even more alarming is the fact that, according to one inside investigator, Hanssen had nearly committed the perfect crime.[14] Among the secrets Hanssen revealed to the Russians were the names of three of their agents who had been spying for the United States. The three were eventually lured back to Moscow and executed.

When top FBI officials learned of the executions, they concluded that there must be a mole inside the Bureau. Ironically, they gave Hanssen the task of finding that mole. As if this web of intrigue were not tangled enough, it turned out that Hanssen also conspired against his own wife by secretly installing a video camera in his bedroom so that his best friend would be able to watch Hanssen and his wife having sex. Finally, he even plotted to drug his wife so that his friend could have sex with her himself.

After Hanssen was arrested for spying in 2001, his story appeared on television, in magazines and newspapers, and in several best-selling books. Called one of the most fascinating and mysterious characters in American history,[15] his story was even turned into a made-for-television movie in 2002 and a Universal Studios film in 2007. In order to understand how much damage Hanssen's story did to the popular perception of Opus Dei, it is necessary to retell that story in some detail.

Robert Hanssen was born in Chicago in 1944, the only child of Howard and Vivian Hanssen. Howard, a policeman, was a cruel disciplinarian at home, constantly abusing his son Bob verbally and physically. After Bob's arrest in 2001, psychiatrist David Charney met with him more than thirty times and concluded that Bob's betrayal of the FBI, a notoriously authoritarian institution, was largely an unconscious expression of the pent-up rage he felt toward his authoritarian father.

Bob graduated from college in 1966. Two years later, he married Bonnie Wauck. After completing a master's degree in business, he took a job in accounting, but he soon lost interest in it and decided to try law enforcement. He became a police officer and worked in the division that investigated police corruption.

This work was engaging, but not engaging enough, so he made yet another career move and, in 1976, joined the FBI.

Not long after becoming an FBI agent, Bob converted from Lutheranism to Roman Catholicism, the religion of his wife Bonnie. This was not a sudden decision. Shortly after marrying Bonnie in 1968, he had asked his mother if she would be hurt if he converted to Catholicism, and she had said no.

Bonnie came from a devout Catholic family. Both of her parents were members of Opus Dei. Her mother called Opus Dei "the best thing that ever happened to the world."[16] Bonnie and three of her seven siblings became members of Opus Dei. Bonnie's youngest brother, John, was ordained an Opus Dei priest in 1999 in a ceremony in Rome attended by Bonnie and Bob. By then, Bob himself had been a member of Opus Dei for more than two decades.

What is Opus Dei?[17] The name itself is Latin for "the work of God." A religious organization established in Spain in 1928 by a Catholic priest, Josemaría Escrivá (1902–1975), its purpose is to offer guidance and support to lay people who wish to lead lives of holiness in whatever work they do. Escrivá believed that one did not have to become a priest or a nun in order to dedicate one's life to God, one could do it in practically any line of work.

In order to stay on the right path, members are expected to attend Mass daily (not just on Sunday), to say traditional Catholic prayers daily, to confess their sins to an Opus Dei priest on a regular basis, to see a spiritual director every two weeks, and to attend various Opus Dei classes and meetings designed to keep their spiritual lives focused and energized. Father Escrivá's book, *The Way*, emphasizes the need for "blind obedience" in the spiritual warfare that characterizes the Christian life.[18]

In *The Da Vinci Code*, Silas, a "hulking albino"[19] who serves Opus Dei as an assassin, repeats Father Escrivá's slogan—"Pain is good"—like a mantra.[20] Although the severe and bloody way Silas inflicts pain on himself with a whip made of cords is clearly pathological, the idea of inflicting some pain on oneself as a discipline—traditionally called "corporal mortification"—is as old as Christianity itself. It has been understood as a means of recalling and identifying with the sufferings Christ endured for the salvation of the world.

Silas is also shown wearing a barbed chain (the cilice) around his thigh. Opus Dei members insist that it is not intended to draw blood, as it is seen to do in the case of Silas. They further point out that the practice of wearing the cilice is not confined to Opus Dei members but was done by some of the most highly regarded Christians of the twentieth century, including Archbishop Oscar Romero of San Salvador and Mother Teresa of Calcutta.

Opus Dei has about 85,000 members worldwide, including 3,000 in the United States. Members of Opus Dei fall into several different categories. Numeraries are lay men and women who live in centers such as the one in Manhattan referred to in *The Da Vinci Code*. Women numeraries, who are strictly separated from the men, do all the cooking and cleaning at these centers. There are about 16,000 numeraries worldwide, all of whom are celibate. It is interesting to note that Bob and Bonnie Hanssen's daughter Sue is a numerary and wears the cilice.[21]

Supernumeraries, who make up roughly 70 percent of Opus Dei's membership, are usually married, live in their own homes, and have professional careers. They are typically well educated and financially well off and, if possible, send their children to Opus Dei schools, which is what Bob and Bonnie did. There are also fifteen Opus Dei universities, including the one in Rome at which Bonnie's brother John teaches.

In the United States, Opus Dei has sometimes been criticized as elitist for attempting to recruit students at top universities such as Harvard and Princeton. Defenders say that if Opus Dei hopes to make its mark on the world, it has every right to recruit people who will one day have wealth and influence. Others have expressed concern that Opus Dei may be manipulating these potential recruits, who are highly vulnerable because of the stress of attending intensely competitive universities. This concern, together with Opus Dei's reputation for secrecy, especially in its financial dealings, has prompted some critics to compare it to a cult.

Opus Dei says that it is not secrecy but privacy that it wants. If so, it cannot have been pleased by Dan Brown's reference on page 1 ("Fact") to Opus Dei's newly built "$47 million National Headquarters" in Manhattan. Whether its finances are labeled "secret" or "private," however, Opus Dei is in conflict with the growing demand for public accountability and financial transparency in a world of conspiracy and corruption.

The strictness with which Opus Dei members adhere to Church teaching has often been noted. In 1999, on the fiftieth anniversary of the coming of Opus Dei to America, the *Chicago Sun-Times* made this observation: "In a world of so-called 'cafeteria Catholics' where Catholics tend to pick and choose which church rules they follow, Opus Dei members are fervent followers of the Pope and church law."[22] Pope John Paul II was a vigorous supporter of Opus Dei and presided over the ceremonies which elevated its founder, Father Escrivá, to the status of "Blessed" in 1992 and finally "Saint" in 2002. The swiftness of his canonization was extraordinary. Kenneth Woodward, former religion editor of *Newsweek*, thought it was a sign of Opus Dei's undue influence at the Vatican and called it "a scandal."[23]

Opus Dei has been criticized for being too right-wing politically. Particularly offensive to many is the fact that several government ministers in Spain under Fascist dictator Francisco

Franco were members of Opus Dei. In the United States, Opus Dei reportedly had strong ties to the Reagan Whitehouse. Today, Republican Senator Sam Brownback acknowledges Opus Dei as instrumental in his conversion to Roman Catholicism. On the U.S. Supreme Court, Justice Antonin Scalia is affiliated with Opus Dei, though he is not a member. Conservative columnist Robert Novak, best known for having exposed Valerie Plame as a CIA operative, owes his 1998 conversion to Catholicism to Opus Dei.[24]

As for Bob and Bonnie Hanssen, they were staunch Republicans who rejoiced in the elections of Ronald Reagan, George H. W. Bush, and George W. Bush to the White House, but groaned under the Presidency of Bill Clinton. It is ironic that, after his arrest, Bob Hanssen had as his defense attorney the same man, Plato Cacheris, who had defended Monica Lewinsky.

But let's return to the career of Bob Hanssen. In 1978, the same year that he became a supernumerary of Opus Dei, Bob Hanssen was transferred to the FBI's field office in New York City. In 1979, he began spying for the GRU, the Soviet military intelligence agency. After his arrest in 2001, he tried to explain why. He said that he had been unable to afford living in the New York area with his growing family—he had three children and a fourth on the way—so he decided to spy just once for the money.

Among the secrets that Bob sold to the Russians at that time was the identity of a GRU agent, Dimitri Polyakov, who had been secretly working for the FBI and the CIA as one of their top spies for seventeen years. Eventually Polyakov was brought back to Russia and executed.

Bonnie Hanssen knew nothing about her husband's work for the Russians until the day in early 1980 when she walked in on him while he was writing a letter. Taken by surprise, Bob hastily tried to conceal the letter, prompting Bonnie to ask if it was a letter to a lover. He assured her it was not, but eventually he did tell her that he had been selling secrets, though not important ones, to the Russians. Bonnie was appalled and insisted that they see Father Robert Bucciarelli, an Opus Dei priest whom she knew. In fact, Bonnie's mother had also known him when he lived in Chicago, where for ten years (1966–1976) he was the head of Opus Dei in the United States.[25]

When Bob and Bonnie met with Father Bucciarelli, Bob confessed that he had divulged FBI secrets to the Russians, for which he had been paid $30,000. At first Father Bucciarelli told Bob he would have to turn himself in to the authorities. But the very next day he called the Hanssens to say he had changed his mind. The situation could be put right, he said, if Bob simply gave all the money to the Church.[26] Relieved, the Hanssens decided to do just that.

When the news of this incident broke in 2001, some people naturally wondered if Father Bucciarelli was guilty of a crime. By not reporting Hanssen's espionage and thus enabling him to escape the law, hadn't Father Bucciarelli made himself an "accessory after the fact"? To anyone thinking along these lines, Dan Brown's portrayal of Opus Dei members involved in a criminal conspiracy can hardly have seemed far-fetched.

It must be pointed out that Father Bucciarelli was not charged under any accessory or conspiracy laws because priests in the United States enjoy a confidentiality privilege. They cannot be required to disclose what has been told to them in professional confidence. Moreover, if Hanssen's statement to Bucciarelli was part of a formal sacramental confession, then the law of the Catholic Church forbids Bucciarelli from ever revealing anything he was told. If he were to do so, he would face automatic excommunication from the Church. Nevertheless, other priests who are experts in Catholic morality have sharply criticized Father Bucciarelli for not exerting extreme pressure on Hanssen to surrender to authorities.[27]

Yet it would appear that Father Bucciarelli was not the only Catholic priest who failed to urge Hanssen to turn himself in. In 1991, while on a trip to Indianapolis, Hanssen confessed his espionage to a priest and was told to stop. He may well have done so for a time, but eventually he began again. After his arrest in 2001, Hanssen told two people who visited him that he had regularly confessed his spying to Catholic priests over a period of twenty years. This claim should not be dismissed as perhaps the attempt of a bitter man to bring others down, since Hanssen still hopes to find forgiveness and redemption in the Catholic Church.

But we need to go back to Father Bucciarelli's phone call to the Hanssens in 1980. After agreeing with Father Bucciarelli that the best solution was simply to give the money from the Russians to the Church, Bob told Bonnie that since he had already spent the money (presumably on their home), he would give monthly donations to Mother Teresa until they equaled the amount he had received. He further promised her that he would never spy again.

It is impossible to know whether he actually did make these donations, but we do know that he eventually started spying again and continued to do so, off and on, until his arrest. During this time, he sold thousands of intelligence secrets. A computer whiz, he obtained much of his information by hacking into top-secret databases.[28] He disclosed the methods, plans, and the latest technology being used by the FBI, the CIA, and the NSA to eavesdrop on Russian intelligence. Among the secrets he sold was one that is particularly alarming in light of the 9/11 terrorist attacks—the secret locations to which the President, the Vice

President, and other top government officials are to be taken in the event of a national emergency.

Bob Hanssen seemed an unlikely spy. Although he had computer skills, he had little else in the eyes of his colleagues. Above all, he lacked social skills, and this probably accounts in large part for his failure to gain the promotions for which he was otherwise well qualified. In conversation, he came across as moralizing and as having an agenda—to persuade people to go to church or to Opus Dei meetings. He became the butt of office jokes, and his sallow complexion, dark hair, and habitual black suits earned him the nicknames "The Mortician," "Dr. Death," and "Dr. Doom." In short, he came across as a deadly dull bureaucrat.

Bob's reputation fared better among his neighbors. In the Virginia suburb where he and Bonnie eventually settled, the Hanssens were admired as a model of family values. True, Bob was not very sociable, and to have to listen to his monologues on computer technology was a fate worse than death, but still he was regarded as a loving husband and a fine father, who with Bonnie raised six wonderful children, three boys and three girls.

All the children attended Opus Dei schools. The boys attended The Heights and the girls attended Oakcrest. The principal of Oakcrest thought Bob was "the most chivalrous man I ever met" and "a perfect gentleman."[29] But of course, Bonnie deserves most of the credit for the glowing image the family had among everyone who knew them. A loving wife and devoted mother, Bonnie was also pretty, vivacious, and sociable on every occasion. In addition to teaching part time at Oakcrest, she often led meetings at her church.

Having Bonnie as his wife filled Bob with joy, but it was the kind of joy a man feels after winning a coveted trophy and displaying it for the admiration of others. But in this case, the display involved another act of betrayal. Starting in 1970, two years after their marriage, Bonnie allowed her husband to take photos of her naked, including ones that were pornographic. He told her that photographing her fulfilled a personal fantasy of his. She did not know that they would also fulfill the fantasies of another man, Jack Hoschouer.

Jack had been Bob's friend since high school days. Although Bob had no brothers or sisters, Jack was "closer than a brother." Jack had been the best man at Bob's wedding. In 1970, Jack was serving in Vietnam when out of the blue he received a packet of photos of Bonnie, with a note from Bob telling him they were intended to boost his morale. At first Jack objected, but his objections soon gave way to his desires. Jack continued to receive photos from Bob long after the war had ended, and long after he had returned home to his wife.

Through the years, Jack regularly visited Bob. He always came without his wife. Bob loved spending time with Jack, but Bonnie felt uncomfortable with him. In 1987, Bob decided to take his fantasies to a new level. Bonnie would now be the unwitting star of a live sex show. When Jack visited that year, Bob arranged for him to hide outside the master bedroom window at night and watch Bonnie having sex with him. A few years later, Bob had an even better idea. He secretly hooked up a video camera in the bedroom so that Jack could watch the couple on closed-circuit television. But Bob's betrayal of Bonnie had still not reached its limit.

As the father of six, Bob felt sorry for Jack because his wife could not have children, so in 1997 he concocted a scheme. He sent an email to Jack, then living in Europe, suggesting that Jack obtain a drug that was illegal in the United States but legal in Europe—Rohypnol (better known today as "roofies," a date-rape drug). If Jack could get it, Bob said, then on his next visit he could drug Bonnie and impregnate her without her ever knowing. Jack could then have a secret son whom he could see every time he visited. Although Jack did go to the Netherlands to confirm that the drug was available, he never followed through with the scheme. As has often been pointed out, in Bob's betrayal of his wife, he demonstrated the same pattern of treachery he had shown toward his country.

The story of Robert Hanssen is so intriguing in part because it is a puzzle that resists any simple solution. Father C. John McCloskey, an eminent Opus Dei priest in Washington D.C. who knew the Hanssens, criticized Bob's espionage severely and at the same time called him a truly pious man. For the purposes of this book, that paradoxical judgment must stand as the last word on the bafflingly complex character of Robert Hanssen.

The end of Hanssen's career can be summarized briefly. He was arrested by FBI agents on February 18, 2001. On July 6, he pleaded guilty to more than a dozen counts of espionage, attempted espionage, and conspiracy. On May 10, 2002, he was sentenced to life in prison without the possibility of parole. Attorney General John Ashcroft and Defense Secretary Donald Rumsfeld originally wanted the death penalty, but in the end a plea bargain was reached, according to which Hanssen would plead guilty and then disclose to the FBI and CIA the full extent of his espionage. It was hoped that these disclosures would help to rebuild an intelligence system that Hanssen had reduced to rubble.

When the story broke, it was reported that he had been spying since 1985. His fervent Catholicism and membership in Opus Dei was also mentioned as a part of the enigma that was his life. But what the FBI did not know at that time was the story of the Hanssens' meeting with Father Bucciarelli in 1980, establishing that the spying had begun a full five years earlier. That story exploded into the news on June 16, 2001 after Bonnie recounted it to authorities. Many who had previously been willing to look upon Opus Dei with sympathy as an organization that had been betrayed by Hanssen now began to think of Opus Dei itself as somehow complicit in an act of treason.

Early in 2002, Bonnie was contacted by Opus Dei in Rome and asked not to make any public statements about her husband. No doubt the publicity being given to Robert Hanssen's membership in Opus Dei would have been unwelcome at any time, but it was especially unwelcome at this time, since the Pope had announced that Josemaría Escrivá would be officially declared a saint in October, an announcement which itself had already stirred controversy. But it was the story of Robert Hanssen that brought Opus Dei into the media spotlight in a way that had never happened before and would not happen again until the publication of *The Da Vinci Code.*

Chapter 6

Classic Voices in American Religion:
Thomas Jefferson, Ralph Waldo Emerson, and William James

> Langdon smiled. "Sophie, every faith in the world is based
> on fabrication. That is the definition of faith—acceptance of
> that which we imagine to be true, that which we cannot prove.
> Every religion describes God through metaphor, allegory,
> and exaggeration, from the early Egyptians through mod-
> ern Sunday school. Metaphors are a way to help our minds
> process the unprocessible. The problems arise when we be-
> gin to believe literally in our own metaphors."
>
> *The Da Vinci Code, 341–42*

American history provides countless examples of individuals who shaped the religious attitudes of the American
people. For this chapter, I have chosen three whose voices are
classic: Thomas Jefferson, Ralph Waldo Emerson, and William
James. Even though they were exceptionally cosmopolitan in
their learning, experience, and outlook, they are viewed from
outside the United States as being quintessentially American
because they devoted all their worldly wisdom to achieving one
supreme goal—nourishing a fledgling nation which they hoped
would carry civilization to new and unprecedented heights.

Europe, by contrast, although it too was trying to advance the cause of civilization, appeared to them to lie partially buried beneath the rubble of decayed institutions, primitive customs, and unenlightened beliefs. To the European masses, the ancient Christian teaching that only God could redeem humanity from its desperate plight seemed all too true. But to the men we are about to consider, it seemed as though God had made a new beginning on the other side of the Atlantic.

This feeling was present from the nation's birth and is reflected in the great seal of the United States which was chosen by the founding fathers and is now engraved on every dollar bill. The seal bears the Latin motto, *Novus Ordo Seclorum,* "The New Order of the Ages." For the first eighteen centuries of its existence, the Christian religion taught that all of humanity needed to be redeemed by God. But now, in America, it was as if God had given one portion of humanity the opportunity to redeem itself. The fullness of time had come. This lofty vision could almost be called "the American religion," with Jefferson, Emerson, and James three of its greatest prophets. For many Americans, the ideals they championed define the essence of what it means to be an American today.

This chapter will attempt to show that some of the claims in *The Da Vinci Code* that drew sharp criticism from Church leaders had long been ingrained in the American psyche, due largely to the influence of our three protagonists.

For all three men, religion was a living, vibrant thing—a source of well-being for the individual and society. But in their view, the Christian churches, with their creeds and dogmas, had drained the sap out of religion, leaving a petrified forest in its place. All three regarded the Christian creeds and dogmas as profound misunderstandings of the message of Jesus and would have agreed wholeheartedly with Dan Brown's Robert Langdon that "problems arise when we begin to believe literally in our own metaphors." In their day, Jefferson, Emerson, and James each endeavored to restore the true meaning of religion and, by so doing, to foster a spiritual freedom consonant with the political freedom of the new nation.

Thomas Jefferson (1743–1826)

The ideas of Thomas Jefferson did more to shape the American form of government than those of any other individual in the nation's history, bar none. Abraham Lincoln said that Jefferson's principles were nothing less than "the definitions and axioms of free society."[1] But Jefferson's achievements extended far beyond government. When President Kennedy addressed the forty-nine Nobel Laureates he invited to the White House in 1962, he wittily remarked that they represented the "most extraordinary collection of talent, of human knowledge, that has ever been gathered together at the White House, with the possible exception of when Thomas Jefferson dined alone."

But Jefferson's dazzling brilliance has often been overshadowed in recent years by charges of sexism and racism, especially over his role as a slaveholder who (as has generally been accepted since 2000)[2] fathered several children by one of his slaves, Sally Hemings. For our purposes, however, those aspects of his complex personality must be passed over.

Jefferson died at the age of 83 on July 4, 1826, the fiftieth anniversary of the Declaration of Independence, which he penned. A few months earlier, he had requested that the following simple words be inscribed on his tombstone: "Here was buried Thomas Jefferson, author of the Declaration of Independence and of the Virginia Statute for Religious Freedom, and Father of the University of Virginia." I will examine each of these achievements in the light of Jefferson's religious thought.

Jefferson's original draft of the Declaration of Independence contained only two references to God, as "Creator" and as "Nature's God." (In their revision, his colleagues at the Continental Congress in Philadelphia added two others at the end: "the supreme judge of the world" and "divine providence.") Jefferson referred to God in order to justify to the world the rejection of British rule by the American people, whose God-given rights to "life, liberty and the pursuit of happiness" had been systematically denied by King George III.

In speaking of God, Jefferson had ample opportunity to refer to Jesus Christ, but did not. His primary reason was political—to include the widest possible range of belief within the purview of the new and religiously diverse nation.[3] But while the Declaration of Independence is one of the most momentous *political* documents in history, its importance as a declaration of *religious* independence should not be overlooked.

Jefferson testified to that significance in his last letter, written eight days before his death. The Declaration of Independence, he said, had been a clarion call to people everywhere "to burst the chains under which monkish ignorance and superstition had persuaded them to bind themselves."[4] The same sentiment underlay the words Jefferson wrote in 1800 and which are now engraved around the inside of the dome of the Jefferson Memorial in Washington D.C.: "For I have sworn on the altar of God eternal hostility against every form of tyranny over the mind of man." As the letter from which these words were taken shows, Jefferson was thinking above all of religious tyranny, which he regarded as the foundation of every other.[5]

The second achievement for which Jefferson wanted to be remembered was the Virginia Statute for Religious Freedom. Its background is as follows. The Church of England had been the established Church in Virginia since 1624, if not earlier. Although Jefferson had been raised an Anglican, his reading in philosophy while in his twenties caused him to lose his faith in Jesus' virgin birth, his resurrection from the dead, and his divinity. Jefferson's abandonment of these beliefs was not only heretical but also dangerous. Under Virginia law, those found guilty of rejecting the Christian faith could be sentenced to three years in prison and risked losing custody of their children permanently. Even Christian "dissenters" (Presbyterians, Baptists, and other non-Anglicans) could be prosecuted.

Some Virginia legislators wanted to do away with legal penalties for dissenters and to grant them toleration for as long as it pleased the state to do so. For Jefferson, this was not enough. Religious freedom, he contended, was not something the state could grant or take away as it pleased. It was a natural right. The state had no business prescribing any specific religion or religion in general. Individuals must not be coerced even if they are atheists. As Jefferson stated in his bill, "Almighty God hath created the mind free . . . [and] being Lord of both body and mind, [he] chose not to propagate [our religion] by coercions on either, as was in his Almighty power to do, but to extend it by its influence on reason alone." The last clause, with its assumption that reason is the ultimate authority in deciding whether to accept or reject the claims of religion, was characteristic of Jefferson but offended many in the Virginia Senate, who deleted that statement from the final version.[6]

Although Jefferson originally drafted his statute in 1777, it met powerful opposition from supporters of the established Church and was not passed until 1786. When it finally did pass, Jefferson told his friend James Madison that Virginia had achieved something that Europeans could only dream of—religious freedom from the slavery of "kings, priests, and nobles."[7]

Jefferson also defended religious freedom in his only book, *Notes on the State of Virginia* (1787). One statement in particular created an uproar among the clergy: "It does me no injury for my neighbor to say there are twenty gods, or no God. It neither picks my pocket nor breaks my leg."[8] A typical indignant response came from a minister in New York: "Let my neighbor once perceive . . . that there is no God, and he will soon pick my pocket and break not only my *leg* but my *neck*."[9]

Such indignation did not fade with time. When Jefferson ran for the presidency against the incumbent John Adams thirteen years later, religious and political opponents were quick to sound the alarm that Jefferson was an atheist. One leading newspaper stated that there were two choices in the election, either "God and a religious President" or "Jefferson and no God."[10]

Despite these charges, Jefferson went on to become the third President of the United States (1801–1809). A public letter he wrote while President provides a succinct statement of his understanding of the relation of the federal government to organized religion. Referring to the words in the First Amendment to the Constitution ("Congress shall make no law respecting an establishment of religion, or prohibiting the free exercise thereof"), Jefferson declared that the First Amendment had built "a wall of separation between church and State."[11]

An even clearer reflection of Jefferson's mind in its full breadth and depth is, of course, the University of Virginia, which received its state charter in 1819 and opened in 1825 with Jefferson as its first rector. Jefferson's idea in founding it was remarkable in many ways, not least in its independence of any religion or church. (The University of Virginia did not even have a chaplain.)[12] This independence made its founding strikingly different from such predecessors as Harvard, Yale, Princeton, and Jefferson's own alma mater, William and Mary, all of which had been founded by religious groups. By contrast, the University of Virginia reflects Jefferson's commitment to the separation of Church and State, to religious liberty for all, and to the intrinsic value of secular learning.[13]

Jefferson's personal religious beliefs were not intended for public consumption. Even as a young man, he had already realized that his hcretical opinions could thwart his political ambitions, and throughout his life he insisted that his friends not disclose them to others. As we have seen, he rejected the fundamental beliefs set out in the ancient Christian creeds, beginning with the belief that Jesus is the divine Son of God. Jefferson called the creeds "the bane and ruin of the Christian church." In his judgment, they were the invention of corrupt churchmen more interested in their own worldly power than in the teaching of Jesus, and they had had disastrous consequences throughout history. In one of his letters he wrote, "On the dogmas of religion, as distinguished from moral principles, all mankind, from the beginning of the world to this day, have been quarreling, fighting, burning and torturing one another, for abstractions unintelligible to themselves and to all others, and absolutely beyond the comprehension of the human mind."[14]

Jefferson was influenced in his views by *The History of the Corruptions of Christianity* (1782) by Joseph Priestley, a renowned scientist (the discoverer of oxygen) and champion of Unitarianism, which also rejected the doctrines of Christ's divinity and the Trinity. Jefferson predicted that such views would come to be shared by all Americans. In his old age, he wrote to a Unitarian minister: "I rejoice that in this blessed country of free inquiry and belief, which has surrendered its creed and conscience to neither kings nor priests, the genuine doctrine of only one God is reviving, and I trust there is not a young man now living who will not die an Unitarian."[15]

Jefferson saw in Jesus the best and wisest man who ever lived, but not one who was God incarnate. Thus, to a surprising degree, Jefferson's view coincides with that of Dan Brown's Leigh Teabing, who calls Jesus "a great and powerful man, but a *man* nonetheless. A mortal." Teabing then goes on to tell Sophie

Neveu: "Many scholars claim that the early Church literally *stole* Jesus from His original followers, hijacking His human message, shrouding it in an impenetrable cloak of divinity, and using it to expand their own power."[16] For Enlightenment thinkers such as Jefferson, the idea that God became incarnate in the man Jesus at a particular moment in history, in an obscure outpost of the Roman Empire, was plainly absurd. God was God of the whole world. Not only that, but the European Age of Discovery (c. 1400–1650) had revealed a world vaster than Christians had ever imagined, one in which the name of Jesus Christ was virtually unknown. Was three-quarters of the human race damned to hell for never having heard the Gospel message?

Not unlike Leigh Teabing, Jefferson believed that the original message of Jesus had been corrupted, not only by churchmen ambitious for worldly power, but also by the biblical authors themselves, who were prone to superstition and irrationality. Jefferson considered the Book of Revelation, for example, to be nothing but "the ravings of a maniac."[17] Since Jefferson believed that the truth about Jesus' words and deeds had been grossly distorted, he decided to make his own briefer version of the Gospels, with all the distortions removed.

To begin with, Jefferson believed that the stories of Jesus' virgin birth, his miracles, and his resurrection from the dead all had to be jettisoned as preposterous fabrications. For Jefferson, they would have qualified as examples of what Robert Langdon was referring to in *The Da Vinci Code* when he said, "Every religion describes God through metaphor, allegory, and exaggeration. . . . The problems arise when we begin to believe literally in our own metaphors."[18] In order to recover the genuine words of Jesus from the four Gospels, Jefferson cut out—literally, with a razor—everything that was not genuine.

He undertook this task with boundless confidence that he

could recognize the authentic teachings of Jesus by their outstanding excellence. So he set about, as he put it, "abstracting what is really his from the rubbish in which it is buried, easily distinguished by its luster from the dross of his biographers, and as separable from that as the diamond from the dung hill."[19] He thought of his work as being similar to that of Jesus, which he described as a recovery of the authentic teachings of Judaism from the rubbish in which the Pharisees had buried it.

The Jesus who finally emerges from Jefferson's Bible is a supremely wise moral teacher who gave to the world precepts which remain, in Jefferson's words, "the most pure, benevolent, and sublime which have ever been preached to man."[20] Despite his denial of Jesus' divinity, Jefferson regarded himself as a Christian. "To the corruptions of Christianity I am, indeed, opposed, but not to the genuine precepts of Jesus himself. I am a Christian," he wrote in 1823, "in the only sense in which I believe Jesus wished any one to be: sincerely attached to his doctrines in preference to all others; ascribing to himself every human excellence, and believing he never claimed any other."[21]

If Jesus was not the divine Son of God, there can be no Trinity, and this is precisely what Jefferson affirmed. He once expressed his views thus: "Ideas must be distinct before reason can act upon them, and no man ever had a distinct idea of the trinity. It is the mere Abracadabra of the mountebanks calling themselves priests of Jesus."[22] He once went so far as to liken the notion of the Trinity to Cerberus, the dog who, according to ancient mythology, had one body and three heads.[23]

Believing as he did that the Creator had bestowed revelation upon people in every time and place, Jefferson sought wisdom not only from Jesus but from other great teachers of the past. Choosing insights from his exceptionally wide reading, he combined them to create a philosophy all his own. His favorite philosopher was the Greek thinker Epicurus (341–270 BC), whose philosophy he regarded as the most rational of all those handed down by the ancients.[24] Among the teachings of Epicurus that Jefferson most admired are these: happiness is the aim of life, virtue is the foundation of happiness, and human beings are free agents. In light of the last of these teachings, it is no wonder that Jefferson repudiated the classical Christian doctrines of the Fall and Original Sin,[25] according to which the sin of Adam and Eve had disastrous consequences for all their descendants, radically reducing their freedom to do good.

The ideas of the Fall and Original Sin have loomed so large in the history of Christian doctrine that it is worth examining them further. The interpretation of the Fall and Original Sin given by the Protestant Reformer John Calvin (1509–1564) was exceptionally harsh. According to Calvin, humanity is enslaved to sin and no longer free to choose or to do what is good. Even seemingly virtuous acts are in fact evil because they proceed from a corrupt heart. Humanity's corruption extends to its ability to reason, so that it is no longer able to know God and God's will from the divine order of creation. To this state, called "total depravity," the only appropriate response is shame and self-loathing.

In Calvinist thought, because God's sovereignty is absolute, God must have willed the Fall and all its consequences. But God also willed the coming of Jesus Christ the Savior, thus revealing the divine mercy. From all eternity, God predestined each and every human being to either salvation or damnation. Nothing they do can alter the divine decree. Moreover, for those predestined to damnation, God predestined not only their damnation but also the sin that leads to their damnation.

Jefferson reacted to Calvin's teaching with abhorrence. Such a God, Jefferson said, is nothing more than "a demon of malignant spirit." Jefferson once said that any attempt to have a rational discussion with someone like Calvin would be pointless. For someone like that there is only one solution: "the strait jacket."[26]

Although he scorned Calvin's doctrine of total depravity, Jefferson was not blind to humanity's corruption and proneness to error. But instead of regarding them as an inheritance from Adam and Eve, he saw them as the results of ignorance, prejudice, and superstition, all of which could be remedied by the proper development of those powers of freedom and rationality with which human beings were naturally endowed by their Creator. Thus education and self-discipline assumed paramount importance for Jefferson because they had the power to mold virtuous individuals, whose lives would be marked by loving service to others, the surest sign that one was following Jesus faithfully.

Jefferson once said that he was his own religious sect,[27] but this is misleading. Other founding fathers, including George Washington, Benjamin Franklin, and James Madison, shared his essential beliefs in Jesus as the greatest ethical teacher, though not divine; in a world created by God with a moral order that reason could apprehend; in free will unencumbered by original sin; in rewards both here and hereafter for a life of virtue; and in the role of the churches in promoting the ethical teachings of Jesus, without which American society could not survive.[28]

Here, for example, is what Benjamin Franklin wrote about his own beliefs a few weeks before his death in 1790:

> As to Jesus of Nazareth, my opinion of whom you particularly desire, I think the system of morals and religion, as he left them to us, the best the world ever saw or is likely to see; but I apprehend it has received various corrupting changes, and I have, with most of the present dissenters in England, some doubts as to his

divinity, tho' it is a question I do not dogmatize upon, having never studied it, and I think it needless to busy myself with it now, when I expect soon an opportunity of knowing the truth with less trouble. I see no harm, however, in its being believed, if that belief has the good consequence, as probably it has, of making his doctrines more respected and better observed.[29]

For all his eloquence, Jefferson could hardly have put it better.

Comparing Thomas Jefferson with Robert Langdon, not to mention Leigh Teabing, is odd—to say the least. But it is still worth considering whether the attitudes toward religion in *The Da Vinci Code* did not resonate with many American readers in part because those attitudes had already been implanted by Jefferson. Jeffersonian ideas that may have resonated with Dan Brown's American readers include the following: that education can help us realize that genuine spiritual insight is not the exclusive domain of Christians but is found among all peoples; that reason and common sense can dispel superstition and enable us to recognize Jesus as a real human being; and finally, that the language of creeds and dogmas distorts our understanding of Jesus and, historically, has been made the basis for needless schisms, conflicts, and wars. Of course, most Americans would not go so far as Jefferson and Langdon do and deny Jesus' divinity. Yet many would agree that the Christian churches, including their own, have distorted his basic message in one way or another.

Finally, Jefferson has one other link to the ideas in *The Da Vinci Code*. One of his many inventions was so ingenious that it was not surpassed until the twentieth century: a decoding device.

Ralph Waldo Emerson (1803–1882)

"The genius of Emerson remains the genius of America: he established our authentic religion, which is post-Protestant while pretending otherwise."[30] Such is the judgment of the great American literary critic Harold Bloom, who has stated elsewhere that Emerson's doctrine of self-reliance is "the fundamental premise of the American Religion."[31] In this section, we will attempt to see how far Bloom's insights can explain the religious appeal of *The Da Vinci Code*.

Emerson's background may be summarized briefly. He studied at both Harvard College and Harvard Divinity School, became a Unitarian minister and, in 1829, was appointed pastor of the Second Church of Boston. Later that year, he married. But in 1831, after only little more than a year of marriage, his wife died of tuberculosis. Emerson's grief and loneliness may have contributed to his growing sense that all that mattered—all that was real—was one's personal relationship with God.

Over the next decade he would suffer the further loss of two beloved brothers, also to tuberculosis, and the supreme loss of his five-year-old son from his second marriage. The fact that he eventually recovered from these devastating losses must have seemed to him nothing short of miraculous, and one of the outstanding characteristics of his writings is his unshakeable faith in the power of the human spirit to triumph over whatever tragedies and hardships life may bring.

But back in 1832, while still mourning the loss of his first wife, Emerson gave up his pastorate and went on a ten-month tour of Europe, from which he would return with renewed sense of purpose to begin a career as an essayist and lecturer. The effect of Emerson's European tour was not what might have been expected. He was not overawed by the magnificent achievements of European culture. Rather, he felt confident that in time American culture could equal them. He reveled in his native land, with its newness and freedom and limitless possibilities. It was a country, he said, that "has no past: all has an onward and prospective look."[32] As the distinguished scholar Jaroslav

Pelikan observed, "The American commonwealth became his one holy catholic and apostolic church."[33]

Even as a minister, Emerson had begun to doubt the purpose of church affiliations, including his own. In his 30s and 40s, he went even further and began to see the basic notion of church tradition—understood as the body of beliefs and practices handed down from previous generations—as dead and deadly, lifeless and crushing the life out of those from whom it demanded obedience. So far as he was concerned, to speak in the mummified language of Christian tradition was to speak "as if God were dead."[34]

As to the Christian creeds, they transmitted "a disease of the intellect."[35] Emerson encouraged people to seek their own direct experience of revelation: "The foregoing generations beheld God and nature face to face; we, through their eyes. Why should not we also enjoy an original relation to the universe? Why should not we have a poetry and philosophy of insight and not of tradition, and a religion by revelation to us, and not the history of theirs?"[36]

But where was such revelation to be found? Not in the established churches. Rather, it was to be found by turning inward. "God builds his temple in the heart on the ruins of churches & religions."[37] The voice of God could be heard within; it did not have to be mediated by priests and prophets. "It is by yourself without ambassador that God speaks to you."[38] Tradition, by contrast, works against this inner voice: "The centuries are conspirators against the sanity and authority of the soul."[39] Every human being has the capacity to consciously share in the divinity of the universal mind, described by Emerson as the "one who is the life of things & from whose creative will our life & the life of all creatures flows every moment, wave after wave, like the successive beams that every moment issue from the Sun."[40]

In a journal entry from 1837 he even went so far as to write, "I behold with awe & delight many illustrations of the One Universal Mind. I see my being embedded in it. As a plant in the earth so I grow in God. I am only a form of him. He is the soul of Me. I can even with a mountainous aspiring say, *I am God.*"[41]

To grasp the meaning of this startling claim, it will be helpful to listen to what Emerson says about the divinity of Jesus in his address a year later to the graduating class of the Harvard Divinity School:

> Jesus Christ belonged to the true race of prophets. He saw with open eye the mystery of the soul. Drawn by its severe harmony, ravished with its beauty, he lived in it, and had his being there. Alone in all history he estimated the greatness of man. One man was true to what is in you and me. He saw that God incarnates himself in man, and evermore goes forth anew to take possession of his World. He said, in this jubilee of sublime emotion, "I am divine. Through me, God acts; through me, speaks. Would you see God, see me; or, see thee, when thou also thinkest as I now think."[42]

Emerson believed that when Jesus laid claim to a divine nature, he was inviting his followers to do the same. He never wanted them to build cathedrals of stone in his memory. But in its blindness, historical Christianity did just that, all but burying his name beneath cold and formal titles that make him seem distant, remote, almost inhuman. Emerson says, "The fear of degrading the character of Jesus by representing him as a man" is a sure sign of "the falsehood of our theology."[43] How did this come about? In short, because the rich, poetic language that Jesus used to express the inexpressible was taken literally. As Emerson says, "The idioms of his language and the figures of his rhetoric have usurped the place of his truth; and churches are not built on his principles, but on his tropes. Christianity became a Mythus, as the poetic teaching of Greece and Egypt before."[44] These sentiments are echoed in the words of Dan Brown's hero, Robert Langdon, quoted at the beginning of this chapter.

Emerson goes on to say in his "Divinity School Address" that historical Christianity has been utterly corrupted by its "noxious exaggeration about the *person* of Jesus,"[45] whereas in fact "it is by his holy thoughts [that] Jesus serves us, and thus only."[46] Emerson praises Jesus as a wise and inspired teacher. But the churches, by insisting that Jesus is the world's one and only Savior, have robbed us not only of the real teachings of Jesus, but also of the spiritual insights of other religious teachers who have been dismissed as valueless or worse.

Emerson was a disciple of Jesus and a disciple of many other wise and inspired teachers, from Goethe to Plato to the Buddha. (Emerson was involved in one of the earliest projects to publish the Buddhist Scriptures in America.)[47] The method employed by all these teachers was not to lay down doctrines and dogmas but to awaken in us a sense of the divine that flows through all things, including our own souls. Fullness of life comes from within, by a process of self-realization. You must discover your authentic self, your true identity. (And here we may pause to note that Dan Brown's entire novel traces Sophie Neveu's slow and painstaking discovery of her true identity.) For Emerson, conformity to any church, to any religion, is life-threatening. What you must always remember, he says, is this: "Nothing is at last sacred but the integrity of your own mind."

Emerson launched a second American Revolution, but it was to overthrow *spiritual* tyrants. The revolution was fought on multiple fronts. On one, Emerson battled against the dominant scientific worldview associated with the name of Isaac Newton. Here Emerson's judgment was in sharp contrast with that of

Jefferson, who saw in Newton the supreme example of the power of reason to dispel the darkness and shadows of ignorance.

To Emerson, the price of Newton's achievement had been too great. It was nothing less than the sacrifice of poetry and feelings, of the imagination and the heart. Newtonian physics had reduced humanity to insignificance in a vast, impersonal, mechanistic universe. The principle which guided Emerson's struggle on this front was the dignity—indeed, the divinity—of the self. In its divine power of intuition, the self had an instrument for comprehending a universe—the spiritual universe far greater in its dimensions and its beauty than the material universe comprehended by Newton's theories.

The same principle of the divine self guided Emerson's struggle with historical Christianity. Emerson pronounced Roman Catholicism—with its demand for submission of mind and will to the authority of the pope—a kind of "despotism."[48] This despotism was made worse by the Church's long history of aligning itself with political power. (This, of course, is a major theme of *The Da Vinci Code*.) Emerson regarded the Church as un-American: "It is the political character of the Roman Church that makes it incompatible with our institutions, & unwelcome here."[49] Submission to papal authority also contradicted Emerson's fundamental belief in nonconformity as essential to the life of the spirit.

As a New Englander, however, Emerson was more concerned to resist the type of Christianity the Puritans had brought to America, which was strongly influenced by John Calvin. Emerson shared Jefferson's utter disdain for the Calvinist doctrine of humanity's total depravity and considered it blasphemous.[50] He believed that every human being possesses an innate capacity for truth which needs only to be awakened from slumber. Once awakened, it guides our inner life to truth, goodness, and beauty.

Emerson thus repudiated the teaching that Original Sin

was a kind of fatal illness all have inherited from Adam. In his view, the real illness was not Original Sin but Christian theology: "Our young people are diseased with the theological problems of Original Sin, origin of evil, predestination, and the like. These never presented a practical difficulty to any man—never darkened across any man's road, who did not go out of his way to seek them."[51] Emerson's conviction that we have God within means that we have no need of a redeemer. We have the capacity to redeem ourselves.

Of course, for Emerson, as for Robert Langdon in *The Da Vinci Code*, the Church is not the only institution which poisons the spirit. Emerson thought all institutions and indeed Western civilization itself had this effect because of their strong tendency to disregard the individual and neglect the spiritual dimension of life. Like Karl Marx, he was appalled by the ravages of capitalism, which he saw firsthand in his travels in England, and he was concerned that the same catastrophe could befall America.

For Dan Brown's Robert Langdon, by contrast, the chief problem with civilization is male dominance. Langdon regards the patriarchal structure of Western civilization, with its relentless efforts to crush the feminine principle, as the source of a pathological imbalance in the human spirit: "The male ego had spent two millennia running unchecked by its female counterpart. The Priory of Sion believed that it was this obliteration of the sacred feminine in modern life that had caused what the Hopi Native Americans called *koyanisquatsi*—'life out of balance'— an unstable situation marked by testosterone-fueled wars, a plethora of misogynistic societies, and a growing disrespect for Mother Earth."[52] Although Emerson and Langdon differ in their diagnoses, these "Harvard men" agree that Western civilization suffers from a chronic spiritual illness.

Another theme emphasized in the writings of Emerson *and*

in *The Da Vinci Code* is that feelings are not peripheral to re-ligious experience—but central. Feelings are signs and instru-ments of our coming into contact with that divine spirit which pervades all things. There is no better expression of this in *The Da Vinci Code* than its closing lines:

> Like the murmurs of spirits in the darkness, forgotten words echoed. *The quest for the Holy Grail is the quest to kneel before the bones of Mary Magdalene. A journey to pray at the feet of the outcast one.*
> With a sudden upwelling of reverence, Robert Langdon fell to his knees.
> For a moment, he thought he heard a woman's voice . . . the wisdom of the ages . . . whispering up from the chasms of the earth.

This epiphany and all the emotions that accompany it mark the culmination of the novel.

The authors of what has been called "the definitive debunk-ing"[53] of *The Da Vinci Code* have accused Dan Brown of cyni-cally playing upon a widespread "distrust with all authority, es-pecially religious authority. . . . Added to these suspicions is an appeal to individualism and the exaltation of the experiential. In negative terms, this means a renouncement of doctrine, dogma, and rules; positively, it is the celebration of self and 'my truth.' Emotion is the preferred guide to spirituality." And where is the reader brought to in the end? To "the worship of the self."[54]

It is interesting to note that in his own day Emerson was the target of strikingly similar criticism. One Harvard professor said of Emerson that he "preached a doctrine which leads man to worship his own nature and himself."[55] Yet this was not at all the impression he made on those who knew him, who referred repeatedly to his deep humility, steadfast courage, and immense integrity. Oliver Wendell Holmes, for example, wrote of him after his death: "Judged by his life Emerson comes very near our best ideal of humanity. . . . What he taught others to be, he was himself. His deep and sweet humanity won him love and reverence everywhere among those whose natures were capable of responding to the highest manifestations of character."[56]

The existence of two such diametrically opposed assessments of Emerson by his contemporaries raises the fundamental question: Did Emerson present Americans with a radiant and original vision of truth, or merely the most beguiling and pernicious of falsehoods? Your answer to this question, I suspect, will be a good indicator as to whether you shouted "Yes!" as you read some of Robert Langdon's speeches—or wanted to soak the novel in gasoline and set it on fire.

William James (1842–1910)

When William James was two months old, his father brought Emerson to see him, and Emerson blessed the infant in his cradle. As William grew up, Emerson often stayed at the James family home in the room his brother Henry, the future novelist, called "Mr. Emerson's room."[57] Through this family connection as well as through his writings, Emerson influenced William James profoundly.

Among the beliefs of Emerson which most influenced James were the supreme importance of personal experience and the deadly peril of institutional conformity. These beliefs were highlighted in the formal tribute James paid to Emerson's memory at the centenary celebration of his birth, in 1903: "The matchless eloquence with which Emerson proclaimed the sovereignty of the living individual electrified and emancipated his generation, and this bugle-blast will doubtless be regarded by future critics as the soul of his message. The present man is the aboriginal reality, the Institution is derivative, and the past man is irrelevant and obliterate for present issues."[58]

James absorbed the ideas of Emerson and of many others and gave them the stamp of his own creative intelligence. One scholar summarized his achievement by saying that he had "formulated in terms of a sophisticated philosophy the essential ideas and convictions of his countrymen."[59] James's friend and fellow professor of philosophy at Harvard, Josiah Royce, remarked that James's philosophy, with its pragmatic outlook on life, is typically American. "It is the spirit of the frontiersman, of the gold seeker, or the home-builder, transferred to the metaphysical and to the religious realm." James both embodied and shaped American attitudes toward religion and life, and may be regarded as a worthy successor of Jefferson and Emerson.

As a young man, James studied at the Lawrence Scientific School at Harvard before entering Harvard Medical School, from which he graduated in 1869. But his studies had drained him to the point that he fell into a deep depression. James identified the cause of his illness as his obsession with science's materialistic worldview, which regarded all of life, including mental life, as nothing more than physical processes. To James this implied that human freedom was an illusion and that life was ultimately meaningless.

He tried desperately to persuade himself of the reality of free will, only to find that the rational arguments against free will were equally valid. James felt trapped in a kind of paralysis of mind. At times he was suicidal. But then he came across the writings of the French philosopher Charles Renouvier (1815–1903), where he found the statement that free will is "'the sustaining of a thought *because I choose to* when I might have other thoughts.'"

This idea set James free. He realized that he no longer needed to find a rational justification for believing in free will. He wrote in his diary on the day he read Renouvier's statement: "My first act of free will shall be to believe in free will."[60] On this basis, he was able to build a philosophy for living: one can choose a belief, act on it, and by so doing add something new and original to the world. Such an accomplishment would itself be sufficient proof of the reality of freedom. Renouvier had revealed to James that philosophy was a method not of arriving at certain knowledge but of coping with life. It would become for James the gospel of life he would preach to the world.

But James did not imagine he now had a license to believe anything. Belief is analogous to a scientific hypothesis, to be tested by its correspondence with life. It should correspond with both our previous experience and our ongoing experience, and give them coherence: "The only test of probable truth is what works best in the way of leading us, what fits every part of life best and combines with the collectivity of life's demands, nothing being omitted."[61] As our experience changes, it is only natural that our beliefs will change also. Thus the truth of a belief is neither absolute nor eternal but provisional, not etched in stone but part of the flow of personal experience, and to be confirmed or disconfirmed by what happens in the future. Only to the extent that it works for good in our lives, is it to be judged reliable, secure, and true. James called his philosophy "pragmatism," pointing out that the term derived from the Greek word *pragma*—meaning "action."[62] For James, the most meaningful questions of philosophy are those that have a significant bearing on the conduct of our lives, whereas questions such as "How many angels can dance on the head of a pin?" are, to put it mildly, less than rewarding.

But what are we to make of the question of the existence of God? Like many philosophers of his day and ours, James felt that God's existence can neither be proved nor disproved. Classical arguments for the existence of God, for example, appear persuasive only to those who already believe in God. Was any unbeliever ever converted by them? Thus the conflict between theism and scientific materialism was at an impasse.

Does that mean that the individual is stuck between belief and unbelief? James thought not. As he had realized from his reading of Renouvier, sometimes one must act as if a belief were true even though there is insufficient evidence. "We cannot escape the issue by remaining sceptical and waiting for more light, because, although we do avoid error in that way *if religion be untrue*, we lose the good, *if it be true*, just as certainly as if we positively chose to disbelieve."[63] Remaining skeptical, in short, has the same effect as choosing atheism.

James famously argued that everyone has a "right to believe." Only by taking a leap of faith, by committing oneself to a belief and acting on it, can one gain any real insight into its validity and truth. James believed the pragmatic method cast fresh light on the dilemma by focusing on the expectations each side generates. With scientific materialism, one expects the universe to be utterly indifferent to human ideals, values, and goals. With theism, one expects there to be an ideal moral order which is being sustained. Thus, from the pragmatist's point of view, there is quite a difference *for us* between theism and materialism, since it affects our expectations and indeed our entire outlook on life.

James held that we have the right to believe in God because such belief corresponds with one of the deepest needs of our nature as moral beings—to find meaning and hope in life. Without these, personality withers and dies. Thus, even if the existence of God cannot be proved by philosophical argument, belief in God's existence seems necessary to human flourishing.

It may well be that James's type of argument from experience accounts for the appeal of *The Da Vinci Code*'s claim that the neglect of the feminine principle has created a sickness in the very soul of Western civilization. For some readers, the passage quoted earlier, with its claim that the "obliteration of the sacred feminine in modern life . . . had caused what the Hopi Native Americans called *koyanisquatsi*—'life out of balance,'" rings true to their own experience of life. No "proof" is necessary; its truth is grasped intuitively.

To the question of how belief in God might be confirmed, James once replied, "I myself believe that the evidence for God lies primarily in inner personal experiences."[64] This leads us naturally to a consideration of his *Varieties of Religious Experience* (1902), widely regarded as one of the greatest books ever written on the psychology of religion. As the title suggests, James examines a broad range of religious experience as recorded in personal accounts from all over the world. He defines religion in this way:

> Religion, therefore, as I now ask you arbitrarily to take it, shall mean for us *the feelings, acts, and experiences of individual men in their solitude, so far as they apprehend themselves to stand in relation to whatever they may consider the divine.* Since the relation may be either moral, physical, or ritual, it is evident that out of religion in the sense in which we take it, theologies, philosophies, and ecclesiastical organizations may grow. In these lectures, however, as I have already said, the immediate personal experiences will amply fill our time, and we shall hardly consider theology or ecclesiasticism at all.[65]

James proceeds to recount numerous cases in which religious beliefs had striking effects, sometimes bringing about total transformations of life—conversion experiences. This phenomenon is so widespread—indeed, it is universal—that we may conclude, says James, that our lives are capable of contact with "higher powers" which work for our good. This is not to say that the person who has undergone a conversion experience is able to give an accurate and detailed account of it, but rather that there exists a beneficent spiritual power, called different names in different cultures, which assists us in saving ourselves from what is wrong with our lives.

In another place, he expresses his view thus: "The drift of all the evidence we have seems to me to sweep us very strongly towards the belief in some form of superhuman life with which we may, unknown to ourselves, be co-conscious."[66] James also refers to this superhuman life as a "cosmic consciousness" which sympathizes with our values and helps us to realize them in our lives. What is called experience of the supernatural may in fact be natural in the sense that there is a part of ourselves—the unconscious—which is in touch with the spiritual realm in a way that our rational thought processes and physical senses cannot be. For James, the unconscious is our channel of communication with the spiritual realm.

In his writings on religion, James attempted to restore religious experience to its rightful place as a subject worthy of serious consideration in an age when many scientists ridiculed religion as mere illusion. By presenting documented cases of religious experiences which had produced profound and permanent results in the lives of individuals, he claimed to be investigating actual evidence that scientists had no right to dismiss out of hand. On the basis of this evidence, James proposed that there is a spiritual dimension to the universe as real as the other dimensions which we refer to in our everyday speech.

At the same time, he felt that religious dogma must also be evaluated in the light of experience. In his opinion, for example, the Christian belief that God is all-powerful does not correspond with our experience of the strength and tenacity of evil in the world. Indeed, even the name "God" goes beyond the evidence, which could be accounted for by presuming one spiritual power or many. As he notes, "The only thing that [religious experience] unequivocally testifies to is that we can experience union with *something* larger than ourselves and in that union find our greatest peace."[67]

James's remarks about Jesus give us insight into his attitude toward official Church doctrine. Jesus' experience of God was so transparent, so dazzling, that it both attracted followers and repelled the religious authorities of his day. After his death, his teaching spread rapidly, gaining vast numbers of disciples. Groups began organizing themselves into churches. But then, almost inevitably, "the spirit of politics and the lust of dogmatic rule" entered in. As a result, the new church became "a staunch ally in every attempt to stifle the spontaneous religious spirit, and to stop all later bubblings of the fountain from which in purer days it drew its own supply of inspiration."[68] New movements of the spirit were denounced as heretical and persecuted. Ironically, if a particular "heresy" managed to relocate and survive, it soon established an orthodoxy of its own and began finding its own "heretics" to persecute.

James's private statements on organized Christianity were even sharper. "It is impossible to believe," he said, "that the same God who established nature should also feel a special pride at being more immediately represented by clergymen than by laymen, or find a sweet sound in church phraseology and intonation, or a sweet savor in the distinction between deacons, archdeacons and bishops. He is not of that prim temper."[69] His attitude toward the Roman Catholic Church in particular rose to the level of active hostility: "I doubt whether the earth supports a more genuine enemy of all that the Catholic Church *inwardly* stands for than I do."[70]

On once being asked whether he believed in the authority of the Bible, James gave this reply: "No. No. No. It is so human a book that I don't see how belief in its divine authorship can survive the reading of it."[71] This is not far removed from what Sir Leigh Teabing tells Sophie Neveu in *The Da Vinci Code*: "The Bible is a product of man, my dear. Not of God."[72] James's attitude toward Christian theology was dismissive: "The theological machinery that spoke so livingly to our ancestors, with its finite age of the world, its creation out of nothing, its juridical morality and eschatology, its relish for rewards and punishments, its treatment of God as an external contriver, an 'intelligent and moral governor,' sounds as odd to most of us as if it were some outlandish savage religion."

In 1909, less than a year before he died, James entertained Sigmund Freud on his one and only visit to the United States. It was a richly symbolic encounter. As James had received Emerson's blessing on coming into the world, so now he gave a blessing of his own to Freud as he was about to leave it, saying, "The future of psychology belongs to your work."[73] James's vision of life falls between those of Emerson and Freud. Though obviously closer to Emerson, a poet of the spirit, James shared Freud's desire to advance the cause of science, but he thought that such advancement could come only if scientists (including Freud) renounced their grandiose pretensions to be the sole arbiters of truth. In his lifelong endeavor to reconcile spirit and reason, religion and science, James sought a pragmatic solution to one of the great cultural conflicts of our time.

There was one last richly symbolic moment in James's life. As he lay on his deathbed in August 1910, he asked his brother Henry to remain in Cambridge for six weeks after his death in order to conduct a scientific experiment for him. He told Henry that he would try to contact him from the world beyond, to provide evidence for belief in immortality. Though Henry waited in vain, the story captures the essence of his brother's lifework.

It is easy to recognize the parallels between James's views and the popular religious ideal of the individual "seeker," the person who searches for spiritual fulfillment wherever it may be found. Unbound to any one tradition, Christian or otherwise, the seeker has become a conspicuous figure in the American religious landscape in recent decades, especially since the 1960s. In the religious smorgasbord of our time, we have come to expect to see people choosing different beliefs according to their taste: Madonna becomes a devotee of Kabbalah, Richard Gere becomes a practitioner of Tibetan Buddhism, and of course Robert Langdon draws upon the wisdom not only of the Hopi Native Americans but of an entire world of religious symbolism and mythology.

Of course, there are questions: When exotic teachings are taken out of context, do they still have their essential meaning? Can they really be understood apart from the traditions on which they are founded, and apart from the communities in which they are an integral part of life? Indeed, the question arises even with respect to James's more thoughtful and considered approach: Is religious experience really as separable from "theologies, philosophies, and ecclesiastical organizations" as he assumes?

Another parallel between James's view and modern attitudes lies in their shared concern to find a practical philosophy of life.

In modern America, this frequently takes the form of reading or listening to self-help literature, in which William James is often quoted—not surprisingly, since he regarded pragmatism as a therapeutic philosophy. Thus, in the American classic *The Power of Positive Thinking*, Norman Vincent Peale refers to James as "one of the very few wise men America has produced" and quotes him enthusiastically.[74]

Perhaps James's most profound influence on spirituality is to be found in the Twelve-Step Movement, which originated with Alcoholics Anonymous. This Movement, which has been called "the greatest spiritual movement of the twentieth century,"[75] drew upon William James for its understanding of reliance upon a "higher power" and the experience of conversion.

James's insistence that our thoughts and beliefs are provisional, not final, that they must be open to constant revision in the light of experience, was exceptionally well suited to a time in American history of accelerating social and economic change. And if, James said, our thoughts and beliefs are merely provisional, then we should not act as if they were infallible and treat others with intolerance. Where there is disagreement, even at the level of fundamental principles, we must aim for compromise above all else. Here it must be recalled that James and his generation had lived through the unspeakable horror of the Civil War, in which more than half a million Americans died. To James and those like him, tolerance and compromise offered the best hope that America might never again have to endure such agony.

Nevertheless, for most of Christian history, the ideas of tolerance and compromise carried extremely negative connotations. How could any Christian compromise with the truth for which Christ himself laid down his life? In the first three centuries of Christian history, when faced with Roman persecution, hadn't Christians preferred to die rather than renounce their faith?

After Christianity became the religion of the Roman Empire in the fourth century, hadn't Church and State deemed it necessary to root out all false religions, in order to preserve from corruption the one that was true? And many centuries later, after paganism had all but disappeared, hadn't Catholics taken arms against Protestants, and Protestants against Catholics, for the sake of what each side regarded as the unadulterated Gospel truth? Thus throughout history, Christians who advocated toleration and compromise were judged as lacking the courage of their convictions. Indeed, to give one clear illustration of this attitude, for four centuries Catholics were forbidden to hold that heretics should not be put to death.

Concluding Remarks

It would be difficult to name three figures whose influence on the American mind has been greater than that of Jefferson, Emerson, and James. During their lifetimes and after, they were widely regarded as national heroes, worthy of comparison with any of the great figures of the European cultural tradition. Their standing was so eminent and their eloquence so captivating that they convinced the nation that the American experiment, which could just as easily have been viewed as an experiment in laissez-faire economics, was in fact a spiritual quest of mythic proportions.

That spiritual quest undoubtedly had its roots in Christian principles enunciated by Jesus himself: the sacredness of the individual, the need to refrain from judging others, the infinite value of spiritual freedom, and so on. Yet in the hands of our three authors, these principles were reshaped into forms that went so far beyond traditional Christianity as to be deeply at odds with the churches of their time. Nevertheless, for many Americans (though by no means all), the depth of the conflict was often lost sight of amidst the devotion and even adulation that was felt for these men. Even now, in a thoroughly anti-heroic age, the mere mention of their names is still capable of conjuring up feelings of national pride.

Despite their real differences, which cannot be explored in this book, these authors shared convictions which are reflected in *The Da Vinci Code.* Each believed in the necessity of individual freedom in matters of religion, a belief which in America today has reached the point where a huge percentage of the population will change their religious affiliation at least once, often several times. Even within particular churches, many pick and choose which doctrines to hold and which to ignore, without giving it a second thought. They simply assume it is their natural right.

Each of our authors also distrusted the Church as a hierarchical institution, regarding ecclesiastical authority as dangerous, especially when linked with political power, as had been the case for most of Christian history. All three men privately considered the Roman Catholic Church to have been one of the greatest hindrances to progress in the history of Western civilization. They would have concurred with the statement originally used by the great Catholic historian Lord Acton to describe the corrupt popes of the Renaissance: "Power tends to corrupt, and absolute power corrupts absolutely."[76]

Of course, it was awareness of this danger that led to the separation of Church and State being guaranteed by the First Amendment to the Constitution, and to the lifelong campaign of Thomas Jefferson on behalf of religious freedom. And yet it would not be until 1965, nearly two centuries after Jefferson began his campaign, that the Catholic Church finally accepted the wisdom of this idea in its *Declaration on Religious Freedom*, one of the documents of the Second Vatican Council. Does this mean that Jefferson was a kind of Christian prophet of religious freedom? It is a question worth pondering.

Like "Harvard symbologist" Robert Langdon, our three authors considered the dogmas of Christianity to be harmful in themselves, quite apart from their use in history to justify the persecution of heretics. Jesus had given his followers a new vision of God as a loving Father. But when the Church decided that this new vision must mean that Jesus was literally God's divine Son, it had mistaken Jesus' poetic language for plain, blunt statements of fact.

All three of the Americans we have considered believed that the poetry of Jesus was never intended to be taken in this way. It was intended to point beyond itself to spiritual truths too wonderful to be captured in ordinary language. Failing to recognize this, Church authorities unwittingly transformed Jesus' spiritual insights into metaphysical abstractions which they called the essential doctrines of the faith, but which were unintelligible to the faithful. If neither reason nor experience nor common sense could clarify their meaning, what was belief in them but a form of superstition?

As heralds of a new nation, the first ever founded on the principle of individual rights, Jefferson, Emerson, and James were naturally forward-looking, future-oriented thinkers. Unlike their Christian contemporaries, they did not believe that the fullness of the truth had been revealed once and for all two thousand years ago.

The words of Jesus, to be sure, were of eternal value for the conduct of life. But other great teachers had contributions of their own to make to the stock of human wisdom. Above all, modern contact with India and China had uncovered a previously unknown wealth of religious wisdom. Jesus did not stand alone at the summit of spiritual consciousness. Krishna and the Buddha were there beside him. Filled with awe at these newly discovered riches, some began to wonder whether Jesus, Krishna, and the Buddha had seen the same inexpressible spiritual reality, which human language could never fully capture, but only point to. If so, there was hope that all humanity might one day be brought together in harmony under the banner of universal truth.

This is the attitude of our three classic authors and of Dan Brown's Robert Langdon, who is their descendant in so many ways. Thus, some of the ideas and attitudes in *The Da Vinci Code* resonated deeply with American readers simply because they too are the heirs of Jefferson, Emerson, and James.

Chapter 7

The Rise of Modern Science as a Challenge to the Catholic Church

An enormous part of the appeal of *The Da Vinci Code* lies in its ingenious plot, in which the hero and heroine must use arcane bits of learning to unravel a mystery—a mystery hidden behind a multitude of fascinating clues but especially those in Leonardo's painting *The Last Supper*. In the course of the novel, the reader is introduced to a dazzling array of esoteric knowledge, from "the Fibonacci sequence" in mathematics to "the Atbash Cipher" in cryptology. Readers can thus experience the thrill of being initiated into secrets, and it was undoubtedly the desire to share in those secrets that drew many readers to the novel in the first place.

In this chapter, we will look at another kind of esoteric knowledge—that acquired by means of the modern scientific method of observation, measurement, hypothesis, and experiment. Nothing has so visibly changed our world as modern science with its endless variety of ingenious applications. It has even made its mark on popular entertainment. The television series *CSI*, for example, with its fictional portrayal of crime-scene investigations, became so successful that it generated two spinoffs, *CSI Miami* and *CSI New York*. What these shows dramatize (with a dramatic license that real crime-scene investigators often find appalling)

155

has already transformed criminal trials in America, most notably in what juries think is required to establish proof beyond a reasonable doubt. And this leads naturally to the most profound impact of all: science has changed our fundamental notion of truth.

How did such a momentous change occur? The question is of vital importance because the change occurred without our being fully conscious of it and because it affected the way people react to Christian claims to having truth that is eternal and unchanging.

In the popular imagination, the progress of science has often been seen as encountering its most stubborn resistance in the Christian religion, a view put forward with great eloquence by Bertrand Russell, Carl Sagan, and (currently) Richard Dawkins. One area where the Catholic Church is currently seen in this light is the debate over embryonic stem-cell research. To many Americans, the Church's implacable opposition to this research is an affront not only to reason but also to the most basic human feelings of empathy and compassion. They cannot understand how the Church can ignore the pleas of people like Michael J. Fox, one of America's most beloved actors and a Parkinson's disease patient, for research which could bring relief to countless numbers who suffer from chronic disease or devastating injury. Once again the Catholic Church finds itself embroiled in the American culture wars.

How did the popular image of the Catholic Church as the enemy of science become so well established? The simple answer is: because it condemned Galileo for claiming that the earth orbits the sun. This answer fails, of course, to do justice to the complexity of the relation between the Catholic Church and modern science, but it is the natural place to begin, and so we begin with the originator of the theory that Galileo defended, Nicolaus Copernicus.

Copernicus

The Polish astronomer Nicolaus Copernicus (1473–1543) is generally credited with having launched the Scientific Revolution of the sixteenth and seventeenth centuries with his then radical theory of the heliocentric universe. (What is not nearly so well known is that Copernicus was also a Catholic priest and even held a doctorate in Church law.) When Copernicus first became interested in astronomy as a university student in the 1490s, the basic picture of the universe given by the Egyptian astronomer Ptolemy c. 140 AD had practically attained the status of religious dogma. According to Ptolemy, the sun, the moon, and the five known planets revolved around the earth, which stood motionless at the center of the universe.

Although the idea that the earth was motionless seemed self-evident, Ptolemy's description of planetary motion contained notorious difficulties. As Copernicus meditated on these difficulties, he realized that they could be drastically reduced if he assumed that the sun, rather than the earth, was at the center of the universe. He then made the further assumption that the earth not only orbited the sun once a year but also revolved around its own axis once a day. The latter, he said, was what made the sun appear to rise and set. Finally, he found it necessary to assume that the distance of the stars from the earth and therefore the dimensions of the universe were far greater than had previously been imagined.

With such potentially revolutionary ideas, Copernicus was hesitant to publish and only agreed to do so at the urging of friends toward the end of his life. In fact, it was as he lay on his deathbed on the very day he died that Copernicus was handed the first printed copy of his masterpiece, *On the Revolutions of the Celestial Spheres*.

Religious opposition did not at first come from the Catholic Church. As a matter of fact, Copernicus's ideas had been presented years earlier in Rome in a lecture attended by Pope Clement VII, who approved of them. The first religious opposition came from the Protestant Reformer Martin Luther, who called Copernicus a "fool" and pointed out that his system was refuted by the biblical book of Joshua (10:13), which says that God made the sun stand still.

Where Copernicus's ideas were not rejected outright, they often raised troubling questions. If the earth really was spinning on its axis, why weren't human beings sent hurtling into space? (No scientist of the time could answer this question.) Even more disturbing was the thought that the earth was no longer the center of all creation, but merely one planet among others in an unimaginably vast universe—a universe whose most striking characteristic was its dark, chilling emptiness. A century later, the French thinker Blaise Pascal expressed his reaction in these words: "The eternal silence of these infinite spaces terrifies me."[1]

If the earth was not the center of the universe, how could the soul of every individual be, as the Church taught, the focus of a cosmic struggle between God and Satan for its eternal destiny? A haunting sense of being homeless in the universe began to creep into Western minds.

Galileo

Copernicus's theory had been based not on new evidence but on a reinterpretation of existing evidence to make it more coherent and intelligible than it had been in the Ptolemaic system. (Remember that there were no telescopes at that time.) Powerful new evidence would eventually come from the astronomical observations of Galileo Galilei (1564–1642), one of the greatest figures in the history of science. Having constructed the first astronomical telescope in 1609, he made a host of major discoveries, of which only a handful can be mentioned here.

He was the first to see that the Milky Way, which to the naked eye was merely a faint glow in the night sky, was actually made up of countless individual stars. Copernicus's bold hypothesis about the vastness of the universe had clearly not been bold enough. Galileo was also the first to see that Venus, like the moon, has phases, confirming Copernicus's hypothesis that Venus (along with the other planets) revolves around the sun, not the earth.

He was the first to see sunspots, which appeared as continually changing marks on the surface of the sun. The very existence of these "blemishes" cast doubt on the traditional belief that the heavens, being the home of angels, were necessarily unchanging and indeed perfect in every way. From the apparent drift of these spots from left to right Galileo deduced that the sun rotated on its axis.[2]

In 1610, Galileo published his discoveries in a book entitled *The Starry Messenger.* The following year, he brought his telescope to the papal court in Rome and gave dazzling demonstrations of its use. The fame that Galileo had already enjoyed for a quarter of a century now grew even greater, but it also sparked opposition from members of the scientific establishment, many of whom feared that their own pre-Copernican views were being discredited. They charged that Galileo's claims contradicted the Bible.

On learning of these charges, Galileo wrote a spirited defense of his work. Quoting the late Cardinal Baronius, Galileo insisted that "the Bible teaches us how to go to Heaven, not how the heavens go,"[3] and noted that the Church traditionally interpreted the Bible allegorically rather than literally in those places where its literal meaning conflicted with scientific truth or was otherwise absurd. (One famous example of absurdity on the literal level concerns the story of Noah's ark in the book of Genesis. As the biblical commentator Origen [185–254] pointed out, if the ark had really taken on board that many animals, in no time at all Noah and his family would have been buried in dung.)

Galileo's self-defense failed to vanquish his enemies, who continued to bring serious allegations against him. In 1616, Church authorities summoned him to Rome to answer some of them. Although he was cleared of the charge of heresy, he was ordered not to hold or defend the heliocentric theory of the universe. To make sure that no one else did either, Copernicus's theory was officially declared to be false and erroneous as science and heretical because it contradicted the Bible, which spoke plainly of the sun's rising and setting and of the earth's remaining fixed in its place.

On the Revolutions of the Celestial Spheres was placed on the Church's Index of Forbidden Books, where it remained until 1835. The condemnation of Copernicus's theory had repercussions that were felt as far away as China. At the time, Jesuit missionaries were teaching the theory to the Chinese, who were fascinated by it. One can well understand their perplexity, therefore, when the Jesuits—suddenly and without warning—refused to talk about it any more.

Why had the Church waited so long to condemn Copernicus's theory? To answer this question it is necessary to view it in the context of the Protestant Reformation. Even though the Reformation is popularly thought to have begun in 1517 when Luther posted his Ninety-five Theses, the Catholic Church was slow to realize the seriousness of its implications. Indeed the Council of Trent, in which the Catholic Church would decide how to respond to the Reformation, had not met when Copernicus's book was published in 1543. (The Council finally got underway in 1545.)

Of paramount importance for both Protestants and Catholics was this question: "Who has the right to interpret the Bible?" The Reformers claimed that *they* had the right *and the duty* to interpret the Bible because the Catholic Church had corrupted the pure Gospel message. In response, the Catholic Church argued that its teaching was the same as it had always been and that neither Luther nor any other individual had the right to interpret the Bible—that right was reserved for the hierarchy of the Catholic Church. What the Reformers were proposing, Catholic officials said, was not the recovery of the pure Gospel but the construction of a new gospel, which was false for that very reason—it was new. By the time Galileo came to Rome in 1616, Catholic officials feared that if they allowed the Church's traditional interpretation of the Bible to be corrected in the light of Copernicus's theory, Protestants would seize the opportunity and say that it was open to correction with respect to weightier matters, such as the authority of the Pope as the successor of Peter.

Moreover, Copernicus's theory created numerous difficulties from a purely scientific perspective. Cardinal Robert Bellarmine (1542–1621), the Church's chief defender of the faith against Protestantism, pointed out to Galileo that although he had amassed a great deal of supporting evidence for the heliocentric theory, he did not have proof.[4] Thus, while he may have demonstrated that Venus orbits the sun, he had hardly begun to do so with respect to the earth.

For the next seven years, Galileo kept silent about the heliocentric theory. But in 1623, Cardinal Maffeo Barberini—Galileo's longtime friend, admirer, and protector—was elected Pope Urban VIII. Galileo went to him and obtained permission to write again about the Copernican theory, so long as he discussed it as something purely hypothetical. Galileo was perfectly happy with this arrangement and decided to write an imaginary dialogue between a supporter of Copernicus and a supporter of Ptolemy, with a neutral observer assessing their arguments.

Cleared by Church censors, Galileo's *Dialogue Concerning the Two Chief World Systems—Ptolemaic and Copernican* was published in 1632 to the acclaim of all Europe. But Galileo still had enemies who told the Pope that the *Dialogue* was a veiled attempt to discredit the Ptolemaic system. The Pope felt betrayed. Moreover, he was told by his Jesuit advisors that if Galileo's ideas were not stopped, they would do more harm to the faithful "than Luther and Calvin put together."

Galileo was brought before the Inquisition in Rome. There, under the threat of torture, his spirit was broken. He capitulated to the demands of the Inquisitors and totally repudiated all that he had previously taught in support of Copernicus's theory. The Church denounced the heliocentric view of the universe once again as heretical, placed Galileo's works on the Index of Forbidden Books (where they remained, alongside Copernicus's, until 1835),[5] and sentenced Galileo himself to life imprisonment. In view of his poor health and his great age (he was 70 at a time when the average life expectancy was 32), his sentence was commuted to house arrest, under which he spent the last eight years of his life. Since that time, Galileo has often been held up as a glorious martyr for the cause of science—and the Catholic Church as its greatest enemy.

The Reopening of the Galileo Case

In 1981, Pope John Paul II, a graduate of the same Polish university as Copernicus himself, set up a commission of historians, theologians, and scientists to investigate the Galileo case anew in order to bring out the whole truth, to acknowledge fully whatever wrongs had been done to Galileo, and to begin to heal the damage that his case had done to the relationship between the

Church and the scientific community. In 1984, all the documents in the Vatican archives pertaining to the case were made public.

In 1992, the 350th anniversary of Galileo's death, the commission reported its findings. The most important of these was that Galileo's ecclesiastical judges had rushed to judgment—not only in hindsight, but even in light of the explicit task they had been given at the time—and were wrong to have silenced Galileo. On accepting the commission's report, the Pope made his own statement. He noted that for centuries the Galileo case had been wrongly but understandably interpreted as proof of a fundamental opposition between science and theology, when in fact science and theology illuminate different but complementary aspects of the one complex truth that exists about the human person and humanity's place in the cosmos. As for Galileo himself, the Pope acknowledged the need for public recognition of and repentance for the wrong that had been done to him and for the immense suffering he had been forced to endure.[6]

But the Pope's forthright statement was not universally applauded. It was even ridiculed by some, as in this headline in *The Los Angeles Times*: "It's Official! The Earth Revolves Around the Sun, Even for the Vatican!"[7] Others shared the reaction of Episcopal Bishop John Shelby Spong: "This confession of error on the part of the Church was 350 years too late." Such remarks led some Catholics to wonder whether the public admission of error should ever have been made at all.

Still others felt the Pope had not gone far enough. In an important and authoritative article published in 2001, George V. Coyne, S.J., Director of the Vatican Observatory, concluded that several of the Pope's statements did not "stand up to historical scrutiny," so that the controversy was not laid to rest once and for all, as the Pope had wanted it to be. Moreover, although the commission had been asked to discover the wrongs that had been done on all sides, Coyne maintained that the Pope's statement, echoing the conclusion of the commission, placed responsibility for the wrong done to Galileo too narrowly on the shoulders of theologians. "There is no mention," he observed, "of the Roman Inquisition or of the Congregation of the Index [of Forbidden Books], nor of an injunction given to Galileo in 1616 nor of the abjuration required of him in 1633 by official organs of the Church. Nor is mention made of [Pope] Paul V or Urban VIII, the ones ultimately responsible for the activities of those official institutions."[8] These criticisms are worthy of serious consideration. At the same time, it is important to bear in mind that they are not attacks on Pope John Paul's personal integrity.

Newton

The man who would bring the Scientific Revolution to its culmination and completion, Isaac Newton (1642–1727), was born on Christmas Day in 1642, a year after the death of Galileo and a century after the publication of Copernicus's masterpiece. Newton's father had died before his son's birth, leaving his mother to raise him alone in straightened circumstances. Shortly after Newton's third birthday, a parson from a neighboring parish, a widower needing to find a mother for his children, proposed to Newton's mother, and she accepted. She left her son to be raised by her own mother, coming back to see him from time to time.

Frank Manuel, the late Harvard historian and biographer of Newton, believed that what Newton's mother did nearly destroyed his ability to trust other human beings, leaving him prey to feelings of paranoia for the rest of his life. On the other hand, he also believed that Newton's deep sense of insecurity may have been the source of his insatiable desire for absolute certainty, which inspired him to make the greatest advances in mathematics in over two thousand years and to produce what is perhaps the greatest single body of scientific work in human history.

For our purposes, it will be helpful to recall a story Newton told toward the end of his life about an incident that occurred when he was twenty-three. While sitting under an apple tree, the fall of an apple made him wonder, "What is the power in the earth that draws the apple downward to the ground?"

Whatever that power is, he intuited, it must be proportional to the earth's mass. And if the earth exercised such a power with regard to the apple, why shouldn't that power extend further, even as far as the moon? (This was a radical idea at the time, since the earth below and the heavens above were thought to operate according to entirely different sets of rules.) Newton then deduced that this power must be proportional to the distance between the earth and the moon—more precisely, to the *square* of the distance between them. Here was the birth of the idea of universal gravitation.

Soon he would invent the mathematics necessary to demonstrate his theory. Years later, Newton elaborated his theory and gave it definitive expression in his *Principia* (1687; the full title is *Philosophiae Naturalis Principia Mathematica*),[9] in which he showed that every material object in the universe attracts every other with a force directly proportional to the product of their masses and inversely proportional to the square of the distance between them. The significance of his achievement has been summarized by Sir Isaiah Berlin: "Newton had performed the unprecedented task of explaining the material world, that is, of making it possible, by means of relatively few fundamental laws of immense scope and power, to determine, at least in principle, the properties and behavior of every particle of every material body in the universe, and that with a degree of precision and simplicity undreamt of before."[10]

The *Principia* is still generally regarded as the greatest scientific work ever written. As Nobel Laureate Steven Weinberg has pointed out, even now, after Einstein's General Theory of

Relativity, "physicists . . . go on using the Newtonian theory of gravitation and motion."[11]

Newton and Religion

At the end of the *Principia*, Newton gave praise to God the creator and sustainer of the universe: "This most beautiful system of the sun, planets and comets, could only proceed from the counsel and dominion of an intelligent and powerful being, a God in fact." This was not mere lip service. Newton regarded his insights into nature as a recovery of knowledge that had been lost in the Fall of Adam and Eve. Now that it had been recovered, Newton hoped that humanity would marvel even more deeply at the beauty, harmony, and grandeur of the universe and give glory to God.

Newton inherited from the Middle Ages the idea of the "Two Books." Nature was one "Book" from which knowledge of God could be obtained, the Bible was the other. Over the course of his life, Newton appears to have devoted far more time to the study of the Bible, especially the prophecies contained in the books of Daniel and Revelation, than he ever gave to physics and mathematics. His biblical learning was so vast that his friend the philosopher John Locke said that he had never known Newton's equal.

Newton's theological writings, estimated at several million words all together, still await thorough scholarly examination and assessment. One fascinating insight that has already emerged is that Newton saw himself not as a scientist but as a prophet, called by God to help restore Christianity to its pristine purity. He considered his discoveries in physics and mathematics to have been revealed to him by God and had no doubt that in ancient times they had been revealed to Moses as well.

But this immediately raises a question. If Moses knew all about gravitation, why did he not refer to it in his account of creation in the book of Genesis? The reason, wrote Newton, was that Moses thought there was no hope of bringing the Israelites up to speed in the higher mathematics necessary to comprehend the law of universal gravitation, so he decided to give them the ancient equivalent of "The Creation Story for Dummies." (Newton hastens to add that dumbing down is not the same thing as lying.) When Newton considered all that God had revealed to him—not only the law of universal gravitation, but also the binomial theorem, differential and integral calculus, and so much else—it seemed to him a sign that the end of the present age must be drawing near, and he predicted that a new age of peace would begin in the year 2060, when Christ would return and establish the Kingdom of God on earth for a thousand years.

Newton kept his theological writings secret. Only a few confidants even knew they existed. The chief motive for his secrecy was to avoid imprisonment; his views were so unorthodox that he could easily have been tried and convicted of heresy.[12] The most unorthodox of all his views was his denial of the doctrine of the Trinity—that the one God exists in three Persons: Father, Son, and Holy Spirit. In Newton's judgment, not only was this doctrine rationally incoherent, it was also gravely sinful because it declared Christ, who was one prophet among many, to be divine, and that was nothing less than idolatry.[13]

Newton (like Sir Leigh Teabing in *The Da Vinci Code*) placed the blame for making Christ divine on the Council of Nicaea in 325, which declared the Son of God to be as fully divine as the Father, or, as the Nicene Creed expresses it: the Son is "one in being with the Father." At that moment the truth was buried beneath a lie, which was believed because of a human weakness Newton diagnosed in these terms: "Tis the temper of the hot and superstitious part of mankind in matters of religion ever to be fond of mysteries, & for that reason to like best what they understand least."[14] Here we are able to discern what led Newton to separate himself (though in secret) from the Church of England and from the "orthodox faith" as it was understood since Nicaea. It was his exalted view of the power of reason.

This is hardly surprising, given what he had accomplished in physics and mathematics. But in the view of traditional Christianity, it led Newton to make a fundamental and catastrophic mistake. He failed to recognize that there are some mysteries which will always be beyond human comprehension because they have to do with the very nature and essence of God. None of these mysteries is more central to Christianity than that of the Trinity. That the one God is three divine persons is something that can come to a believer only by revelation and be apprehended only by faith. The role of reason is to help Christians to understand this revelation, so far as it can be understood, but it is ultimately beyond human comprehension.

In the view of traditional Christianity, Newton's mistake was to treat the mystery of God's nature as if it were of the same kind as some mystery of physical nature—capable in principle of being solved by human reason. In rejecting the doctrine of the Trinity, Newton showed that he had elevated human reason to the point where he had given it the authority to pass judgment on divine revelation.

Newton's denial of the Trinity was kept secret. But some interpreted his public statements as undermining traditional Christianity. Despite Newton's emphatic statement at the end of the *Principia* that God was present always and everywhere to uphold the order and harmony of creation, only an infinitesimally small number of people were capable of reading and understanding the *Principia*, and a vague, misleading impression of his worldview gained currency—he had propounded a view of the universe as a machine and of God as remote and impersonal.

God was the creator of the universe, to be sure, but once created, the universe basically ran by itself according to the laws God had built into it. It was like a great clock. Once the master clockmaker had built it and got it started, it could go on indefinitely. If the universe operated in this mechanical way, and Newton had proved that it did, not only did God seem impersonal, but the fixed and unalterable laws of the universe seemed to leave God with little or no room to act in it. The universe was, in effect, a closed system.

This was a profound change from the traditional view of God intervening in history to guide some nations to victory and others to defeat, to answer the prayers of those who petitioned Him, and to grant His saints the power to perform miracles. Some even feared that Newton's theories, according to which both the heavens and the earth are composed entirely of "dead" matter moving according to fixed laws, would lead inevitably to the assumption that the universe was devoid of spirit, and eventually to the spread of materialism and atheism.

If the universe could be explained without bringing God into the picture, then perhaps God was a negligible player in the world—perhaps God was nonexistent. How far this view can be carried is shown by these haunting words of physicist Steven Weinberg: "The reductionist worldview *is* chilling and impersonal. It has to be accepted as it is, not because we like it, but because that is the way the world works."

It is interesting to note that Pope John Paul II gave an address on the occasion of the three hundredth anniversary of the publication of Newton's *Principia*. In it he stated that science cannot by itself compel anyone to accept an atheistic view of the world. Such a view (Weinberg's would be a good example) proceeds from assumptions which are independent of science. But the Pope also stated that science cannot be used in a simplistic way as the basis for accepting belief in Christianity. "Christianity," he said, "possesses the source of its justification within itself and does not expect science to constitute its primary apologetic." The danger of using science as a primary ground for believing in God is that it can all too easily lead to a notion that God is remote and impersonal or even that God does not exist at all.

The final point I would like to make has to do with Newton's influence on our basic assumptions about knowledge and truth. As stated above, while only a handful of people in Europe could follow Newton's reasoning in the *Principia*, it was widely understood that his scientific method had revealed the rational order of the entire material universe. The discovery of this order was so thrilling that it immediately inspired the hope that Newton's method could be adapted and applied not only to the other sciences (then in their infancy) but to every aspect of life. There seemed to be no limit to the possible benefits that science could bring.

The prestige that Newton's achievement gave to science was so great that society's very definition of knowledge started to change. Knowledge now began to be understood as the power to transform the world. In many ways, science became a new belief system, spreading like Christianity itself until it encompassed the world.

Of course, this faith in science is now under fire even within science itself, as for example in the sphere of medicine, where it is recognized that for far too long doctors have tended to view patients as a bundle of symptoms rather than as whole human persons. But what has led to this recognition? Many would say that it is just better science. Diagnoses have been found to be more accurate when the patient is allowed to speak freely and at length, rather than being merely prodded and probed with medical instruments.

But I hardly need to give examples. We look to science to solve every problem in the world, from scarcity of food to the depletion of oil to the environmental crisis. And even in our most trivial everyday purchases we look for the label that says. "Scientifically proven to . . . [fill in the blank]." All this has led to the assumption among the public at large that Christianity is not dealing with knowledge and truth in the strict (that is to say, the scientific) sense.

Rather, Christian claims are best categorized as belonging to the realm of opinion. Those who defend this view point to the disagreements in doctrine that separate the Catholic, Orthodox, and Protestant churches. Indeed, among Protestants alone it has been estimated that there are more than thirty-three thousand denominations.[15] By contrast, when one turns to science, one does not find the Americans using one kind of science to launch a rocket into space, the Russians another, the French a third, and the Chinese a fourth. No, at the most elementary level, all are following Newton's laws. The popular view, according to which science offers the only genuine truth, with everything else being a matter of personal opinion, has been regarded by religious leaders such as Pope John Paul II and Pope Benedict XVI as having brought disastrous consequences for Western civilization.

Darwin

Having looked briefly at the Scientific Revolution which culminated in the work of Isaac Newton, we turn now to the work of Charles Darwin (1809–1882), for what Newton achieved in the realm of physics, Darwin was destined to achieve in the realm of biology. Both men demonstrated that a vast realm of experience could be explained by simple laws comprehensible to human intelligence without having to invoke the activity of God. Both came to symbolize the power of science and reason to solve the great mysteries of the world. But unlike Newton, Darwin would not portray nature as one beautiful and harmonious system, though his portrait did give a prominent place to beauty and harmony. Darwin's portrait was ultimately darkened by the realization that the beauty and harmony we see in nature is all too often the outcome of fierce struggle, savage cruelty, and pointless suffering.

As a boy, Darwin showed little promise at school, and when he was sixteen his father told him, "You care for nothing but shooting, dogs, and rat catching, and you will be a disgrace to yourself and all your family." Like many other unremarkable but wealthy young men of the time, Darwin ended up studying at Cambridge to become a priest in the Church of England. While there, however, he met John Stevens Henslow, a professor of botany, who encouraged his interest in that field and later recommended him for the job of naturalist aboard the Royal Navy's HMS *Beagle*. Darwin got the job, which entailed studying and collecting specimens of the rocks and organisms of the places they visited on the ship's voyage around the world from 1831 to 1836. It would prove to be the decisive event in Darwin's life.

When the voyage began, Darwin held the common Christian view that all forms of plants and animals had been created individually by God and had remained basically the same ever since, although some species had become extinct as a result of natural disasters such as volcanic eruptions. But that view would slowly change over decades as he reflected on the fossils he had found and the various plants and animals he had observed on his voyage. His most important observations were made when the ship landed in the Galápagos Islands, five hundred miles off the coast of Ecuador.

Among the creatures he observed there were the giant Galápagos tortoises. Weighing up to 770 pounds, they had no difficulty in carrying Darwin when he tried to ride them, but their ungainly steps made it almost impossible for him to keep his balance. Darwin learned that the tortoises on the different islands were quite similar in many respects, but the shape of their shells was distinctive for each of the islands. Years later he would realize that the shape of the shell represented an adaptation. While some had rounded shells, others had shells that curved upward at the neck, enabling them to reach the higher plants on their particular island. Whether these tortoises represent different species or merely different subspecies is uncertain. At the very least, they exhibit the sort of transformations that over long periods of time could *become* different species.

When he left the Islands, Darwin took with him three baby tortoises, whose shells were only the size of dinner plates. One of them is widely believed to have ended up in the Australia Zoo in Queensland. There Harriet (as she was called), who had grown to weigh 330 pounds, was the most beloved of all the animals. One of the last great events of her long life was the Zoo's celebration of her 175th birthday in 2005. She died peacefully on June 23, 2006, ending her reign as the oldest known living animal in the world.

In 1859, Darwin published *The Origin of Species* in which he argued with overwhelming supporting evidence that life on earth had evolved from a few simple forms to the abundant varieties of living things we see today. The mechanism by which this had taken place he called "natural selection," a concept often misunderstood and requiring some clarification.

If we take any species of animal, let us say the cheetah, it will typically produce more offspring than can survive. Among these offspring, each of which is unique, some will have variations that are disadvantageous. A cheetah that is relatively slow will be at a disadvantage when it comes to catching its natural prey, the gazelle. In a time of scarcity of prey, it is less likely to survive and to pass on its traits to offspring. If scarcity persists, perhaps becoming permanent, the number of slow-moving cheetahs will tend to decrease. Darwin called this process "natural selection" because it is analogous to "artificial selection" as practiced by breeders of farm animals, for example. Darwin also called it "the survival of the fittest."[16] (By "fittest" Darwin merely meant "best adapted to its particular environment.") Over long periods of time, an accumulation of favorable variations will lead to new life forms—the origin of species.[17]

How could so many changes have taken place if, as Darwin claimed, life originated from very few or perhaps just one original form? Darwin's theory depended on the newly calculated age of the earth, which made it far older than anyone had previously imagined. Two centuries earlier, a learned Anglican archbishop, James Ussher (1581–1656), had calculated the age of the earth by summing up the chronology of the Bible and, where the Bible was silent, drawing upon other historical records. His results, published in 1650, indicated that creation began early on the night of October 22–23, 4004 BC, with Adam being created on Friday, October 28.

Four years later, Dr. John Lightfoot of Cambridge University was able to be even more precise, pinpointing the exact time of Adam's creation to 9:00 o'clock in the morning. On a more somber note, November 10 would go down in infamy as the day when Adam and Eve ate the forbidden fruit and brought misery upon all their descendants. Ussher's dating was considered so authoritative that it was printed in the margin of the King James Version of the Bible for the next two centuries, leading many readers to assume it was actually part of the original Bible.[18]

In 1830, however, Charles Lyell published the first volume of his masterpiece, *Principles of Geology*, which argued that the age of the earth must be reckoned not in thousands but in hundreds of millions of years. (The best current estimate is about 4.6 billion years, with the origin of life thought to have occurred at least 3.6 billion years ago.) Lyell's work met fierce opposition from conservative scientists, but it provided Darwin with the vast expanse of time he needed for evolution to have developed from one species, or very few, to the incalculable number on earth today.

Let's look at two of the most notorious difficulties that Darwin faced, difficulties which fundamentalists still refer to as fatally undermining the theory of evolution. The first has to do with Darwin's outrageous claim that in the course of its evolution the whale, being a mammal, must once have walked on land. The idea that the whale was a mammal, not a fish, had been proposed by the Swedish biologist Carl Linnaeus in 1735 for the following reasons: they are warm blooded, they nurse their young, and they breathe air through their lungs.[19]

Linnaeus did not, however, suggest that whales had evolved. He believed they had always been in the forms in which we find them now. But even so, the idea that whales were mammals proved a hard sell to the public. Not only did the whale look like a fish and appear to behave like a fish, but the words of Jesus himself, as they appeared in the King James Bible, were thought to have ended the matter once and for all. Jesus said plainly that Jonah had spent "three days and three nights in the whale's belly," referring to the passage in the Book of Jonah where it says that Jonah spent three days and three nights in the belly of "a great fish." It followed therefore that the whale is a great fish.

Nevertheless, Darwin was convinced that whales must have evolved from land mammals. In *The Origin of Species* he even suggested that they might have evolved from bears that hunt fish in water and can swim. This struck some critics as preposterous and they said so, with the result that Darwin silently deleted this suggestion from later editions. For more than a century, biblical literalists maintained that God created whales as part of his original act of creation, just as their Bible says he did (Genesis 1:21 in the King James Version). If whales had evolved, they asked scornfully, where was the fossil evidence of "walking whales"? This taunt continues to this day.

But in 1979, while hunting for fossils of mammals in Pakistan, paleontologist Philip Gingerich discovered the fossilized remains of a wolf-like creature that had inner-ear bones with a particular shape found in no other vertebrate except the whale. He called it *Pakicetus*, which means "the whale of Pakistan." Here was an ancestor of modern whales that walked on land fifty million years ago. Since 1979, the fossilized remains of several more species of whales with legs have been discovered, and these species have been assigned provisional places in a chronological sequence going all the way up to the whales of today. This tree, though only a construct, suggests how a four-footed land animal with hoofed feet could have evolved into a semi-aquatic seal-like animal, then into a creature that lived entirely at sea but still retained tiny hind legs just a few inches long, and finally into a creature without hind legs at all.

And there is further evidence that calls into question the idea that God designed whales in essentially the forms in which we see them today, as biblical literalists insist. Take for example the flippers on the sides of every whale, from the dolphin to the 150-ton blue whale. In each flipper, we find the same bones in the same order as we find in the front legs of land mammals and indeed in our own arms. Attached to a whale's shoulder blade there is the upper arm bone, followed by two forearm bones, wrist bones, hand bones, and finger bones (making up five "fingers"). But they are incapable of serving as forelimbs. Where there was once an elbow joint, the bones have fused together, making the flipper stiff. If God made the great whales on the fifth day of creation, why did he place such a complex bone structure in their flippers?

Biologists prefer to see it as further evidence that the remote ancestors of whales were land mammals with forelimbs, which gradually evolved over ten million years into flippers which can be used to steer and brake in the water. It is a striking but typical example of evolution making use of what was available from an earlier form of life.[20] More evidence comes from the fact that some whales have tiny hind-leg bones concealed within their sides. Biologists believe that hind legs eventually came to serve no purpose in the oceans and indeed were a disadvantage, so they were "selected against" by evolution and have now become mere vestiges. Such anatomical evidence makes today's whales living fossils.[21]

The second difficulty to be considered is the one Darwin himself regarded as the most formidable of all—how to explain the design of the human eye. The eye had been used before as an example of divine design by Isaac Newton and most famously by the English clergyman William Paley (1743–1805). Darwin had read Paley's *Natural Theology* while studying for the ministry at Cambridge University, where he happened to reside in Paley's old rooms at Christ's College. Darwin had admired the clarity and cogency of Paley's argument so greatly that he learned it by heart.

Paley himself had been especially moved by Newton's statement that the order of the universe showed the hand of its Creator. In his *Natural Theology*, Paley followed Newton's line of thought and gave compelling evidence of design in nature in order to argue for the existence of God. In the most famous passage in the book, Paley argued that if one found a watch while walking across a desolate heath, one would presume it was the work of a watchmaker. Similarly, he said, the human eye, with its many intricate parts all working together in harmony, all essential to the functioning of the whole (what good would an eye be without a lens, for example), shows it to be the work of a supreme designer, God. Moreover, the eye has exquisite and variable powers to see things near and far, large and small, in relative darkness and in bright light. It is inconceivable that such an amazing anatomical structure could have come about by chance. This line of argument continues to be used to this day by fundamentalists who aim to discredit the theory of evolution.

Though Darwin had once found Paley's argument utterly convincing, his study of animals over many years led him to doubt the need to presume the activity of a divine designer. Darwin could not of course expect to find evidence in the fossil record of the evolution of the eye, made as it is entirely of soft tissue. But the evidence provided by living organisms in Darwin's day suggested to him how the eye might have evolved, step by tiny step, over vast expanses of time. Darwin's argument has been confirmed so many times that it is now generally accepted by scientists.

As Darwin observed in the animal kingdom in his day, so we see even more clearly today representatives of the kind of steps that must have been taken for the eye to have evolved. At one end of the spectrum is the flatworm, with a few light sensitive cells, capable of detecting light and darkness but not of forming any image. At the other end, there is the falcon, which, if it could understand English, would be able to read *The New York Times* at a distance of one hundred yards. Between these two are many thousands of species whose power of vision has been tested and which can each be assigned its place in relation to the others. In each case, that species' vision was naturally selected as advantageous in its particular environment.

Thus, evolutionary biology is *not* saying that the human eye came about by sheer chance, which is the only alternative to divine design recognized by William Paley and by today's fundamentalists. Rather, the eye has evolved by little bits of "tinkering" which have given its owners some temporary advantage in the struggle for survival. Over time, the accumulation of millions upon millions of advantages gives the undeniable appearance of design, indeed of miraculous design. But closer inspection suggests the error in this way of thinking. According to scientists, the human eye has what would be considered by any reasonable standards "design flaws." Among these flaws is the connection between the eye and the optic nerve. The connection is so placed as to cause a blind spot in each eye.

But isn't it possible that the connection is not a "flaw" but rather an essential part of some more sophisticated design that scientists have not yet recognized? The trouble with the implied argument here can be demonstrated by comparing the human eye with the eye of an octopus. Its eye is structured much like our own, but because it took a different evolutionary path, its optic nerve is connected differently and creates no blind spot. Does the connection of its optic nerve prevent it from gaining some visual benefit that we enjoy? If so, scientists have not found it, and the vision of the octopus is considered to be just as good as ours.

The conclusion biologists draw is that our blind spot is a typical result of the way evolution proceeds, by tinkering with whatever it has at hand, and in some cases having to make the best of a bad situation. And the example of the octopus leads to another important point. Just as the eye of the octopus evolved independently from ours, scientists now believe that eyes have evolved independently at least forty times in the history of life on earth, suggesting that the process of creating an eye is not nearly so difficult for nature as the finished product might lead us to imagine.

Darwin was painfully aware that his theory undermined the argument from design and the biblical account of creation, then assumed to be basically correct both as history and as science. Darwin himself had assumed this until his voyage around the world began to raise doubts in his mind. As he wrote *The Origin of Species* he wanted to avoid shattering the faith of his family and friends, and this may be part of the reason that he used Christian language and ideas in significant ways.

At the very beginning of the book, opposite the title page, Darwin placed a quotation from Sir Francis Bacon commending lifelong study of both the Bible and Nature—"the book of God's word" and "the book of God's works." A subtle but revealing aspect of the body of the work is that Darwin did not use the term "evolution" once, but the terms *Creator, creation*, and variants appear over a hundred times.[22] And in the famous last sentence of *The Origin of Species*, where he speaks of "life . . . having been breathed by the Creator into a few forms or one," he is clearly echoing the story of creation in Genesis where it says, "The Lord God formed man of the dust of the ground, and breathed into his nostrils the breath of life" (Genesis 2:7 King James Version).

Darwin did not dare to apply his theory to human beings in *The Origin of Species*, but the implication was inescapable that we too were the product of evolution. When *The Origin of Species* succeeded far beyond Darwin's expectations, and the general idea of human evolution was gaining acceptance, Darwin decided to publish his research on human evolution in *The Descent of Man* (1871). In it, he claimed that human beings are closely related to chimpanzees and gorillas, indeed that we differ from them only in degree and not in kind. Our proudest boast—that our lives at their best are guided by noble moral values—was undermined by Darwin's claim that these values are essentially social instincts that we have inherited from the great apes, adapted to our own circumstances and elevated to the status of moral laws.

Among those who criticized Darwin's view of human evolution was the one person in the world best qualified to do so, Alfred Russel Wallace (1823–1913). Wallace had discovered the principle of natural selection independently of Darwin in 1858, but when he learned that Darwin had been working on an elaborate theory of evolution for many years and had gathered a prodigious amount of supporting evidence, he graciously allowed Darwin to take the lion's share of the credit. After studying Darwin's books, Wallace grew increasingly dissatisfied with Darwin's idea that the human mind could be explained as the product of evolution by natural selection.

Natural selection, Wallace argued, favors slight variations which are directly advantageous to survival in a particular environment. But the powers of the human mind go so far beyond mere survival needs that the principle of natural selection seems altogether inadequate to explain them. When we contemplate the human mind, he said, we realize we are in "the world of spirit." Although natural selection was able to explain the evolution of the human body, only divine intervention could account for the human soul. Wallace was not a Christian, but much the same view soon began to be expressed by Catholics and other Christians, as we will see.

Darwin suffered from severe stomach problems from the time he returned from his voyage around the world until the day he died, and this contributed to his being unable and unwilling to enter into public debate about his theory of evolution. In retrospect, there was really no need for him to do so anyway, since in *The Origin of Species* he had already anticipated and answered every major objection to his theory that has been raised in the century and a half since its publication.[23]

So Darwin left the work of public debate to others, especially Thomas Henry Huxley (1825–1895), who came to be known as "Darwin's bulldog." Huxley particularly liked to upset the clergy and claimed that the theory of evolution showed humanity to be the result of purposeless forces and thus cast serious doubt on the existence of God. With friends and supporters like Huxley, Darwin feared he might be ostracized from Victorian society. So he was delighted and amused when, late in his life, he received an unexpected invitation to become the Honorary President of the Cat Fanciers Society of London. He accepted without a moment's hesitation. As he told a friend, he hoped it might soften his image among the general public.

Over the years, Darwin slowly and almost imperceptibly lost his faith, eventually becoming an agnostic. He explains how this happened in a very moving passage in his autobiography, written for his grandchildren when he was sixty-seven years old. It is particularly moving because many of the beliefs he says he cannot accept are ones that are no longer held by most Christians, apart from fundamentalists. These include the literal truth of the Old Testament story of the origin of the world and the Old Testament's frequent portrayal of God as a vengeful tyrant.

He was appalled by the Christian doctrine that "men who do not believe, and this would include my Father, Brother and almost all my best friends, will be everlastingly punished."[24] But again, most churches would not view the matter so simply today. The Catholic Church, for example, officially teaches that nonbelievers can receive eternal salvation if they have sought to live a good life and acted according to their conscience.[25]

After his death, Darwin's wife published his autobiography, but with the passage dealing with his loss of faith heavily edited. That passage was not restored in full until 1958. It is now widely believed, moreover, that there was another reason for Darwin's loss of faith which may have been more decisive than any of those he discusses—the death of his eldest daughter Annie, the second and most affectionate of his ten children.

Annie suffered a long and agonizing illness of unknown origin before dying at the age of ten. Her symptoms were so like those of Darwin's own chronic illness that he thought she must have inherited it from him. Her loss, he wrote to a friend, was "bitter and cruel," and his daughter Henrietta would later say that he never really got over it.[26] Writing in his *Autobiography*, twenty-five years after Annie's death, he could only say, "Tears still sometimes come into my eyes, when I think of her sweet ways."

The Reaction of Fundamentalists
and Others to Darwin's Theory

As we have noted, Darwin's theory was challenged in his day by biblical literalists. Among them were many scientists. By the end of the nineteenth century, however, Darwinism had triumphed among scientists generally, and the theory of evolution began to be included in American school and college textbooks. But in the early decades of the twentieth century, the American Fundamentalist movement rose up to defend the authority of the Bible and its literal truth, declaring Darwinism its mortal enemy. Their position was known as Creationism for its teaching that God created all the different forms of life on earth separately in the beginning, just as it says God did in the opening chapter of Genesis.

Fundamentalists/creationists believed (and still believe) that because Darwin denied that humanity was a special creation of God, but claimed instead that humanity shared common ancestors with the great apes, the teaching of evolution would shake the foundations of Christian belief and especially Christian morality. So in 1922, William Jennings Bryan, one of America's most famous politicians, declared that Darwinism would be driven out of America's public schools.

In 1925, the state of Tennessee made it illegal "to teach any theory that denies the Story of Divine Creation of man as taught in the Bible, and to teach instead that man has descended from a lower order of animal." The American Civil Liberties Union sought to challenge the Tennessee law as a violation of free speech as guaranteed under the First Amendment to the Constitution, and they persuaded a young high school science teacher named John T. Scopes to stand trial in a test case.

Scopes had the most famous defense attorney of the day, Clarence Darrow. William Jennings Bryan was the prosecutor. The Scopes trial was hailed in the press as "the Trial of the Century." In one of the most dramatic moments in the trial, Darrow called Bryan himself to the stand, and proceeded to tear him to shreds by asking him questions that he was unable to answer, despite claiming to be an expert on the Bible. Darrow asked just the sort of questions that literalists stumble over, such as, "How was Cain able to find a wife, as the Bible says he did (Genesis 4), when at the time there was not a single woman in the world except his mother Eve?"

But Bryan and the prosecution team held the trump card. They had managed to persuade the judge to limit the trial to the single question—"Did Scopes break the law?"—rather than the question that the ACLU wanted to raise, "Was the law itself null and void because it violated the First Amendment?" By that standard, Scopes was easily found guilty and fined $100. (The verdict was later overturned on appeal on the grounds that the fine imposed had been excessive.)

Although the antievolutionist position had been made to look foolish in the press, the court's decision had a chilling effect on the teaching of evolution for decades to come. For one thing, publishers knew that other states were working to pass similar laws, so they immediately began downplaying evolution or eliminating it altogether from their science textbooks. As a result, the teaching of evolution largely disappeared from public high schools in America.

But in the late 1950s, after the Soviets launched the first space satellite, science education suddenly rose to prominence on the national agenda. Scientists from universities were enlisted to upgrade high school textbooks, and evolution was emphasized as the indispensable foundation of the biological sciences. A strong reaction to this new emphasis on science teaching came from fundamentalist circles. In the 1960s, their creationism morphed into "creation science," which claimed that there was powerful scientific evidence to support the biblical creation account.

Creation science became a force to be reckoned with in the 1970s and 1980s as its proponents introduced bills in a number of state legislatures, including Arkansas and Louisiana, requiring that the teaching of evolution in public schools be balanced by the teaching of creation science. But in 1987, the Louisiana "equal time for creationism" law was struck down by the U.S. Supreme Court as a violation of the First Amendment's requirement of separation of Church and State. Part of its decision reads as follows: "The preeminent purpose of the Louisiana Legislature was clearly to advance the religious viewpoint that a supernatural being created humankind."[27]

The Supreme Court's decision did not end the matter, however, because the supporters of creation science see themselves as being under the jurisdiction of a court far higher than any earthly court, to be judged ultimately by the One whom the Bible calls "the Judge of all the earth." For this reason, they have not abandoned the fight, but since 1987 have put forward dozens of proposals—from the Kansas State Board of Education to the New York State Assembly—challenging in a variety of ways the place of evolution in the public school curriculum. I have selected one recent case which garnered attention not just nationally but worldwide, and was even attended by Darwin's great-great-grandson. The case is that of *Kitzmiller v. Dover Area School District* (2005).

In October 2004, the Dover (Pennsylvania) Area School Board voted to amend the district's science curriculum to include discussion of gaps and problems in the theory of evolution and to introduce the theory of Intelligent Design as an alternative scientific theory. Their view was in agreement with legislation proposed in 2001 by U.S. Senator Rick Santorum of Pennsylvania and with views publicly expressed by President George W. Bush.

Intelligent Design theory, according to Professor Michael J. Behe of Lehigh University, one of its leading proponents, does not deny that evolution has occurred, but says that it cannot account for every aspect of life on earth. In particular, it denies that evolution can account for certain life processes at the cellular level. For example, in order for our blood to clot when we cut ourselves, a dazzlingly complex series of chemical reactions must take place. If even one link in the chain is missing, we may bleed to death.

This is what Behe calls "irreducible complexity." By that he means that there is no way that the clotting of blood can have evolved gradually, one infinitesimally small step at a time, in the blind and clumsy way that natural selection is supposed to proceed. For blood to clot requires the complete program of chemical events to occur, or it will not happen at all. At this point, Behe insists, we must be open to the possibility that we are looking at evidence of intelligent design.

Behe is quick to add he is not saying that we must proclaim, "This is the work of God!" That would be going well beyond the bounds of science. All that Intelligent Design theory wants to be able to say is that some life processes cannot be explained in terms of evolution by natural selection and must be interpreted as having been designed by some unspecified intelligent agent or agents.

In December 2004, a group of eleven parents of Dover school children led by Tammy Kitzmiller sued the Dover Area School District, charging that by adding Intelligent Design theory to the curriculum it was promoting religion and thus violating the First Amendment's guarantee of separation of Church and State. A month later, the school board, undeterred, ordered science teachers at Dover High School to read a brief statement to their ninth-grade biology classes pointing out that evolution is not a fact and describing the theory of Intelligent Design as an alternative scientific explanation for the origin of life. The statement recommended that students learn more about Intelligent Design theory from a textbook on the subject entitled *Of Pandas and People*, multiple copies of which were available in the school library. When the teachers refused to read the statement to their classes, school administrators did it themselves.

The trial began on September 26, 2005, with Judge John E. Jones III presiding. He had been appointed as a U.S. District Judge by President Bush at the recommendation of Senator Santorum, so one would have thought he would be sympathetic to Intelligent Design theory. One of the most stunning revelations to emerge in the course of the trial concerned the book *Of*

Pandas and People, which the prosecution was able to show had originally been drafted by creationists to promote creationism. Then, immediately after the 1987 Supreme Court ruling that it was unconstitutional to teach creationism in a science classroom, the draft was edited so that all references to "creationism" were replaced by "Intelligent Design."

In his decision, rendered on December 20, 2005, Judge Jones ruled that to present Intelligent Design as an alternative to evolution in public school biology classes was a violation of the First Amendment to the Constitution because Intelligent Design is simply "creationism relabeled." And the reason for the relabeling was clearly to get around the 1987 Supreme Court ruling. "The writings of leading [Intelligent Design] proponents reveal that the designer postulated by their argument is the God of Christianity."[28] Moreover, Intelligent Design fails to meet the basic definition of science for a variety of reasons, one of the most important being that it gives supernatural explanations for natural phenomena, whereas science limits itself to natural explanations. Judge Jones added that in an age when science is attempting to cure deadly diseases and to prevent pandemics, it made no sense to try to introduce bad science into the classroom.

Dr. Michael J. Behe, who had served as the chief expert witness for the defense, said afterward that Judge Jones was unqualified to pronounce on the scientific validity of Intelligent Design. But Judge Jones's decision was based not upon his own scientific expertise but on that of the overwhelming majority of scientists who have examined Intelligent Design theory and concluded that it is not science. Indeed, Dr. Behe's own webpage at Lehigh University contains an "Official Disclaimer" which states that most of his colleagues in the Department of Biological Sciences strongly disagree with his ideas about Intelligent Design. Dr. Kenneth R. Miller, a professor of biology at Brown University who served as an expert witness for the prosecution, felt Judge Jones's opinion hit the bull's-eye. (Miller, incidentally, is a Catholic.)

Few, however, imagined that they had seen the last of Intelligent Design. Eugenie Scott, executive director of the National Center for Science Education, said in an interview, "I predict that another school board down the line will try to bring Intelligent Design into the curriculum like the Dover group did, and they'll be a lot smarter about concealing their religious intent."[29] This comment may sound cynical, but Judge Jones himself said he was convinced that at least two of the original School Board members who took the stand lied under oath about their actions and motives and should therefore be tried for perjury.

In the immediate aftermath of the court's decision, Judge Jones received death threats, and he and his family had to be placed under round-the-clock protection.

Catholic Reaction to Darwin's Theory

Although it will require us to go back to the time when Darwin's theory was first published, we need to consider the Catholic reaction separately because it follows its own path. Many Catholic leaders initially reacted with alarm at the popular reports of the theory of evolution which interpreted it as an attack on Christianity. But this interpretation did not necessarily follow from the theory itself, and the theory was accepted by some of the most acute Catholic thinkers of the day, including John Henry (later Cardinal) Newman (1801–1890) and Gregor Mendel (1822–1884), whose plant experiments laid the foundation for modern genetics. (Genetics, in turn, would take evolutionary theory one enormous step forward by showing how heredity works, something which Darwin had been unable to do.)

The Catholic anatomist, St. George Mivart (1827–1900), sought to reconcile theology and evolution (though without the mechanism of natural selection), and in his book *The Genesis of Species* (1870), he proposed that evolution was divinely guided. He also made a crucial point that has been central to Catholic teaching on evolution ever since: while the human body may be the product of evolution, the soul is directly infused into it by God. In recognition of his work, Mivart was awarded a medal by Pope Pius IX in 1876. (Incidentally, St. George was his first name. He was never declared a saint. In fact, he was excommunicated by the Catholic Church toward the end of his life.)

Not every effort to reconcile theology and evolution was looked upon so favorably by the Vatican. When Father John Augustine Zahm (1851–1921), a professor at the University of Notre Dame, published *Evolution and Dogma* in 1896, it was condemned in Rome. Its condemnation, however, seems to have been elicited not so much by the contents of the book as by Zahm's reputation as a liberal at a time when the Vatican was clamping down on liberal tendencies in American Catholicism.

It is important to note that while there was often suspicion of the theory of evolution at the Vatican, there was never any blanket condemnation of it. The first official acceptance of evolution by the Catholic Church appeared in the encyclical *Humani Generis*, issued by Pope Pius XII in 1950. The Pope acknowledged that evolution was a hypothesis worthy of careful consideration and encouraged dialogue between scientists and theologians. But he also emphasized the limits of such discussion: God's direct creation of every human soul, which is spiritual and immortal, must be affirmed unconditionally. The further hypothesis proposed by some evolutionary biologists, that humanity originated from several independent pairs of ancestors, not just one (Adam and Eve), was ruled out. The Pope said it was hard to see how such a hypothesis could be reconciled with the Church's teaching that original sin, with which all human beings (except Jesus and the

Virgin Mary) are born, derives from "a sin actually committed by an individual Adam."[30]

Pius XII's tentative and conditional acceptance of the theory of the evolution of the body, while flatly denying any evolution of the soul, was reiterated and deepened by Pope John Paul II, especially in an address he gave in 1996. In it he noted that, since the promulgation of *Humani Generis*, the theory of evolution had been confirmed by work across a broad spectrum of the sciences and could no longer be regarded as a mere hypothesis. At the same time, he said the Church must preserve the truths about human nature that it has received through revelation, above all that humanity is created in the image of God,[32] and that this image is made fully manifest in Jesus Christ.

The theory of evolution was compatible with Christianity so long as biologists did not stray outside their area of expertise and try to claim that spirit could evolve from matter or, in extreme cases, that there is no such thing as spirit at all. The view that matter is the only reality is based upon certain philosophical assumptions, he said, not science. The Pope called for continued dialogue between scientists and theologians, working together to deepen our appreciation of human nature and its unique dignity.

The Catholic Church's attitude toward the creation stories in the Bible had also undergone development since the pontificate of Pius XII, as may be seen in this statement made by John Paul II in 1981:

> The Bible . . . speaks to us of the origin of the universe and its make-up, not in order to provide us with a scientific treatise, but in order to state the correct relationships of man with God and with the universe. Sacred scripture wishes simply to declare that the world was created by God, and in order to teach this truth it expresses itself in the terms of the cosmology in use at

> the time of the writer. . . . Any other teaching about the
> origin and make-up of the universe is alien to the in-
> tentions of the Bible, which does not wish to teach how
> heaven was made but how one goes to heaven.[33]

There can be no doubt that the Pope was consciously echoing the words of Galileo in the last of these sentences. But the
main purpose of the Pope's statement was to counter and correct erroneous views such as those associated with creationism.
The Catholic Church rejects creationism on two grounds. First,
it judges that creationism misinterprets and indeed degrades the
Bible insofar as it refuses to read the opening chapters of Genesis on their own terms and instead reads them as if they were
modern science. As a result, their value as revealed truth about
the relation between God and humanity is obscured.

Second, creationism willfully refuses to accept one of the
most important contributions of modern science to our knowledge of humanity and the universe. The theory of evolution is
not one theory among many that offer credible explanations
of the development of life on earth. As Francisco Ayala, one of
America's most highly respected biologists, has put it, "The evolutionary origin of organisms is today a scientific conclusion established with the kind of certainty attributable to such scientific
concepts as the roundness of the Earth. . . . [It] is accepted by
virtually every biologist."[32]

The Catholic Church, in turn, accepts this consensus of experts, just as it accepts the consensus of experts in every field
of knowledge, believing that truth ultimately cannot contradict
truth, because all truth comes from God. Conflict typically arises
when experts step outside their field of expertise and pass judgment on another, as when scientists claim science can disprove
the existence of God, or when biblical scholars claim the Bible
disproves evolution.

The Catholic Church and Biotechnology

Despite the valiant efforts of Pope John Paul II over more than a quarter of a century to foster dialogue between scientists and theologians, the Catholic Church is still widely perceived as the most stubborn opponent of progress in the biological sciences. In the United States, this is largely because the Catholic Church often appears to be allied to the Christian Right in the culture wars.

Even in the case of *Kitzmiller v. Dover Area School District*, in which the Board was convicted of attempting to promote creationism, the defense was conducted by the Thomas More Law Center, an organization which considers itself Catholic to the core. Named after the Catholic martyr and patron saint of lawyers, the Center was founded as "the sword and shield for people of faith" in the culture wars. Its existence was made possible by the extraordinary generosity of businessman Tom Monoghan, the founder of Domino's Pizza, who has launched a number of conservative Catholic projects using his *Mater Christi* ("Mother of Christ") fund.

Two ongoing struggles in which the Catholic Church and the Christian Right have joined forces are those over abortion and embryonic stem-cell research, which they both regard as homicide. Their opposition is considered by many, including many scientists, as a case of particular religious groups trying to impose their beliefs on the entire nation by federal law, thus violating the separation of Church and State. These and other issues in medical ethics are likely to remain in the forefront of the culture wars for many decades to come because, following the "completion" of the Human Genome Project in 2003, we have entered what is being called a "biorenaissance."

The Catholic Church has already reached conclusions in medical ethics which are officially regarded as absolute and unalterable. But the story of Molly Nash, as spotlighted in an important book by Leo Furcht and William Hoffman, *The Stem Cell Dilemma: Beacons of Hope or Harbingers of Doom?* (2008), gives an example of the complex issues raised by advances in biomedicine.[34] It shows the sort of battle we can expect to see the Catholic Church engaging in with increasing frequency.

In 1999, Molly Nash, a six-year-old Colorado girl and the only child of Lisa and Jack Nash, was diagnosed with Fanconi anemia, a rare and deadly genetic disease that causes catastrophic failure of the bone marrow to produce healthy blood cells. She was not expected to live to see her seventh birthday. Doctors said the only hope of saving her life was to perform a bone marrow transplant from a sibling who was a perfect match.

Molly's parents were both carriers of the genes for Fanconi anemia and the chances of another child having the disease were one in four, so they decided to use in vitro fertilization (IVF) followed by genetic testing. They produced a dozen embryos by means of IVF. Two of these were shown by genetic testing to have the Fanconi anemia genes and were discarded. Several other embryos were suitable matches but in each case implantation into Lisa's uterus failed. Finally one embryo was successfully implanted and nine months later, in September 2000, a healthy baby boy was born. They named him Adam.

Doctors took stem cells from Adam's umbilical cord and implanted them into Molly. Within three weeks, these stem cells had rebuilt Molly's bone marrow to a point where Molly was able to resume her favorite activity, dancing. Lisa Nash said, "We have two miracles!"[35] Not only did she and Jack have a new son, but their daughter had been rescued from certain death.

But not everyone approved of what had been done. The official teaching of the Catholic Church is absolutely opposed to IVF for several reasons. At least three of them are applicable here. First, IVF typically involves destroying embryos, and since embryos are human persons from the moment of conception,[36] destroying them is a form of homicide. Second, it obtains semen by means of masturbation, which is always objectively evil. (Precisely how evil a particular act of masturbation is depends on *subjective* factors, as for example whether the man acted with full knowledge of the grave evil he was doing.) And third, it produces children without the "conjugal act, which God willed to be the only means of their production."[37] IVF, for this reason too, is always objectively evil.

The Church's teaching could hardly be clearer. Still, Lisa and Jack Nash never expected the Vatican to comment on their particular case. Yet, as Lisa Nash told *The Denver Post*, the Vatican actually sent her and her husband a personal letter, telling them that they were excommunicated from the Catholic Church. This puzzled them, since they are Jewish.[38] In another interview, Lisa, who is a nurse, told CNN that embryos are not capable of living beyond day five but will die unless they are successfully implanted in the womb. "And 'die' isn't even a good word. They start degenerating."[39] For this reason she does not believe that cells in a Petri dish can be called a "person."

But even if the Nashes had been Catholics, would they necessarily have acted any differently? We know that a slim (but growing) majority of American Catholics make moral decisions regarding such things as abortion and contraception primarily on the basis of their own inner beliefs. Their ultimate authority in dealing with such questions is their own conscience, not the teaching of the Church. This is not to say that they don't think the Church has wise teaching, it is just that they don't think its teaching is equally wise on every issue.

On learning of the Vatican's reaction to Molly's story, one person responded, "Don't those people have any idea what agony parents of a dying child go through?" He then raised the question of whether priests and bishops would be more compassionate if they had children of their own. Another asked, "What would Jesus do?" and proceeded to relate what Jesus *did* do, by referring to the Gospel story in which a man named Jairus came to Jesus and begged him, "My little daughter is at the point of death. Come and lay your hands on her, so that she may be well and live." Jesus went and saved her. He did not let her die.

For its part, the Catholic Church would answer that mere sentiment, even one as noble as compassion, cannot be relied upon to decide moral questions. Furthermore, if we focus on one aspect of this case apart from the others, namely, the destruction of human embryos, this is more than a violation of Catholic moral law, it is a violation of a law that transcends any one religion—the law that one should never deliberately take an innocent human life. For every human being walking the earth today was once a cluster of cells less than five days old.

Nevertheless, for some the story of the Nashes recalls the Galileo case and rekindles the suspicion that the Catholic Church is blind to the march of scientific progress. The conflict between the Vatican and biotechnology will doubtless continue, as scientists around the world promote the potential benefits of embryonic stem-cell research. As Furcht and Hoffman put it, "No new approach to dealing with the monumental suffering and social costs of major diseases comes close to the promise of stem cell therapy."[40] The promise extends to juvenile diabetes, cystic fibrosis, multiple sclerosis, Parkinson's disease, various cancers, and even to spinal cord injuries. Such potential benefits have already led many mainline Protestant churches to approve embryonic stem-cell research.[41]

At the same time, the danger posed by biotechnology is recognized well beyond the bounds of traditional religion.

Political philosopher Francis Fukuyama has sounded the alarm that genetic engineering may create a "posthuman future" in which our species, *Homo sapiens*, is transformed into another species entirely. What effect would this have on fundamental Christian beliefs—the belief that humanity is created in God's image, and that in Jesus Christ that image finds its fulfillment and perfection, in accordance with the eternal purpose of God? Can the purposes of God be thwarted? These are bewildering questions.

From a Christian perspective, what *can* be said is that humanity, by virtue of its freedom, is capable of bringing about its own destruction. Even the sovereignty of God appears to be no bulwark against this *human* capacity.

Chapter 8

The Rise of Modern Psychology as a Challenge to the Catholic Church

In the twentieth century, psychology rose rapidly to become one of the dominant ways of understanding human nature, rivaling and often surpassing Christianity in that regard. Vast numbers of people in the Western world began to think of themselves first and foremost as psychological beings. To them, psychology offered better solutions to life's problems than did traditional Christianity, and even where psychology offered no solution, it could discuss the problem in more realistic terms. Christianity began to look archaic and out of step with the changing times.

Even among those who held on to their faith, psychology often served as the criterion for judging which religious teachings to follow and which to leave behind. Personal happiness and emotional well-being became the primary goals of life, and some of Christianity's moral teachings seemed to block the path to these goals by setting up impossible standards which could only result in feelings of guilt or shame or both. To the extent that psychology triumphed over religion as the ultimate guide to life, it paved the way for *The Da Vinci Code*'s claim that much of traditional Christianity can finally be abandoned.

For this chapter, I have chosen to concentrate on Sigmund Freud (1856–1939), the founder of psychoanalysis, because no other figure in the history of psychology did more to shape and mold twentieth-century thought. By the time he died, not only had he transformed psychology and psychiatry, but he had also made his mark on sociology, criminology, anthropology, biography, history, film, art, literature, and literary criticism.[1] In his elegy on Freud, the poet W. H. Auden put it this way, "To us he is no more a person now but a whole climate of opinion."[2] Half a century after Freud's death, the literary critic Harold Bloom said that "No twentieth-century writer . . . rivals Freud's position as the central imagination of our age."[3] And in 2006, psychiatrist and best-selling author Peter Kramer titled his biography *Freud: Inventor of the Modern Mind*. Yet none of this would have impressed Freud, who wanted to be thought of strictly as a scientist.

Albert Einstein was one of Freud's most ardent admirers and told Freud on a number of occasions how much he enjoyed reading his writings because of their wonderful clarity and beauty, even though he could not make up his mind about the validity of Freud's theories. When he wrote to congratulate Freud on the occasion of his eightieth birthday, Freud replied, "But I have often asked myself what indeed there is to admire about [my theories] if they are not true, that is, if they do not contain a high degree of truth."[4]

Yet truth in the scientific sense is precisely what critic Bloom and biographer Kramer find lacking in Freud's body of work. Controversy surrounding the scientific standing of psychoanalysis has raged from the beginning and shows no sign of dying down for the foreseeable future. Whenever pundits predict its imminent demise, new studies are published which claim to offer empirical evidence supporting aspects of Freudian theory. No doubt Freud would have been particularly pleased with the evidence from neuroscience, his own original field of study, that MRIs are confirming the existence of unconscious mental processes. Yet the dominant view today is undoubtedly that most of Freud's ideas have not stood up to scientific scrutiny.

Freud has been criticized on a number of grounds. Among the most severe criticisms have been those directed against his method, especially his reliance on case studies of individual patients, which by their very nature cannot be repeated and empirically verified by others. The philosopher of science Karl Popper famously pronounced Freud's theories unscientific because they are not open to being disproved. Others have faulted Freud for trying to capitalize too much on evolutionary theory and thus reducing the human mind to mere biological processes, or for wildly exaggerating the importance of the sexual aspect of human personality. In these and other ways, Freud has been viewed with skepticism and even dismissed. Critics have compared him to a traveler at night who took a wrong turn and became hopelessly lost. But his disciples insist that the critics are mistaken; all along Freud had been guiding his journey by the stars.

The scientific standing of Freud's theories is not what ultimately matters for the purposes of this book, which is rather the scope of his influence on twentieth-century thought and beyond. One gauge of that influence is provided by a study published in 1993 comparing writers in terms of the number of times they have been quoted or referred to, which showed that Freud surpassed all other writers except Plato, Aristotle, Shakespeare, and Lenin.[5] Even in our everyday speech, we pay homage to Freud whenever we speak of "acting out," "being in denial," "libido," "defense mechanisms," "the unconscious," "narcissism," "rationalization," "passive-aggressive behavior," and of course "Freudian slips." It is probably fair to say that the vast majority of those who have read *The Da Vinci Code* think of human behavior at least partially in Freudian terms.

How did Freud gain such enormous influence, especially in America, when indeed his was a bleak, atheistic vision of the individual caught in a never-ending conflict between the incessant demands of desires within and the ironclad restraints of civilization without? Yet he did gain such influence and, by doing so, helped psychology to become for many a source of wisdom superior to traditional Christianity. The following section lays a foundation for understanding how this came about by providing an overview of the development of some of Freud's ideas. Readers who feel no need for such an overview may want to skip this section and proceed directly to the section on Freud's attack on religion.

So, how *did* Freud, with his dark, forbidding vision, gain such a hold on the American imagination?

The Development of Freud's Ideas

The most momentous of Freud's ideas was that our lives are motivated and directed by irrational forces of which we are largely unaware. This was his concept of the unconscious. Freud did not discover the unconscious, but he was the first to recognize its central importance in understanding human behavior, feelings, and thoughts. Prior to Freud, psychologists and philosophers had focused almost exclusively on *conscious* mental processes.

How did Freud come to his theory of the unconscious? To understand that, it is necessary to trace his career from its beginning. After obtaining a medical degree from the University of Vienna in 1881, Freud began his career as a physician specializing in nervous disorders, eventually becoming a world authority on cerebral palsy in children.[6] In time, however, his interest shifted to a baffling syndrome then called "hysteria." What made hysteria baffling to the medical establishment was that its physical symptoms, such as paralysis, did not appear to be caused by nerve damage, as would have been expected. Yet neither was there evidence that the patient was faking her symptoms.

For Freud, the mystery deepened when his friend and mentor Josef Breuer, an eminent Viennese neurologist, told him the story of a young woman whom he had treated for hysteria. Breuer had noticed that when, under hypnosis, the woman recalled and described all of the circumstances in which each of her symptoms first came about, and relived the original emotions she had experienced, the symptom went away.[7] Breuer called this "the cathartic method"; the patient herself called it "the talking cure." Breuer concluded that at the root of hysterical symptoms were buried memories of distressing incidents in the patient's life. Later, when Freud wrote about the case of "Anna O."—as she was called, to safeguard her anonymity—he called the cathartic method "the immediate precursor of psychoanalysis."[8]

In his own treatment of hysteria, Freud soon gave up hypnosis, for which he had little talent, and replaced it with a technique that was actually far more effective, "free association." His procedure was to encourage patients to relax and speak to him openly about whatever came into their minds, however trivial or embarrassing it might seem to them. Freud observed that when the patient's flow of words reached an impasse, unconscious forces seemed to be at work, blocking the way. Freud called this blocking mechanism "repression." Often, what was repressed was the memory of a traumatic experience whose conscious recollection would cause acute distress. And yet the memory was, in one sense, crying out for release. Keeping such memories from conscious awareness used up an immense amount of psychic energy and in this way was preventing the patient from living a full and productive life.

As a therapist, Freud wished to remain a blank screen to his patients. This is reflected in the way he conducted therapeutic sessions, including his sitting behind the couch on which the patient lay, totally out of his or her sight. The patient's role was to speak freely; the therapist's role was to maintain an "alert passivity."[9] Freud would always say that the therapist's motive for being a blank screen should be to allow a patient to develop strong feelings toward the therapist (which inevitably happens), and then to help the patient see that these feelings really have nothing to do with the therapist as a person, but are unconscious repetitions of emotional patterns established early in life. This phenomenon he labeled *transference*. Recognition of the emotional pattern could provide an insight of immense value in cases where the pattern was destructive, as for example when a patient's romantic relationships were really unconscious searches for the love of a parent—a love that was never satisfied when the patient was growing up.

Following the death of his father in 1896, Freud's experience of a whole range of conflicting emotions led him to undertake a lengthy and difficult analysis of himself, including dream analysis, much of which would be incorporated (without acknowledging that the dreams were his) in his *Interpretation of Dreams*. Though he published it in November 1899, he had it postdated to 1900 to signify what he hoped would be the dawning of a new era in the history of science. He always considered this book his masterpiece. Thirty years later, when he was seventy-five, he said of it, "Insight such as this falls to one's lot but once in a lifetime."

Freud regarded dreams as "the royal road to a knowledge of the unconscious activities of the mind."[10] They were powerful expressions of unconscious drives, overlaid by veils of symbolism. If this symbolism could be interpreted and its overarching patterns discerned, dream analysis could give profound insight into the subterranean wishes, hopes, and fears that unconsciously guided an individual's life.

The goal of therapy was to bring to light this unconscious motivation, as revealed by dream analysis and by the analysis of a whole range of other psychological phenomena. Once in the light, this motivation could be examined and evaluated by the patient and therapist together to determine its harmful and helpful effects.

Freud constructed several theoretical models of the mind to help explain how the mind works from a psychoanalytic point of view. The most famous of these is the tripartite division of the mind into the *id*, the *ego*, and the *superego*. (They are not really three "parts," but such language is convenient.) The id refers to the reservoir of biological instincts or drives—such as the sexual drive and aggression—that a child is born with. These are unconscious.

As the child grows in awareness of the world around her and learns from her experiences, she develops a sense of the reality around her. The ego is the largely conscious aspect of the mind that tries to mediate between the drives of the id and the demands of reality.

The superego (an idea which overlaps to some extent with that of conscience) is made up of those notions of right and wrong learned, both consciously and unconsciously, from parents, teachers, and other authority figures. It is largely unconscious and is the source of feelings of guilt, for example.

Conflicts may arise between the different "parts" of the mind. For instance, a man who has a deep fear of anger owing to his own terrifying experiences in childhood of his father's anger may be incapable of expressing anger as an adult even when it is appropriate and necessary. The natural flow of anger is blocked by repression. In its place, an extremely gentle and unassertive mask may emerge, which in fact hides from others and from the individual himself his fear that an expression of anger will result in retaliation. These unconscious strategies are called defense mechanisms.

In such a case, the task of the analyst would be to help the patient recognize the root conflict and consider more healthy ways of resolving or at least mitigating it. The ideal therapeutic result would be that the patient's ego would have greater freedom to deal with reality.

The psychological concept of defense mechanisms, referring to any of a number of unconscious mental processes that protect the conscious mind from painful thoughts or feelings, has proved to be one of Freud's most helpful insights for interpreting human behavior. One defense mechanism that has become very familiar in our time is denial. If a practicing alcoholic is accused of being an alcoholic, she will typically deny it and say her drinking is not as bad as her accuser thinks it is. Another common response is, "I know, and I'm going to do something about it." But she doesn't do anything about it, and the firm conviction of *recovering* alcoholics is that she can't recover because she can't accept that she *is* an alcoholic. This denial is so powerful because it is unconscious. *Recovering* alcoholics say that it takes a very great deal of time and help to break through the barrier of denial.

Another defense mechanism of immense power is projection, which consists of attributing to others qualities that we cannot face in ourselves. Projection has been proposed as one key to interpreting racist beliefs, for example, since these beliefs tend to follow patterns, regardless of the race in question. For example, it is striking how similar the beliefs about Blacks held by white racists in America were to the beliefs about Jews held by Nazis in Germany.

The parallels included the following: Both Blacks and Jews were considered intellectually inferior. Yet, while deficient in terms of real intelligence, Blacks and Jews did have a kind of animal cunning which enabled them to lie, cheat, and steal.[11] It also enabled them to avoid hard work, thus reinforcing their innate laziness. They were greedy and materialistic. The typical Black man drives a Cadillac while his children starve; the typical Jewish moneylender would be willing to sell his own daughter.[12] Filled with insatiable lust, Blacks and Jews were sexual predators just waiting to attack.

The stereotyped pattern of qualities attributed to very different groups points to the common origin of those qualities—not the hated groups themselves but rather the racist mind-set. A closer look reveals that the very qualities the racist despises in others are precisely those which he or she cannot acknowledge in himself or herself. The clarity with which the concept of projection enables us to unmask the psychological origins of racism makes it a tool of immense potential benefit for society.

A third example of a defense mechanism is displacement, in which one obsesses about a trivial matter in order to prevent becoming aware of a serious matter. For example, a man might reproach himself for using foul language in front of his children but not care or even notice that he is squandering his paycheck on alcohol while his family's needs are being neglected. By focusing on the former, he unconsciously avoids facing the latter. But at the conscious level he imagines that he is taking responsibility for his wrongdoing.

Thus the idea of displacement provides potential insight into the role of guilt feelings in our lives. Of course, the danger of analyzing guilt feelings as displacement is that one may imagine that every manifestation of them is illusory. (The trouble is that no sooner is self-deception kicked out the front door than it creeps in through the back door, but that is not Freud's fault.)

The most shocking and scandalous part of Freud's theory

was his emphasis on sexuality, which evoked widespread condemnation even from the medical establishment when he introduced it in his *Three Essays on the Theory of Sexuality* (1905). What was particularly shocking was his insistence that a person's sexual life begins in infancy, not at puberty as was widely assumed. This clashed with the Victorian myth of "childhood innocence." Freud's theory required a broadening of the definition of sexuality.

"It is a mistaken belief," he wrote, "that sexuality coincides with 'genitality.' The sexual instincts pass through a complicated course of development, and it is only at the end of it that the 'primacy of the genital zone' is attained."[13] Redefining and recontextualizing human sexuality in this way had far-reaching implications for the way sexuality would be viewed by culture at large.

Let us take for our example masturbation, one of the great taboo subjects of the Victorian Age. Physicians had occasionally referred to instances of masturbation in early childhood, but, Freud observed, "these [were] always quoted only as exceptional events, as oddities or as horrifying instances of precocious depravity."[14] Freud was the first to regard masturbation as a normal and nearly universal phenomenon of early childhood.[15] Thus masturbation in a five-year-old boy was not a sign of gross moral corruption but an innocent expression of a natural sexual drive, no more to be condemned than thumb-sucking at an earlier age.

Freud's view of masturbation may be contrasted with the one found in an authoritative guide for women published in 1901, *Maiden, Wife, and Mother,* by Mary R. Melendy, M.D., Ph.D. Dr. Melendy's lengthy discussion of what a mother should do with a little boy who masturbates includes the following advice:

> Teach him that when he handles or excites the sexual organs, all parts of the body suffer, because they are connected by nerves that run throughout the system. This is why it is called "self-abuse." . . . Don't think it does no harm to your boy because he does not suffer now, for the effects of this vice come on so slowly that the victim is often very near death before you realize he has done himself harm. . . . It lays the foundation for consumption, paralysis and heart disease. . . . It even makes many lose their minds; others, when grown, commit suicide.[16]

Dr. Melendy goes on to commend the example of a mother who cured her five-year-old son of "this loathsome habit" by terrifying him into believing that if he continued he would soon die a horrifying death. (Her method was to put an ointment on his abdomen as he slept at night that caused a stain, and then tell him in the morning that the stain was the first sign of the deadly disease.)

The dire consequences of masturbation in later years that Dr. Melendy refers to are illustrated in a report contained in a very popular Catholic work of the time, *Educating for Purity*, in which a physician describes an interview with a boy of eighteen (whom he refers to as a young masturbator): "'A young masturbator narrates that all of his twelve or fifteen companion onanists died early in frightful torments. At eighteen years he was afflicted with frequent nightly pollutions which occurred in spite of himself. "I never sleep soundly, and the whole day I am sad.'"[17]

With respect to little girls who masturbated, one medical solution recommended by European doctors was to have the clitoris cauterized, leaving it incapable of being stimulated. Freud's *Three Essays on the Theory of Sexuality* brought a halt to this form of genital mutilation.[18] We will return to the question of attitudes toward masturbation later in this chapter, but for now I would like to turn briefly to Freud's attitude toward homosexuality, another subject toward which he showed extraordinary tolerance for his day and age.

When he was about eighty, Freud received a letter from an American woman whom he did not know asking him for advice about her son. He replied to her in English: "I gather from your letter that your son is a homosexual." He noticed that she herself did not use the word *homosexual* and could understand why, so he said to her, "Homosexuality is assuredly no advantage, but it is nothing to be ashamed of, no vice, no degradation, it cannot be classified as an illness; we consider it to be a variation of the sexual function, produced by a certain arrest of sexual development." He goes on to mention that "many highly respectable individuals of ancient and modern times have been homosexuals, several of the greatest men among them. (Plato, Michelangelo, Leonardo da Vinci, etc.) It is a great injustice to persecute homosexuality as a crime—and a cruelty, too."

Freud told her that while he could not answer her question about whether her son's condition could be changed, he hoped psychoanalysis might be able to bring the young man "harmony, peace of mind, [and] full efficiency, whether he remains a homosexual or gets changed." Years later this woman recalled Freud as "a great and good man."[19]

The late Anthony Storr, the distinguished Oxford psychotherapist and author, considered this tolerance of what society condemned as one of Freud's greatest legacies.[20] A further example of that tolerance, which reveals much else about Freud as well, is the case of the "Wolf Man," whose pseudonym comes from a haunting dream he had as a child involving white wolves. The man was Sergei Pankejeff, a young Russian aristocrat who came to Freud in 1910 with a number of severe symptoms. His bizarre childhood history had included the torture of small animals.

His first period of psychoanalysis extended for more than four years and brought considerable improvement, which Freud thought was due to the patient's coming to awareness of psychic trauma suffered in childhood. The key to uncovering that trauma was Freud's analysis of the dream of the white wolves. Freud's crediting psychoanalysis for the improvement is questionable, however, especially in light of the reflections of the "Wolf Man" himself more than sixty years later, a long-term follow-up unparalleled in the history of psychoanalysis.[21]

The "Wolf Man" had profound doubts about the validity of psychoanalysis, but he believed that Freud had helped him just the same. Anthony Storr sums up the significance of the reflections by the "Wolf Man" that were published in 1971: "The 'Wolf Man' attributes his improvement wholly to his relationship with Freud; to his having discovered a new 'father' who was more tolerant and accepting than his own; one who was prepared to listen to his intimate and sometimes shocking revelations for four years without criticism, revulsion or repudiation of him as a person."[22] In a letter to Carl Jung, Freud wrote that psychoanalysis was "in essence a cure through love."[23] There may be more truth in this statement than Freud himself realized.

Freud's Attack on Religion

Freud was a Jew and proud of his Jewish ancestry. He regularly attended meetings of the Jewish fraternal organization B'nai B'rith and refused to accept royalties from the publication of his works in Hebrew and Yiddish.[24] His strong identification with the Jewish people was partly an act of defiance in the face of the hostility he encountered in his native Vienna, a city in which "anti-Semitic politics flourished, anti-Semitic organizations proliferated, anti-Semitic writing and propaganda poured forth in an unending stream."[25] (It was the anti-Semitism of Vienna that converted young Adolf Hitler.) And this was happening even though Vienna, the capital of an Empire that was officially Catholic, was controlled by the Catholic hierarchy.

The Cathedral of St. Stefan, with what Freud called "its abominable steeple,"[26] dominated the city of Vienna, and became to Freud a symbol of the Church's oppressive yet irresistible presence. Living in a city soaked in racist hatred of the Jews engendered in him a resentment and hostility toward the Church that was deepened by his growing awareness of the history of Christian persecution of the Jews. This explains the conversation (quoted in the Introduction) between Freud and a visitor that took place in the 1930s: Finding that Freud looked sullen and gloomy, the visitor asked him why. "It's because I've been thinking about my mortal enemy," Freud said. "Oh, you mean the Nazi Party?" his visitor asked. "No," Freud said, "the Roman Catholic Church!"

Yet Freud's identification with the Jewish people did not go so far as to accept a belief in God. According to his disciple and biographer Ernest Jones, Freud "went through his life from beginning to end as a natural atheist."[27] Freud often described himself as "a godless Jew."[28] He viewed religious belief as an illusion unconsciously created in the psyche to fulfill childhood wishes which would otherwise be crushed by the harshness of reality. But the maintenance of this illusion came at a price; the amount of psychic energy needed to keep reality at bay was immense. Freud hoped that by exposing the psychological origin of religious belief, both in the individual and in the human race, he might hasten the decline of religion, alleviate the neurotic suffering that it caused, and free individuals from the irrational fears held over from childhood.

Freud's writings on the origins of religion in general (*Totem and Taboo*) and of Judaism and Christianity in particular (*Moses and Monotheism*) are wildly speculative and have not stood the test of time. Of *Totem and Taboo*, Freud himself once said, "Oh don't take that seriously. I made that up on a rainy Sunday afternoon."[29] Far more interesting, though still controversial, are his explanations of the psychological origins of religion in the individual (*The Future of an Illusion*) and of the role of religion in society (*Civilization and Its Discontents*). Although Freud's main focus was the Judaeo-Christian tradition, in the discussion that follows we will focus more narrowly on Christianity and especially Roman Catholicism. Freud's interpretation of religion is closely correlated with his theory of personality development. In what follows, we will focus on Freud's thoughts on male as opposed to female development, as his statements on female development have been largely discredited.

According to Freud, the roots of an individual's belief in God may be traced back to early childhood. The very description of God as Father suggests that God's real identity is the child's own father. The infant experiences feelings of helplessness, of utter dependence upon his parents, and of fear of losing his parents' protection and care. The infant boy is more closely bonded to his mother, who breastfeeds him, than he is to his father. The father is more distant and, to that extent, more awe-inspiring. By about the age of four or five, the boy's attachment to his mother is so intense that he desires exclusive possession of her, but he cannot have it because the father also enjoys the mother's love. The boy experiences feelings of jealousy and hostility toward his father and wishes to replace the father in his mother's affections. Freud called this the "Oedipus complex" after the Greek tragic hero who unwittingly murdered his father and married his mother.

But the boy can hardly hope to triumph over his "all-powerful" father and instead begins to fear that he might lose his father's love and incur his father's wrath. So great is this threat perceived to be, that the child unconsciously begins to let go of his obsessive desire for his mother, while at the same time turning his earlier admiration for his father into identification. The father represents an ideal for the child to realize in his own life. At the same time, however, the father is the ultimate authority for the boy.

Through his identification with the father, the boy internalizes the father's will, which becomes part of the voice of conscience within, telling him, "You must do this, but you must not do that." Obedience to the voice of conscience brings its own internal rewards: pride, peace, self-satisfaction. Disobedience in turn brings its own punishment in the form of guilt, while failure to live up to the ideal in his mind produces shame. The benefit of this complex process is the stability and security of knowing what behavior will be rewarded and what will be punished.

Over time, the boy becomes increasingly aware of his father's imperfections and disappointed with him as a parental figure. He unconsciously longs for an ideal father figure as a replacement. Moreover, he begins to perceive that his parents cannot protect him from the terrors of the world and above all from death. Unable to face these terrors squarely, he turns to religion, the seeds of which have already been planted in him by the earlier religious teaching he has received. God is the all-powerful protector who will save him even from death if only he will obey God's commandments. Thus, by regressing to an earlier attitude toward life—one in which certain behaviors will ensure his father's protection—he is able to attain some measure of peace in an otherwise fearfully unpredictable and uncontrollable world.

According to Freud, it is hard to break free from the infantile narcissism in which we see ourselves as the apple of God's eye.

He regarded this to be emotional maladjustment, the retention of an infantile way of thinking in adult life. Ultimately, it is an inability to accept life on life's terms. That is why he called religious beliefs "illusions, fulfillments of the oldest, strongest and most urgent wishes of mankind."

After Freud, some found it hard to maintain the biblical view that God had made humanity in the divine image. Freud had argued (following the philosopher Feuerbach) that it was really the other way around. Humanity had made God in its image. It was equally hard for these people to uphold the traditional Christian belief that God had endowed human beings with reason to enable them to make free, rational decisions in accordance with divine law. Freedom and rationality were but surface phenomena of a mind driven and dominated by instinctual processes inherited from the animal world through evolution. Humanity's chief endowment now appeared to be those irrational drives passed on through evolution, which had left its stamp on the mind every bit as much as on the body. Even humanity's noblest achievements, from works of art to acts of charity and justice, had roots in unconscious impulses which were at best morally ambiguous.

Freud recognized how profoundly unacceptable was his view of humanity:

> In the course of centuries the naïve self-love of men has had to submit to two major blows at the hands of science. The first was when they learnt that our earth was not the centre of the universe but only a tiny fragment of a cosmic system of scarcely imaginable vastness. . . . The second blow fell when biological research destroyed man's supposedly privileged place in creation and proved his descent from the animal kingdom and his ineradicable animal nature. . . . But human megalomania will have suffered its third and most wounding

blow from the psychological research of the present
time which seeks to prove to the ego that it is not even
master in its own house, but must content itself with
scanty information of what is going on unconsciously
in its mind.[30]

It is not a consoling picture.

After Freud, even John Henry Newman (1801–90), one of the
most subtle and penetrating minds in the history of Christianity, suddenly seems naïve when he writes of recognizing God
through conscience:

> If, on doing wrong, we feel the same tearful, broken-
> hearted sorrow which overwhelms us on hurting a
> mother; if on doing right, we enjoy the same sunny se-
> renity of mind, the same soothing, satisfactory delight
> which follows on our receiving praise from a father, we
> certainly have within us the image of some person, to
> whom our love and veneration look, in whose smile we
> find happiness, for whom we yearn, towards whom we
> direct our pleadings, in whose anger we are troubled
> and waste away. These feelings in us are such as require
> for their exciting cause an intelligent being.[31]

For anyone familiar with Freud's ideas, this passage from Newman appears to reveal far more than its author was consciously
aware of. Whether this appearance will stand up to careful scrutiny is, of course, another matter, because both men, Freud as
well as Newman, are trying to persuade us of positions based
on deep-seated personal beliefs which for them had the status
of self-evident truths: Freud, that there is no God; Newman, that
there is.[32] Those who have reacted most strongly against Freud
have argued that his atheism blinds him to the inner realities of
Christianity.

On the other hand, Freud's skeptical attitude can be an aid in ridding ourselves of false and even idolatrous images of God. One image which many have rejected as false is that of the God of wrath—a.k.a. the "punishing God," an image that was widespread among Catholics in modern times. In this image, God is seen as being ever on the lookout for any sin (however slight), quick to condemn, and willing to send his children to hell for all eternity if by chance they happen to die suddenly without having confessed and repented. Those who came to reject this image posed the rhetorical question, "What kind of stable relationship could ever be possible with a God such as this?"

Freud's Influence in America

In 1909, at the age of fifty-three, Freud was invited to receive an honorary doctorate and deliver a series of lectures at Clark University in Massachusetts. He regarded the invitation as the first official recognition of the psychoanalytic movement.[33] His five lectures were delivered in his customary style, without notes, and gave a clear and engaging introduction to psychoanalysis. They made a very favorable impression on a distinguished audience which included William James from Harvard and a number of other leading American thinkers. Although they were given in German, they were important enough to be reviewed in the daily press, which spoke highly of them. When they were translated into English and published several months later, they accelerated the spread of his reputation in America.[34] Meanwhile, in 1911, both the New York Psychoanalytic Society and the American Psychoanalytic Association were founded.

Freud's name became even more familiar in other ways. In 1914, *The Psychopathology of Everyday Life*, which would prove to be his most popular book, was published. A London magazine pinpointed one aspect of his appeal when it described him as "the

Sherlock Holmes of the Mind."[35] This would not be the last time this comparison was made, and Freud did not reject it. It testifies to his talent for compelling narrative, which he exhibited in so many of his writings, and especially in his case histories. Freud's ideas even began to be disseminated in popular magazines, such as *Ladies' Home Journal*, and they were often portrayed in detective stories as helping to solve crimes.

When the First World War ended in 1918, large numbers of American soldiers came home suffering from what we would now call post-traumatic stress disorder. Psychiatrists turned to psychoanalysis for help in treating them, and Freud's stature grew. By the mid-1920s, Freud was a household name, so much so that in 1924 the publisher of the *Chicago Tribune* offered Freud the then considerable sum of $25,000 to psychoanalyze Leopold and Loeb, the defendants in what was being hailed as the trial of the century. Freud declined the offer.

Later that same year, film producer Samuel Goldwyn, who called Freud "the greatest love doctor in the world," offered him $100,000 to be a consultant in the making of "a really great love story." Again Freud declined.[36] Although he was in financial straits after the War, Freud was also worried that such popularization of his views in America might do more harm than good. The danger was real. By the end of the 1920s, some two hundred popular books on Freud had been published. (There were also serious attempts by competent psychiatrists such as Karl Menninger to meet the growing hunger of the American public for authoritative books on psychoanalysis.)

Meanwhile, in the mid-1920s, the New York Psychoanalytic Society declared that only medical doctors could be psychoanalysts. Though Freud himself had an M.D., he strongly opposed this requirement. He thought medical training unnecessary and feared psychoanalysis would be relegated to a branch of medicine, whereas he considered it "a cure for souls." Freud's wishes were defeated. But the requirement that American psychoanalysts have medical degrees resulted in their gaining the added prestige that went with having an M.D. after one's name.

In the 1930s, the rise of Nazism drove many Jewish psychoanalysts to the United States, resulting in the establishment of a number of training institutes. Psychoanalysis became a movement in America which would attain dominance in the 1950s. In addition, variations of psychoanalytic theory began to be disseminated by "neo-Freudians" such as Erich Fromm, Erik Erikson, and Karen Horney, whose writings became widely known and respected.

Changes in psychoanalytic practice were brought about by the huge numbers of veterans who needed treatment after the Second World War. In 1946, there were forty-four thousand inpatients in Veterans Administration hospitals.[37] Psychoanalysis was deemed to have been successful in the treatment of soldiers after the First World War, and it was only natural that the U.S. Government should turn to it again.

But in order for it to be used on such a large scale, a radical reduction in the amount of time that could be given to each soldier was required. (Freud had normally met with patients six times per week over a period of several years.) Nevertheless, even in small doses, it was regarded as effective. Stories about soldiers being successfully treated for post-traumatic stress disorder appeared in a wide variety of newspapers and popular magazines (*Life*, *Time*, *Newsweek*, *Scientific American*, *House and Garden*, *Ladies' Home Journal*, and *Woman's Home Companion*). Readers were fascinated by tales of brave soldiers traumatized in battle who were helped by speaking freely of their experiences, their nightmares, and the guilt they felt for surviving the battle when their fellow soldiers had died.

Freud was becoming a hero. Another flood of popular books on him began appearing in 1950, together with the three-volume biography by his disciple Ernest Jones. The review of the biography in the *New Yorker* noted that by the age of forty Freud had achieved neither fame nor fortune. Yet, it went on to say, "If his discoveries prevail, he will have reached out to touch and perhaps in some measure to save every other life on earth."

It is interesting to note that three decades later the *New Yorker* would once again praise Freud to the skies, likening Freud's message to an invitation to undertake a "spiritual journey of self discovery":

> To become acquainted with the lowest depth of the soul—to explore whatever personal hell we may suffer from—is not an easy undertaking. Freud's findings and, even more, the way he presents them to us give us the confidence that this demanding and potentially dangerous voyage of self-discovery will result in our becoming more fully human, so that we may no longer be enslaved without knowing it to the dark forces that reside in us. By exploring and understanding the origins and the potency of these forces, we not only become much better able to cope with them but also gain a much deeper and more compassionate understanding of our fellow man.[38]

This was published in an article in the *New Yorker* in 1982 which was then expanded and published in book form a few years later. But it was really in the 1950s and 1960s that Freudianism reached the zenith of its popularity, and to that time we must return. In 1953, the Standard Edition of Freud's works in English began to be published. Several of Freud's major writings were included in Encyclopædia Britannica's *Great Books of the Western World*. And on college campuses across America, Freud was all the rage.

The effect of psychoanalytic ideas on younger people was subtle but widespread. By dominating the mental health field for decades, psychoanalysis inevitably influenced the counselors who in turn influenced the children in the American public school system. Most influential of all were the psychoanalytic ideas underlying the advice given by Dr. Benjamin Spock in his *Common Sense Book of Baby and Child Care* (1946). Spock, an analyzed pediatrician, based a number of his ideas on Freud's theory of child development. Selling more than twenty-four million copies between the late 1940s and the 1970s, it became "the most important single vehicle by which Freudian psychology influenced American society.[39]

Let us pause briefly to consider one of the questions with which we began. (We will consider it again later in the Concluding Remarks.) How did Freud, with his dark vision of the individual caught in a never-ending conflict between the incessant demands of desires within and the ironclad restraints of civilization without, gain such a hold on the American imagination? It is at the very least paradoxical. The great historian of Freudianism in America, Nathan Hale, offers this useful historical insight:

> In one of the few popular analyses of *why* Freud and psychoanalysis had achieved such a vogue in America, [literary critic Alfred] Kazin argued in 1956 in the *New York Times* that it was because of Freudianism's "insistence on individual fulfillment, satisfaction and happiness." Harking back to the popular Freudianism of the 1920s, Kazin insisted that psychoanalysis emphasized the "truths of human nature" against "the hypocrisies and cruelties of conventional morality," and stressed the role sex played in the imagination. "No one can count the number of people . . . who turn to a psychoanalyst or to psychoanalytic literature for an explanation of their

suffering where once they would have turned to a minister or to the Bible for consolation."[40]

Yet Freud himself would have regarded his triumph in America as having been gained at too great a cost—sacrificing the most disturbing truths of psychoanalysis for the sake of the relentless American quest for "happiness."

In the 1960s, Freudianism began to go into decline for a wide variety of reasons. The repeated failure of scientists to obtain experimental confirmation of psychoanalytic claims undermined its credibility. At the same time, drugs were being invented that offered cheaper, quicker, and often more reliable help than psychoanalysis. (Freud had predicted that pharmaceuticals would one day replace psychoanalysis to a large extent.) Feminists insisted that his understanding of female sexuality was not only deficient, as Freud himself had acknowledged, but had exerted a positively harmful influence on women by reinforcing the idea that women were inferior to men.

Nevertheless, Freud had brought about lasting change in human self-understanding. His emphasis on child development led to a deeper awareness of the emotional needs of children and of the lifelong damage that could be done by neglecting them. His emphasis on sexual development from infancy onward led to the removal of some of the taboos surrounding the subject of sexuality and to more open discussion of it. The sexual aspect of human personality came to be recognized as foundational.

The Catholic Church itself affirmed this in its *Declaration on Certain Questions Concerning Sexual Ethics* (1975): "The human person, present-day scientists maintain, is so profoundly affected by sexuality that it must be considered one of the principal formative influences on the life of a man or woman. In fact, sex is the source of the biological, psychological and spiritual characteristics which make a person male or female and which thus considerably influence each individual's progress towards maturity and membership of society." It is questionable whether this statement could have been made if the Freudian revolution in ideas had not taken place.

But earlier Catholic attitudes persist. As we will see in Chapter 9, there is a thread running through the history of Catholic preaching and teaching which associates sex with sin. The most shocking expression of this tendency is the statement of Pope Gregory the Great (c. 540–604) that all sexual pleasure is sinful, which includes the sexual pleasure involved when a devout Catholic couple conceives a child. A stern warning about marriage was given by St. Bernardino of Siena (1380–1444), who said that 999 of 1,000 marriages are of the devil's making. And he was referring to marriages in the Church![41] Even giving a kiss could be perilous. A Vatican decree issued in 1666 and never revoked stated that a kiss given for pleasure was a mortal sin.[42]

However extreme these statements may be, they reflect an underlying attitude of fear toward sexuality that has darkened a significant part of the Christian tradition. And as Shakespeare observed, "In time we hate that which we often fear."[43] Sexual temptation has frequently been seen by clergymen as the chief and greatest danger in their quest to lead holy lives, especially holy *celibate* lives. Sexual temptation included masturbation, and one measure of the Catholic Church's attitude toward masturbation is the judgment of St. Alphonsus Liguori (1696–1787), one of the most highly regarded teachers of morality in the history of the Church, that sexual "impurity is either wholly or partly to blame for most people's damnation."[44]

In the 1940s and 1950s, scientific studies—most notably those of Professor Alfred Kinsey and his colleagues—lifted the last taboos surrounding sexuality for many Americans. The

Kinsey Reports showed that Americans engaged in far more sex in far more ways than anyone had imagined. A free-for-all of open discussion followed, leading the way to the sexual revolution of the 1960s. One piece of telling evidence was the launching of *Playboy* magazine in 1953, which founder Hugh Hefner claimed was prompted in part by the Kinsey Reports. The Kinsey Reports indicated, among other things, that masturbation was extremely common in both males and females of all ages. In the decades that followed, masturbation came to be viewed by many psychologists and much of society at large as harmless and even beneficial in some cases (such as those involving frigidity).

This evaluation conflicts sharply with the official teaching of the Catholic Church, as is clear even from the following brief excerpt from the article "masturbation" in the *New Catholic Encyclopedia*: "Masturbation is considered to be objectively disordered or intrinsically evil . . . that is, no circumstances or intentions can render the action of masturbation 'morally good.' The degree or seriousness of the moral culpability of a particular act of masturbation, however, can be judged only in the light of the degree of the moral actor's knowledge, freedom and intentions; full moral guilt requires a fully deliberate choice of what the person fully realizes is seriously evil, which can then be evaluated as gravely, or mortally sinful."[45]

The Church teaches that what makes masturbation "intrinsically evil" is the fact that the individual is seeking sexual pleasure outside of marital intercourse open to procreation, which is the only place where it may legitimately be sought. When done freely and knowingly, masturbation is a contradiction of the will of God and mortally sinful. Indeed, even within marriage, if a couple freely and knowingly engage in mutual masturbation as an alternative to intercourse, that too is mortally sinful. The

Catechism of the Catholic Church spells out the destiny of those who die in a state of mortal sin: "Immediately after death [their] souls . . . descend into hell, where they suffer the punishments of hell, 'eternal fire.' "[46] Since sexual fantasies also fall under the heading of sexual pleasure sought outside of marital intercourse open to procreation, they too, if freely and deliberately indulged in, are worthy of eternal hellfire.

Since the 1960s, and especially since *Humanae Vitae* in 1968, the vast majority of Catholics have rejected the Church's official teaching on masturbation, even if they are willing to acknowledge that in some instances it can be a sign of emotional immaturity or self-centeredness or a degree of loneliness which is unhealthy. This widespread rejection of the official Church teaching on masturbation prompted Pope John Paul II to insist that it be reaffirmed in the revised *Catechism of the Catholic Church* (1994). Nevertheless, it is still only a small minority of Catholics who accept this teaching, making it another point at which the majority of Catholics (and ex-Catholics) reject the authority of the Church's moral teaching.

For the majority of Catholics (and ex-Catholics), it is difficult to see how masturbation, which is regarded by the medical profession as an ordinary and normal phenomenon, could totally shatter one's relationship with God. Such a view makes it seem that as far as God's love is concerned, we live our lives perched on a knife edge—only a slip away from everlasting damnation. In recent decades, other perspectives on masturbation have been proposed to the Vatican by Catholic psychologists and theologians, but they have invariably been weighed in the balance and found wanting.

Meanwhile, without the moral guidance of the Catholic Church and other churches, large segments of American society find themselves lost in a sexual wilderness. One sign of this, which has been sensationalized by the media, is the widespread phenomenon of young people, often as young as thirteen or fourteen, engaging in recreational sex with multiple partners, sometimes even strangers, without having any qualms about it so long as it does not reach the level of genital intercourse. Here sexual intimacy is entirely separated from personal intimacy, commitment, and love. One wonders what will happen to these people when they begin to long for an exclusive, lifelong commitment. Will it still be possible for them to give themselves totally to another human being? Or did they come from broken backgrounds where loving commitment was unknown and perhaps unimaginable in any case?

Another sign of trouble is pornography. In America today, porn shops outnumber McDonald's restaurants. Far more insidious, however, is the availability of porn on the Internet, where the costs of (predominantly male) sexual fantasies extend far beyond any credit-card payments, to addiction and broken marriages. Thus, within little more than a century, sexuality outside of marriage went from being forbidden and condemned, to being reclaimed by psychology and deemed normal and healthy, to becoming the symbol of the Sexual Revolution of the 1960s, to being increasingly recognized as highly dangerous and, in the age of HIV and AIDS, potentially lethal. We have come full circle.

Once again, dialogue between the Catholic hierarchy and American culture would surely bring enormous benefits, but the problem of authority weighs heavily on both sides. Official Catholic teaching is often couched in terms of moral absolutes, as when acts such as contraception and masturbation are said to be "objectively evil" always and everywhere. The very idea of moral absolutes is almost unintelligible to many Americans, especially young Americans, among whom a vague moral relativism is widespread. For these people, the only thing that even approaches the idea of a moral absolute is individual freedom.

Concluding Remarks

Freud launched a revolution in human self-understanding. As a result of it, many Americans came to take it for granted that human nature and human relationships had to be interpreted in psychological terms if they were to be understood in any depth. Freud was not only the father of this revolution by virtue of his ideas, he was also its most brilliant propagandist. Hailed as the "Sherlock Holmes of the mind," he made readers feel as though they were reading a mystery thriller, only the mysteries he was unraveling were not limited to the story he was telling, they were mysteries about human nature itself.

Freud convinced readers that their lives were influenced by unconscious forces of which they had previously been unaware. At the same time, he demonstrated that those forces could be brought into the light, rationally evaluated in terms of their effects on our lives, and changed. By focusing on these unconscious forces, Freud made other guides to life seem naïve.

People's true motives, said Freud, were often hidden behind masks that even they were unaware of. Kindness could mask unconscious hostility. Appearances were not to be trusted. Of course, "trust not appearances" is an old saying. What made Freud's version of it seem startlingly new was that these false appearances were not being deliberately put on; the deceiver himself was deceived.

Freud's impact was to promote an attitude of suspicion toward human motivation. This struck at the very foundation of traditional claims made by authorities such as the Catholic Church. Was the torture carried out in the name of the Spanish

Inquisition just a way of trying to save a heretic's soul by forcing him to confess his mortal sin, as its defenders had claimed? Or was it a horrific expression of sadism? After Freud, simply to have formulated the question was at once to have answered it.

Freud's vision of humanity was one of endless conflict within the individual and within civilization as a whole. But after the Second World War, America entered an economic boom that seemed to open up limitless opportunities for prosperity and happiness. Psychology quickly adapted to meet the needs of a people who were upwardly mobile. It now promised to enable them to discard neurotic patterns of behavior and find happiness and fulfillment.

And here we reach one of the most important developments of all. Like virtually everything else in America, psychology became—at least to some significant extent—assimilated to the culture of consumerism. It became a tool to be used in building the good life, but in so doing it lost some of the depth that Freud had originally given it. Those who sought to benefit from it were often looking for more than a way of living with less psychic pain and suffering, which is what Freud had offered. They were looking for a way of living without any psychic pain or suffering at all.

In the 1940s, many Christian churches in America began incorporating psychological insights into their preaching and teaching. Norman Vincent Peale incorporated the psychology of the unconscious into his *Power of Positive Thinking* (1953). His combination of a highly diluted Freudianism and full-blooded American optimism attained immense popularity. Imitators are everywhere in America today. Among the most conspicuous are those who preach that Jesus wants you to be rich. My guess is that they rarely preach on Jesus' saying, "It is easier for a camel to go through the eye of a needle, than for a rich man to enter the kingdom of God."

The Catholic Church was extremely cautious about incorporating psychological insights into its teaching, not least because Catholic psychologists in America had been among the most discerning critics of Freud from the start. There was, however, a sense in which that caution came to be perceived as typical of the Church's failure to read the signs of the times. That perception riveted the minds of many Catholics in 1968, when Pope Paul VI issued *Humanae Vitae*, which reaffirmed the Church's absolute ban on artificial contraception. Many suspected the real purpose of the encyclical was to safeguard the Church's teaching authority in matters of sexuality, for if the Church changed its teaching, its image as eternal and unchanging—"the rock of ages"—would be undermined, and with it the obedience of millions.

Pope John Paul II, acknowledging that many Catholics had not found *Humanae Vitae* convincing, pleaded with Catholic theologians and philosophers to find more powerful ways of bringing its truth home to the faithful. Over the quarter century of his pontificate, no one did more in this regard than the Pope himself. His teachings on the meaning of marital love and sexuality have been hailed as among the most profound in the history of the Church. Yet, critics say, it still does not justify the claim that contraception is intrinsically evil.

It is sometimes said that the Church is more concerned with sexual matters than with things like nuclear war, environmental pollution, or the oppression of the poor by military dictatorships in Latin America. Armchair Freudians have raised the question: Why does the Vatican talk about sex incessantly? And they have an answer: Obviously, because it is obsessed with sex. Why would it be obsessed with it? Obviously because the people who run the Vatican are celibate, and celibacy requires the repression of sexuality. And as Freud often said, whatever is repressed will come out in one way or another, even if it is just in obsessive talking.

Thus, both the Church's teaching and its claims to authority are frequently viewed with distrust in America. It is true that growing numbers are now turning to authoritative Catholic teaching because they are appalled by the moral chaos they see in so much of American society. But many others, while seeing the moral chaos, no longer trust the Catholic Church, perhaps in part because they feel the Catholic Church no longer trusts them. They feel unable to give obedience to moral teaching which makes no sense to them.

In the past, Catholics would have been expected to give obedience in principle even though a particular teaching seemed to make no sense. Catholics were taught that difficult teachings would make sense in due time, so they should be accepted in good faith. For many, that bridge of trusting acceptance has collapsed. If they are invited to join in a dialogue which is free, open, and respectful, and in which they feel they are genuinely loved, perhaps that bridge can be rebuilt.

Chapter 9

Mary Magdalene, the Place of Women in the Catholic Church, and the Sexuality of Jesus

On March 16, 2005, the Vatican ended its two-year silence on *The Da Vinci Code* with a series of thunderous denunciations by Cardinal Tarcisio Bertone, a friend of Pope John Paul II and the former deputy to Cardinal Joseph Ratzinger (the Church's chief guardian of orthodoxy, who is now Pope Benedict XVI). Speaking from inside the Vatican, Cardinal Bertone called *The Da Vinci Code* "a sack full of lies against the Church and against the real history of Christianity" and deplored Dan Brown's "shameful" behavior.

With a countenance more in sorrow than in anger, he reminded his audience that "great writers did not behave this way," apparently forgetting Dante's depiction of popes in hell[1] and Milton's depiction of hell itself as the Vatican writ large. Ironically, even as the Cardinal issued an impassioned plea to booksellers to remove *The Da Vinci Code* from their shelves, the novel was being sold in the very hospital where Pope John Paul lay dying.[2] In the year that followed, sales of the novel hardly abated, even in Catholic countries where reading is nearly a lost art. Thus in Brazil, the São Paulo Book Fair in March 2006 featured *O Código Da Vinci*.[3]

Meanwhile, in the United States, as the date for the release of the much anticipated film version of the novel drew near, the Vatican launched a new campaign to immunize Catholics against this potential avian flu of the mind. Among the claims being challenged, the most explosive concerned the relationship between Jesus and Mary Magdalene. Halfway through the novel, the claim is made that not only were Jesus and Mary Magdalene married, but their marriage is a matter of historical record,[4] having been explicitly affirmed in the Gnostic *Gospel of Philip*. Moreover, in a claim especially designed to pique Catholics, the novel claims that it was through Mary Magdalene—not upon Peter, the rock—that Jesus intended to found his Church.

Despite all the attempts to expose historical errors in *The Da Vinci Code* and all the claims to offer the definitive refutation of it—there were some fifty debunking books published—*The Da Vinci Code* continued to strike a chord with millions of readers and film-goers. It is my contention that one of the primary reasons for this phenomenon is the satisfaction many people experienced in seeing Mary Magdalene finally recognized for her importance in the life of Jesus, and cleared of the centuries-old charge of having been a prostitute.

As Brown himself said in an interview, "She's a historical figure whose time has come. People sense that."[5] Perhaps more importantly, people also sense that the recognition and rehabilitation of Mary Magdalene provides a firm basis for what they see as the long overdue recognition and rehabilitation of the value of the feminine itself. For as they see it, the time has finally come to put to rest the negative mythologies with which Mary Magdalene and women in general have been saddled since the earliest days of Christianity. Simply put, though a case can be made that much of *The Da Vinci Code* is based on speculation, it is unmistakably true that prejudices against women are part of the history of the Church. The delight over *The Da Vinci Code* was at least as much about those prejudices being exposed as it was about any more dubious matter.

Mary Magdalene

So, who was this Mary Magdalene, what do we know of her, and how have mainstream Christianity and other sources treated her?

For the past twenty-five years, scholars have been drawing attention to the prominence of Mary Magdalene among the followers of Jesus, not only in the four Gospels of the New Testament, but also in the Gnostic Gospels, most of which have only recently been made readily accessible to the public. On the basis of her name, scholars believe Mary Magdalene came from Magdala, a city on the western shore of the Sea of Galilee. The Gospels of Mark and Luke tell us that Jesus cast seven demons out of her. Since the number seven is symbolic, signifying completeness, "seven demons" means that her life had been under complete demonic control.

Some scholars suggest she may have suffered from psychosis or a severe form of clinical depression. In any case, Jesus healed her and allowed her to join him as he traveled from town to town, preaching and healing. Thus, Mary, whose illness had once made her a social outcast, was given a community to belong to and a new status as a disciple of Jesus. Many other women also joined this community and ministered to Jesus and his male disciples out of their own resources.[6]

For a Jewish teacher to have had women disciples was unprecedented. For a Jewish teacher to have allowed them to travel with him was scandalous.[7] When Jesus' mission came to an end in Jerusalem and virtually all the male disciples fled in fear for their lives, these women did not abandon Jesus. They stood in sorrow before the cross, eyewitnesses of the crucifixion.[8]

Mary Magdalene was also a witness of the burial of Jesus[9] and later of the empty tomb, where she went before dawn on Sunday morning to anoint Jesus' body with fragrant oil.[10] In one of the most moving passages in all of Scripture, Mary Magdalene became the first person to see Jesus after his resurrection. As she wept before the tomb, Jesus came to her and called her name. She immediately recognized his voice and cried out, "Teacher!" She must have reached out to embrace him, but Jesus told her not to hold on to him, perhaps because the process of transformation whereby he had risen to new life was not yet complete. He then told her that she must go to the other disciples and announce his resurrection—the cornerstone of the Christian faith. For this singular honor given to Mary by Jesus, the Catholic Church calls her "the Apostle to the Apostles."

But despite this honor, after Mary makes her announcement, the New Testament says no more about her. Why? What role did she have in the early Christian community that gathered in Jerusalem? Surely she must have been greatly revered and sought after for her unique eyewitness testimony about Jesus. If so, then it is surprising and even disturbing to read what St. Paul says in his First Letter to the Corinthians, when he presents the official form of the Good News as he himself originally received it, presumably at Jerusalem when he met Peter for the first time after his conversion on the road to Damascus.

He says that Christ died for our sins and was buried. Then on the third day he was raised and appeared to Peter, then to the Twelve, and so on, but there is no mention of Mary Magdalene. Why not? The hypothesis that Peter and the other members of the Twelve in Jerusalem envied her and omitted her name out of spite lacks any supporting evidence. The most probable explanation is that the Good News of the coming of the Messiah was first proclaimed to Jews, and according to Jewish Law women could not serve as official witnesses, just as in our own time and country, children still cannot serve as official witnesses in some states.

So the absence of Mary Magdalene's name makes sense when we consider the Jewish audience to whom the Good News was first proclaimed. Still, the fact that the risen Jesus chose to appear first to a woman and told her to bear witness to the disciples must give us pause. Didn't he realize that technically women weren't allowed to bear witness? Or could it be that he was once again disregarding a Jewish law that had outlived its usefulness, in order to establish a new precedent? I think there can be little doubt that this is precisely what John thought when he wrote his Gospel. After all, earlier in his Gospel he also shows the Samaritan woman, after her encounter with Jesus, witnessing to the people of her village and making many converts. John obviously wishes to emphasize that the witness of women to Jesus—and especially the witness of Mary Magdalene—was valid.

When we turn from the New Testament to the literature produced by the so-called Gnostics,[11] we see that many of these writers also sought to highlight Mary Magdalene's special relationship with Jesus. In one of these texts, *The Dialogue of the Savior,* Mary is one of three recipients of special teaching, along with Matthew and Judas (not Iscariot). But she excels the other two because she "understood completely." In another text, the *Pistis Sophia,* Jesus reveals that Mary and John are destined to become the greatest of the disciples. In *The Gospel of Mary,* Mary receives a special revelation from the risen Lord before his ascension into heaven. His ascension leaves the other disciples feeling despondent and fearful that if they preach the gospel they will be put to death. Mary assures them that Christ's spirit will protect them and shares with them the private revelation she has received. But on hearing this, Peter becomes jealous and angry and says (in a passage quoted in *The Da Vinci Code*), "'Did the Saviour really speak with a woman without our knowledge? Are we to turn about and all listen to her? Did he prefer her to us?' And Levi answered, 'Peter, you have always been hot-tempered. Now I see you contending against the woman like an adversary. If the Saviour made her worthy, who are you indeed to reject her? Surely the Saviour knows her very well. That is why he loved her more than us.'"[12]

Here we reach a crucial point in understanding the popular fervor for *The Da Vinci Code*. What seems to be implied in *The Gospel of Mary* is made plain in *The Gospel of Philip* when it says in another passage quoted in *The Da Vinci Code*, "The companion of the Saviour is Mary Magdalene. Christ loved her more than the other disciples and used to kiss her often on the mouth. The rest of the disciples were offended by it and expressed disapproval."[13]

In *The Da Vinci Code*, Sir Leigh Teabing interprets this passage for Sophie Neveu: "The word *companion*, in those days, literally meant *spouse*." Given the statement that Christ "used to kiss her often on the mouth," Teabing's claim seems credible, until we look at other Gnostic documents from the same collection, called the Nag Hammadi Library.[14]

The Second Apocalypse of James, for example, says that Jesus embraced his brother James and kissed him on the mouth. What this kiss signifies is the imparting of secret revelation, as is made clear a few lines later when Jesus says, "Behold, I shall reveal to you everything, my beloved." The kiss is a sign not of physical but of spiritual intimacy. The same must be true for *The Gospel of Philip*, especially in light of the fact that elsewhere it refers to physical sex as something disgusting and degrading—an attitude typical of the Gnostic documents in the Nag

Hammadi Library. This understanding helps us to make sense of the statement found in both *The Gospel of Mary* and *The Gospel of Philip* that Jesus loved Mary Magdalene more than the others.

Paradoxically, while "demoting" Mary Magdalene from the possibility of being Jesus' wife, this reference also elevates her into the highest ranks of the disciples. The meaning is that she understood Jesus better, that she had deeper insight into his message.[15] To use the vernacular, she "got it" when even the leading men of Jesus' entourage did not. How could this be unless Jesus had given Mary special revelation, which was naturally viewed as a special sign of his love? We find the same hint of special knowledge in John's Gospel, where one disciple (presumably John the son of Zebedee) is closest to Jesus, displays greater insight than Peter,[16] and is called "the disciple whom Jesus loved."

But let us return to the question of a possible marriage between Jesus and Mary Magdalene. Even Elaine Pagels, a Princeton professor who believes that some Gnostic documents may reflect alternative forms of Christianity that were eventually suppressed by the Catholic Church—and whose *New York Times* best seller *Beyond Belief* talks about how these documents helped her on her own spiritual journey—does not believe that the Gnostic texts quoted above are referring to a romantic relationship, let alone marriage, between Jesus and Mary Magdalene. Rather, she believes that Mary serves as a symbol of a form of Christianity that was opposed by the Catholic Church, partly because it valued visionary experience as new revelation, partly because it accepted the spiritual authority and leadership of women.[17]

This symbol was counterpoint to that of Peter, which embodied the value of institutional authority, the one which eventually held sway. The historical conflict is discussed at length by Irenaeus, Catholic Bishop of Lyons c. 180, who deplored the fact that one Gnostic sect allowed women to prophesy and to serve as priests in the celebration of the Eucharist.[18] Thus we may regard Mary in *The Gospel of Mary* and other Gnostic documents as symbolizing a movement of protest against the Catholic Church. It may not be too much to say that the enthusiasm for *The Da Vinci Code* is just the latest episode in that movement.

Here I might add that indirect evidence from the New Testament all but rules out the possibility that Jesus was married to Mary Magdalene. First, we have seen that her name refers to her hometown of Magdala. In that culture, if a woman was married she was known by the name of her husband, not by the name of her hometown, so the Gospels would have called her Mary the wife of Jesus if they had been married. A second bit of indirect evidence that Mary and Jesus were not married comes from St. Paul, who claimed that he had the right to take a wife along with him in his travels, just as Peter and the other apostles and the Lord's brothers all took their wives with them. If Jesus had been married to his traveling companion Mary Magdalene, wouldn't Paul have mentioned him in order to clinch his argument? The best explanation for the omission is that Jesus and Mary Magdalene were not married.

But could Jesus have been unmarried? Sir Leigh Teabing rightly says that Jewish males were expected to marry, so that if Jesus had been unmarried, the Gospels ought to have explained why. What Dan Brown and his source, *Holy Blood, Holy Grail*, forget is that Matthew's Gospel *does* explain why: Jesus says that there are those who are celibate for the sake of the kingdom of heaven. The distinguished Oxford scholar Géza Vermès has no difficulty with the idea that Jesus took on celibacy as certain prophets before him had done, in order to fulfill a divine mission.[19]

If Mary Magdalene cannot be honored as the bride of Christ,

she has been honored for her insight, for her discipleship, and for her role as "Apostle to the Apostles." For all these things, the Orthodox Churches further honor her with the title "Equal to the Apostles."

How did we move in Church history from this high status for Mary Magdalene to the current need for her to be reha- bilitated? Honored though she has been in the history of the Catholic Church, Mary Magdalene has also been the victim of mistaken identity, as *The Da Vinci Code* rightly points out. The fateful mistake occurred in the year 591 when Pope Gregory the Great gave a homily in which he identified the unnamed sinful woman in Luke 7:36–50, who wet Jesus' feet with her tears, dried them with her hair, and anointed them with ointment, as Mary Magdalene, from whom seven demons had been cast out.

Assuming that the unnamed woman's sinfulness must have taken the form of prostitution, he sees in the anointing of Je- sus signs of the woman's past life: "It is clear, brothers, that the woman previously used the ointment to perfume her flesh in forbidden acts. . . . She had coveted with earthly eyes, but now through penitence these are consumed with tears. She displayed her hair to set off her face, but now her hair dries her tears."[20] Ba- sically what Gregory did was to combine two of the women in the Gospels, and then assign to the one who is named (that is, Mary Magdalene) the supposed flaws of the other.

The reference to the seven demons cast out of Mary Mag- dalene occurs in Mark 16:9 (the verse Gregory is thinking of), but also in Luke, and in fact in the passage immediately follow- ing the one in which Jesus' feet are washed, dried, and anointed. Luke says, "The twelve were with [Jesus], as well as some women who had been cured of evil spirits and infirmities: Mary, called Magdalene, from whom seven devils had gone out, etc."[21] The inclusion of specific details makes it obvious that Luke is here introducing Mary Magdalene to the reader for the first time, and that therefore she cannot be the unnamed sinful woman discussed a few verses earlier, as Gregory mistakenly thought. The Greek-speaking Churches, which carefully discriminated among the various women of the canonical Gospels, never made Gregory's mistake.

This mistaken identification of Mary Magdalene with Luke's sinful woman, and the unquestioned assumption that she was called sinful because she was a prostitute, rather than a liar or a thief, would be repeated so often in the West that it took on a quasi-official status, and went on to do incalculable harm to the image of women in the Western Church. To doubt it was to risk excommunication, as one sixteenth-century Dominican friar discovered to his sorrow.

As the Bishop of Paris remarked at the time, if the Church admitted an error on this matter, not only would she leave herself open to questioning on other matters, she would risk being publicly disgraced.[22] Erasmus tried to correct the error by holding it up to ridicule, as did Calvin,[23] but it was all to no avail. It was not until more than four hundred years later, in its revised Lectionary of 1969, that the Catholic Church changed Mary Magdalene's designation from "penitent" to "disciple," but it did not give the slightest indication that the earlier designation had been wrong.[24] It comes as no surprise, therefore, that up until the publication of *The Da Vinci Code*, most Catholics were unaware that the view of Mary Magdalene as a prostitute was erroneous, and in the population at large, films such as *Jesus Christ Superstar* and *The Last Temptation of Christ* did not help matters by continuing to portray her as a prostitute.

Here we begin to see why *The Da Vinci Code* has been so powerfully embraced by so many, women and men alike. It has taken fourteen centuries for the tide of presumption against

Mary Magdalene to turn. As Dan Brown said, her time has come. What has come with it is a tidal wave of demand for redress from the negative views of women which the Magdalene's false story was used to undergird.

Let's look more closely at what is being overturned. At first sight, Gregory's mistake seems innocuous enough. After all, the whole point of the passage in Luke about the sinful woman is often said to be that the worse the sinner, the more deeply he or she will love Jesus once forgiven. And for many this message is full of truth and beauty. Thus Dante compares Mary Magdalene purified of sin to "a sunbeam in clear water." Some also find in the portrayal of Mary as a great sinner who becomes a great saint an apt parallel to the story of St. Paul, who was once the "chief" of sinners.[25]

So, what's the big deal? Why not let Gregory's error stand, and make the best of it by focusing on what good can be drawn from it . . . or at least not make the matter into a federal case? Those who reject this suggestion say that their reason for doing so is simple. Mary has been unjustly condemned for something she never did, and denied her rightful place in Church history, while Paul has been exonerated of his own sins and held up as a model for all. If Paul deserves the honor, does not Mary Magdalene then deserve *at least* the clearing of her name?

Small things are telling here. In the history of art, Paul has rarely been depicted in his role as Saul, "breathing threats and murder against the disciples of the Lord" (Acts 9:1). But Mary Magdalene has often been depicted as a voluptuous prostitute, flaunting her breasts for every man to ogle. Moreover, in his former life as a persecutor, Paul has not been viewed as emblematic of his sex, but in her former life as a prostitute, Mary has often been viewed as emblematic of *hers*, at least in the Catholic imagination. This is not to say that all women have been viewed as prostitutes *per se*, but rather that there has been a strong tendency to see women in general as temptresses. Sadly, as small things often presage big ones, this seemingly minor issue of artistic portrayal points to the massive power of the symbolism—which sharply conflicts with the symbolism highlighted by Elaine Pagels in her discussion of *The Gospel of Mary*, that Mary enjoyed special insight into Jesus and his teaching.

The Place of Women in the Catholic Church

The condemnation of women in general on charges of tempting men to sin finds an early but by no means isolated voice in the African Church Father Tertullian, writing around the year 200. Expressing his disapproval of women's desire for fancy hairstyles and bling, Tertullian equates this with the sin of Eve in the Garden of Eden: "*You* are the one who opened the door to the Devil, *you* are the one who first plucked the fruit of the forbidden tree, *you* are the first who deserted the divine law; *you* are the one who persuaded him whom the Devil was not strong enough to attack. All too easily *you* destroyed the image of God, man. Because of *your* desert, that is, death, even the Son of God had to die."[26]

What is so tragic about this view of women as temptresses is that Jesus had repeatedly challenged it. Jewish rabbis frequently warned men not to be seduced by a woman's charms. But because Jewish society was already deeply patriarchal, such teaching tended only to reinforce the degradation of women. Jesus sought to redress the imbalance by teaching that adultery begins when a man gazes at a woman and allows his imagination to fan the flames of lust. Jesus also defended the dignity of women by his actions. When scribes and Pharisees brought him a woman who had been caught in the act of adultery and asked him if he dared to challenge the law of Moses that such a woman should be stoned to death, Jesus replied, "Let anyone among you who is without sin be the first to throw a stone at her." When they had all walked away, Jesus assured her he did not condemn her but told her not to sin again, thus treating her as a responsible adult.

It is unfortunate that Jesus' attitude was forgotten so many times in the early Church, but it is even more unfortunate that it was forgotten in the New Testament itself. The most notorious instance is found in the First Letter of St. Paul to Timothy: "I permit no woman to teach or to have authority over a man; she is to keep silent. For Adam was formed first, then Eve; and Adam was not deceived, but the woman was deceived and became a transgressor. Yet she will be saved through childbearing, provided they continue in faith and love and holiness, with modesty."[27]

This text was used again and again in the history of the Church to support male power and to suppress female equality and leadership. In fairness to the author, it may well have been a belief he took over, without thinking, from the culture of the time, since the subordination of women both in theory and in practice was already ancient when Christianity first appeared. Or, as many scholars believe, it may be that the proscription pertained to only a very isolated and particular situation, unfortunately later elevated by those in Church authority who saw the advantage to themselves of making it a general rule.

The Church's problem with women continued when Christianity became the dominant religion of the Roman Empire in the fourth century. To understand why, we must recall that at this time some of the most eloquent voices in the history of the West—including Saints Jerome, Ambrose, Augustine, and John Chrysostom—were proclaiming ideals of monasticism and asceticism for the Church. These ideals called for continual warfare against the desires of the flesh, as Jerome testifies from his own experience. And who were the instigators of these desires? Women, of course:

O how often, when I was living in the desert, in that lonely waste, scorched by the burning sun, that affords to hermits their primitive dwelling place, how often did I fancy myself surrounded by the pleasures of Rome . . . though in my fear of Hell, I had condemned myself to this prison house, when my only companions were scorpions and wild beasts, I often found myself surrounded by bands of dancing girls. My face was pale with fasting; but though my limbs were cold as ice, my mind was burning with desire, and the fires of lust kept bubbling up before me while my flesh was as good as dead.[28]

Along with their call to a more ascetic life, the early Church Fathers also promoted the ideal of priestly celibacy, to which women were seen as posing the ultimate danger. Writing on the priesthood, John Chrysostom said: "There are in the world a great many situations that weaken the conscientiousness of the soul. First and foremost among them is dealings with women. . . . For the eye of woman touches and disturbs our soul, and not only the eye of the unbridled woman, but that of the decent one as well."[29]

Many more examples could be given. It is impossible to overstate how these views, very much the norm during this period of Church history, colored the perception of women generally, even in the context of Christian marriage. Thus, Augustine could write this: "I know nothing which brings a man's mind down from the heights more than a woman's caresses and that joining of bodies which is essential to marriage."[30]

The sense that marriage itself was somehow a lower state of life was used not only to coax men away from it but also to limit women. Thus, Jerome sent a letter to a newly widowed woman to tell her that however much she might mourn the loss of her husband, she should mourn the previous loss of her virginity even more. Once again Scripture itself was used to give warrant, as for example in the vision of the Book of Revelation in which those closest to Jesus are the one hundred forty-four thousand virgins, "who have not defiled themselves with women."[31] Thus when Gregory the Great identified Mary Magdalene as a prostitute in 591, and elsewhere taught that all sexual pleasure is sinful, he was building on a tradition which already had a tendency to identify sin with female sexuality.

When we turn to the thirteenth century—the Golden Age of Catholic theology—and to the Dominican friar Thomas Aquinas, widely regarded by Catholics as the greatest teacher of the Church after the apostles, we find an attitude towards women which is nothing short of alarming. Although we have seen that the risen Jesus chose Mary Magdalene to bear witness to his resurrection to the Apostles, Aquinas, speaking about women in general as witnesses, says that their witness, owing to a defect in the reason, is weak, like that of children and imbeciles.[32]

According to Aquinas, it was woman's natural inferiority of mind and will that prompted the serpent to speak to Eve rather than Adam. It was likewise her weakness that opened her to the temptation of believing in the serpent's slander of God. When Eve ate the fruit it was because she wanted to usurp God's place, whereas when Adam ate the fruit it was to avoid being separated from his wife. Thus, while acknowledging Adam's guilt, Aquinas insists that that of the woman is greater.[33] Elsewhere, Aquinas endorses Aristotle's teaching that male is to reason as female is to sensuality,[34] and that women's minds are simply not strong enough to resist concupiscence.[35] The natural inferiority of woman even has implications for the performance of the conjugal act—the only natural and therefore proper position is for the man to be on top.[36]

One of the worst statements on women comes from Aquinas's revered teacher, fellow Dominican Albertus Magnus, whom Pope

Pius XI declared to be a Doctor of the Church in 1931. Here is what Albertus wrote:

> Woman is less qualified [than man] for moral behavior. . . . When a woman has relations with a man, she would like, as much as possible, to be lying with another man at the same time. Woman knows nothing of fidelity. . . . Woman is a misbegotten man and has a faulty and defective nature in comparison with his. Therefore she is unsure in herself. What she herself cannot get, she seeks to obtain through lying and diabolical deceptions. And so, to put it briefly, one must be on one's guard with every woman, as if she were a poisonous snake and the horned devil. . . . Her feelings drive woman toward every evil, just as reason impels man toward all good.[37]

Nowadays scholars often excuse such statements as the product of historical conditioning, but in this case it is hard to see how any amount of historical conditioning could have so overridden the teaching and example of Jesus. After all, few at that time had studied the Scriptures more thoroughly than Albert.

Two centuries after their deaths, Albert and Thomas Aquinas would become two of the chief authorities cited in the *Malleus Maleficarum* (*The Witches' Hammer*), referred to in *The Da Vinci Code* as "arguably . . . the most blood-soaked publication in human history."[38] At a quarter of a million words, it was a veritable encyclopedia of witchcraft, designed to be the definitive guide to the interrogation, prosecution, and execution of witches. It was published in 1486 by two Dominican Inquisitors, Heinrich Krämer and James Sprenger, with the papal seal of approval. The time of its publication coincided with the beginning of the European witch craze, which continued for another two centuries, by which time it had spread all the way to Salem, Massachusetts.

The *Malleus* begins by establishing the reality of witchcraft and its nature. One of the first questions addressed is why witchcraft is predominantly a female phenomenon. The Inquisitors answer this way: "Since [women] are feebler both in mind and body, it is not surprising that they should come more under the spell of witchcraft. For as regards intellect, or the understanding of spiritual things, they seem to be of a different nature from men." Presumably by "different nature" the reader is meant to infer "bovine."

But her deficiency of intellect is not the principal reason for woman's susceptibility to witchcraft. That, the Inquisitors inform us, is due to the fact that "she is more carnal than a man, as is clear from her many carnal abominations." In short, "all witchcraft comes from lust, which is in women insatiable." As a consequence of their insatiable lust, some women go so far as to have sexual intercourse with demons.[39]

Intercourse with demons made witchcraft the most heinous of crimes because it signified total surrender to the devil and the utter repudiation of God. Given this premise, it comes as no surprise that witches' sexual activities are described in lurid and obsessive detail. One might have hoped that after Freud, readers would recognize here the psychological mechanism of projection—the unconscious attribution of one's own unacceptable desires to others, making them scapegoats. But this may be hoping for too much. The editor of the standard English edition of the *Malleus Maleficarum*, Rev. Montague Summers, wrote of this book in 1948: "One turns to it again and again with edification and interest. From the point of psychology, from the point of jurisprudence, from the point of history, it is supreme. It is hardly too much to say that later writers, great as they are, have done little more than draw from the seemingly inexhaustible wells of wisdom which the two Dominicans . . . have given us."[40]

In the two centuries following its initial publication, the *Malleus Maleficarum* went through twenty-nine editions, outselling all other books published in Europe except the Bible. For the history of the papacy, this had the embarrassing consequence that the papal bull against witchcraft that served as the book's preface became the most widely disseminated papal document ever. One might have expected that the preface alone would cause the book to be rejected by Protestants in the Reformation, but in fact it was immensely popular with them as well, thus giving the *Malleus* a unique place in the history of ecumenism.

The evidence necessary to determine the precise number of those executed for witchcraft during the European witch craze of 1450 to 1700 is lacking. The number given in *The Da Vinci Code*—five million—seems wildly exaggerated, though it is far lower than the baseless nine million often cited. The most conservative estimates place the number between thirty and fifty thousand, of whom eighty to eight-five percent were women. It is telling that almost all the men executed were relatives of "witches" (husbands, sons, etc.). The prescribed methods of interrogation included torture, often prolonged over many days, sometimes resulting in death. The purpose of the torture was to obtain a confession and the names of other witches. If the suspect did not confess, even under torture, it was presumed that her silence was maintained with the devil's help. Thus, whether or not she confessed, she was likely to be found guilty and executed.

In light of this evidence, we can begin to see clearly why scholars, especially feminist scholars, have expressed concern over the error of Gregory the Great and its continual repetition through the centuries. And perhaps we can understand just why *The Da Vinci Code* has sold over sixty million copies. Labeled a prostitute, Mary Magdalene became a symbol of woman in her role as temptress, and women generally came to be considered the greatest single threat to men trying to lead lives pleasing to God.

Moreover, feminist scholars say, by elevating Mary Magdalene to a position among women second only to that of the Virgin Mary, the Catholic Church reinforced the tendency to define women narrowly in terms of sexuality, a category which is at best ambiguous, at worst associated with corruption. Thus, over time, even the Virgin Mary's perpetual virginity[41] came to be viewed by Catholics less as a matter of purity of heart—meaning singular focus on God and God's will—than as freedom from the defilement and degradation believed to be inherent in sexual relations.

But is it prudent to listen to the voice of feminists? With that discretion which has become his hallmark, televangelist Pat Robertson counsels otherwise: "Feminism encourages women to leave their husbands, kill their children, practice witchcraft, destroy capitalism and become lesbians."[42] While few would go quite so far, the Catholic Church *has* rejected the kind of feminist interpretation given above of its devotion to Mary Magdalene and the Virgin Mary. Indeed, as religious symbols, both are far too rich and complex to be interpreted as mere symbols of sexuality.

Mary Magdalene has been venerated not only as a penitent but also as one who stood at the Cross and became the first to see the risen Jesus. The Virgin Mary is venerated not only as Virgin but as *Mater Dolorosa*, the sorrowful mother who stood at the Cross as her son slowly died and cradled him in her arms when he was taken down (a scene rendered by Michelangelo in perhaps the most moving sculpture ever made, the Pietà in St. Peter's Basilica in Rome). The Virgin Mary is also venerated as Maria Regina, the Heavenly Queen who shares eternal life with her son,[43] and as the great Intercessor, whom Catholics call upon in the Hail Mary to "pray for us now and at the hour of our death."

So the meanings symbolized by Mary Magdalene and the Virgin Mary are many and tangled. Yet one of these entangled meanings is now widely regarded as having done immense psychological and spiritual harm through the ages. This meaning, which was already deeply embedded in the mainstream of Western culture and civilization long before Christianity was born, and which the Church often reinforced, is that women and sexuality are to be feared.

Undoubtedly, not all the history of the Catholic Church is negative towards women. In many ways, the Catholic Church has fought valiantly and successfully for the dignity of women when cultural forces stood firmly against it. Equally, we must not forget all the good that Gregory the Great accomplished during his pontificate, at a time when Italy was devastated by flood, famine, and plague—an accomplishment that in the aftermath of Katrina puts our own government agencies to shame.

But this does not erase the unintended and tragic consequences of Gregory's error regarding Mary Magdalene. That is why so many feel that until the Catholic Church is willing to redress Gregory's error openly and publicly, and to acknowledge the damage done to the dignity of women as a consequence, it will neither comprehend nor be able to fully address what is erroneous in *The Da Vinci Code*.

The Sexuality of Jesus: The Ultimate Taboo

Many of those for whom the claims of *The Da Vinci Code* struck a chord spoke of their delight in the idea that Jesus was a sexual being who knew from his own experience the love that can flourish between a man and a woman. In some almost inexpressible way it made Jesus seem more fully human to them.

What does it say about Christian teaching on sexuality when the very idea of Jesus as a sexual being hit so many readers of *The Da Vinci Code* with the force of new revelation? And an even more disturbing question is this: Why did others find the idea outrageous, even blasphemous? Part of the reason must be that during most of Christian history the subject of sexuality has been taboo, and the subject of Jesus' sexuality has been the greatest taboo of them all.

Many Catholics through the centuries appear to have assumed that Jesus' celibacy meant that he was asexual. One example of this in the past hundred years, which was especially prominent up to the Second Vatican Council, was the portrayal of Jesus as apparently sexless in popular pictures associated with devotion to the Sacred Heart of Jesus. (I do not wish to denigrate such devotion, which has its place.) Catholics have often turned to Jesus as they have to the Virgin Mary as representing the total transcendence of sexuality and freedom from all the tempestuous desires and bitter disappointments associated with sexuality. In Jesus and Mary they have found, however fleetingly, that peace which is a foretaste of the peace they hope to enjoy forever in heaven.

This attitude is irreproachable. The need for peace arises in every aspect of our lives, and is one reason why pastors continually exhort their congregations to be faithful in prayer and worship. The attitude becomes problematic only when sexuality begins to be looked upon as a relentless enemy from whom one must seek not just an oasis of peace but a permanent refuge, with walls ten feet thick and a hundred feet high. And that, as we have seen, has been a recurrent (some would say dominant) attitude in the history of Christianity. One of the consequences of it has been to view Jesus (and the Virgin Mary) as symbols of the total rejection of sexuality. Moreover, Jesus is thought to have supported this view when he said, "The men and women of this age marry, but the men and women who are worthy to rise from death and live in the age to come do not marry."[44]

One implication of this saying is that human sexuality is not ultimate. But does it follow that sexuality ought to be rejected, which has sometimes been the inference drawn from this saying? When that inference has been drawn, it has encouraged a tendency toward dualism—toward viewing the body and its natural impulses as corrupt and corrupting, and the soul as needing to be separated and protected from those impulses. This dualism has colored the popular view of Jesus himself, leading to an unintentional neglect of the central belief of the ancient Church that Jesus was not only fully divine, but fully human as well.

This central belief, rooted in the statement in John's Gospel—"The Word became flesh and dwelt among us"[46]—is officially held to be a mystery, meaning that it is ultimately beyond the power of human comprehension. Because the idea that Jesus is both fully human and fully divine is so baffling, it is not surprising that since the earliest days of Christianity there has been an unconscious tendency to emphasize one or the other—humanity at the expense of divinity or divinity at the expense of humanity. Even John's Gospel, which did more than any other Gospel to shape the Church's understanding of Jesus, so stressed Jesus' divinity as to obscure his humanity in the minds of many readers. This may be one reason why the Church insisted that no fewer than four Gospels be included in the New Testament.

One of the most influential statements on the full humanity of Jesus outside the four Gospels is found in the Letter to the Hebrews. In it, the unknown author, comparing Jesus to a high priest and contrasting him with Jewish high priests of old, says, "For we do not have a high priest who is unable to sympathize with our weaknesses, but we have one who in every respect has been tempted as we are, yet is without sin."[46] The Council of Chalcedon in 451, which further clarified the Church's belief in the full humanity of Jesus, developed the statement from Hebrews and spoke of Jesus as being "like us in every respect apart from sin."

If Jesus was like us in every respect apart from sin, then he must have had sexuality as an integral aspect of his personality, just as we do. After all, the Catholic Church has now officially stated that sexuality is part of the very foundation of our personalities.[47] This raises questions that *The Da Vinci Code* has made not only unavoidable but pressing. Father Andrew Greeley has stated them plainly: "Was Jesus sexually attracted to women? Did he feel sexual desire for some of them?" Here is his own response: "One can answer 'no' to that question only if one wants to deny the humanity of Jesus or argue that sexual feelings are in themselves evil."[48]

Father Greeley accepts the traditional belief that Jesus never married, despite the fact noted earlier that it was extremely rare for a Jewish man not to marry. But for Greeley the key question is this: How are we to think about Jesus' celibacy? Greeley's suggestion will not please those who cast their copies of *The Da Vinci Code* into the bonfire. "If Jesus did not marry, the reason was not that he could not marry, but that he chose not to marry. As a true man in all things, sin alone excepted, he could imagine married intimacy and sexual love with a woman and enjoy those images."[49]

Greeley then turns to the love that existed between Jesus and Mary Magdalene, which makes the story in John's Gospel of their encounter after the resurrection so moving.[50] Here are his thoughts:

> Did she love Jesus? How could she not have loved him? He had saved her from the emotional troubles that had paralyzed her. He was certainly the most attractive man she had ever encountered. And also the kindest,

the most gentle, and the most respectful. Better to say
she adored him.

And did he love her? Again one must ask how he
could not have responded with love to a woman so utterly dependent on him and devoted to him. Could he
have imagined the possibility of making love with her?
If he were human, he certainly could have and would
have.[51]

If we find Greeley's comments arresting, it may be because
for us sexuality is profoundly ambivalent. It is associated with
some of the most exalted moments in life and with some of the
most shameful. For that reason, the idea of Jesus feeling sexual
desire seems somehow wrong. Yet could it be that this vague
sense of wrongness is simply a projection of our own ambiva-
lence, and that is why these reflections on Jesus have the power
to shock and even repel?

Before we try to answer this question, let's recall some of the
comments made in the previous chapter on Catholic attitudes
toward sexuality and on attitudes found in American society at
large. Many Catholics over many generations have associated
sex with sin, guilt, and shame. Sex is the supreme example of the
proverbial "forbidden fruit." In American society at large we see
what at first appears to be an almost opposite attitude.

Sex is, for example, one of the principle motifs used in advertising to drive the consumer society, and therefore our
culture is saturated with sexual images. So far from being hidden in shadows, sex is in the spotlight. Women are presented as
eye candy, conjuring up the adolescent fantasies of heterosexual
males, whether they are still adolescents or only wish they were.
In fact it hardly matters, because when women are presented
in this way, men of all ages can drink from the mythic fountain

of perpetual adolescence. It is a world in which the thought of emotional intimacy and commitment (not to mention STDs) is rarely even hinted at.

One of the things I find most remarkable is how little magazine advertising has changed over the years with regard to depicting women as mere sexual objects or degrading them in some other way, especially by portraying them as having an IQ equivalent to that of an average dairy cow. (You can easily prove this to yourself by flipping through a range of magazines at your local supermarket or public library.) What is equally remarkable is how many people—women as well as men—don't even notice it.

My point is that the consumer society (and if one had to describe American society with just one adjective, it would be hard to do better than *consumer*) has thoroughly conditioned us with regard to our attitudes toward women and sexuality. What does our tendency to reduce women to objects of male sexual desire mean? If we take, for example, one of the icons of the sexual revolution—Hugh Hefner's *Playboy* magazine—we can see the meaning very clearly. It signifies men's fear. For what could possibly be a clearer symbol of the fear of women and sexuality, and the need to assert control over them, than the silent, motionless, air-brushed body of a *Playboy* centerfold?

I suspect Jesus' sexual feelings for Mary Magdalene, which Andrew Greeley has spoken of, are beyond our comprehension, beyond our imagining, largely because of our social conditioning. (And this applies even if we have never been served a whisky sour by a Playboy bunny.) Not only that, but assume for a moment that we weren't so profoundly conditioned. I think we would still want to acknowledge—as such great religious figures as the Hindu Mahatma Gandhi have done—that Jesus reached the highest pinnacle of human spirituality. If so, why should it be so hard for us to acknowledge that Jesus' sexuality was both deeply human and beyond our imagination?

Let me use an analogy. We readily acknowledge that we cannot conceive how Einstein made the mental leaps he made in order to arrive at his general theory of relativity. Indeed, some of the greatest physicists in the world today have said the same. Why then shouldn't we be able to acknowledge that Jesus must have experienced erotic desire in a way that ultimately eludes us, though we still hope to glimpse it.

The consumer society aims at creating forms of addiction, so that we will buy beyond our needs and even beyond our means. Sex is one of its most effective instruments of this effort to attract and addict. Evidence of this is provided by the Internet porn industry, long the most successful moneymaker on the Web. If sex is used to fuel addiction, then by definition it has become inextricably connected with obsession and compulsion. Yet what a contrast there is when we turn to the example of Jesus, who was supremely free of obsession and compulsion in his dealings with women.

There is no sign of fear when he speaks with them, no sign of a need to control them, no need to establish his superiority over them. He interacts with them with a freedom which shocks his disciples, who thought Jewish teachers were not supposed to engage in public discussions with women.[52] He listens to them, and—as shown by the encounter with the Gentile woman mentioned in the Introduction—he even learns from them.

In no respect does he treat them as virtual children, as was often done by Jewish men at that time. Instead, Jesus accepts women as being on a level of equality with men. And in a culture in which Jewish men prided themselves on being "sons of Abraham," Jesus takes the unprecedented step of calling a Jewish woman a "daughter of Abraham" (Luke 13:16), which must have shocked his male hearers. This recognition of women as worthy of being treated as responsible adults on a par with men is a lesson our society is still struggling to learn. But increasing numbers are learning it and recognizing that equality, particularly in a marriage, is essential if the relationship is to thrive.

Donal Dorr, a Catholic missionary priest who has been a consultor to the Pontifical Council for Justice and Peace, has pointed out that we can learn much about intimacy and therefore about sexuality from Jesus' attitude toward power. Jesus did not dominate and manipulate others. This, Dorr says, contrasts with what has often happened in the Catholic Church, and he is not referring here to the specific problem of child sexual abuse. "It has to be admitted that in recent centuries church leaders and theologians frequently exercised a quite oppressive power in the sexual sphere."[53]

To oppress, to control, or to manipulate others by making them fear sexuality or feel shame and guilt about it would be regarded by many today as a form of sexual abuse.

What other lessons can be drawn from the example of Jesus? For one, there is the need for forgiveness, without which no loving relationship can survive. In offering forgiveness, Jesus enabled individuals to experience healing and the possibility of beginning anew. He also had a healing touch, which he extended even to the untouchable of his society, the lepers. Although psychologists have established how necessary touch is for human well-being, "white Anglo-Saxon" males in America and elsewhere have ambivalent attitudes with regard to touching. Not only that, they have ambivalent feelings about those emotions and behaviors that could be regarded as feminine—gentleness and sensitivity, openness and vulnerability, and above all the capacity to grieve. All of these are exhibited in the Gospels by Jesus, without embarrassment. Yet they are a source of embarrassment for many men in American culture, who seek to keep them under strict control. But such emotions, when buried, do not disappear. They return in some disguised form—often that of an avenging fury, wreaking havoc and destruction.

Though he was celibate, Jesus offers lessons in sexuality our own society is desperately in need of. He was not goaded by his sexuality, as we so often are, nor was his sexuality overshadowed by negative emotions. His sexuality was integrated into his personality. Had it been otherwise, he could not have been so magnificently free. Although he chose not to express his sexuality in the narrow way our society often thinks of it—namely, genital intercourse—that does not mean his sexuality was repressed. On the contrary, it was expressed in all the other ways love could be expressed in the context of his chosen mission. It drew countless numbers of people to him, men as well as women. So far from being stifled, his sexuality was part of the radiance of his personality.

If this is true, then the failure to appreciate Jesus as a sexual being has not been simply a colossal failure of imagination in the history of the Church. It has been an implicit denial of Jesus' full humanity—and our own. In that case, it becomes easier to see why so many people have found the Church's image of Jesus unsatisfying. Of course, they couldn't consciously link their dissatisfaction to the subject of Jesus' sexuality because the taboo surrounding that subject had made it unthinkable. That is why the idea of Jesus' being married to Mary Magdalene and having a child with her electrified and satisfied so many readers of *The Da Vinci Code*.

Chapter 10

The Quest for the Historical Jesus

"Almost everything our fathers taught us about Christ is false."

Sir Leigh Teabing to Sophie Neveu[1]

Sir Leigh's remarks would not have come as such a shock to Sophie if she had bothered to read any of a number of recent and not-so-recent bestsellers on Jesus, several of which he points out to her in his library.[2] These were also among the actual sources Dan Brown used in writing his novel. My primary concern, however, is not with Brown's immediate sources, which are discussed in most of the debunking books. I am much more interested in tracing the deeper roots of some of the novel's radical claims about Jesus, since, as Brown himself has stated, they have been around for centuries.[3] To find these deeper roots, we will need to go back to the beginning of the modern era, to about 1500, and the cultural forces that were operating at that time.

Renaissance Humanism

The rebirth of learning that was one of the defining characteristics of the Renaissance sought to recover the "more-human" wisdom of antiquity (hence the term *humanism*). This wisdom, contained in the literature of ancient Greece and Rome, was contrasted with the abstract and lifeless speculations of the later Middle Ages, when philosophers and theologians were said to have debated how many angels could dance on the head of a pin, and scorned the pagan literature of antiquity as "the literature of the damned."[4]

The Renaissance humanists knew that to understand the ancient civilizations of Greece and Rome in any depth, it was necessary to study their literature in its original languages. One of the most brilliant humanists was the Italian priest and scholar Lorenzo Valla (1407–57). We discussed in Chapter 1 his demolition of papal claims to power based on a legal document known as *The Donation of Constantine*, which he showed to be a forgery. Later in his career, Valla undertook another bold project—that of comparing the Latin translation of the New Testament contained in the Vulgate, which had been the official version of the Bible in the West for more than a thousand years, with the original Greek. This was a perilous undertaking in the context of the time.

No one had ever dared to put the revered Vulgate to the test. Indeed, few Western scholars and theologians of the Middle Ages knew enough Greek to be able to do so.[5] By careful comparison with the original Greek, Valla was able to show that the Vulgate was often misleading. For example, according to the Vulgate, when the angel Gabriel came to announce to the Virgin Mary that she would conceive a child, he greeted her with the words "Hail Mary, full of grace: the Lord is with thee" (Luke 1:28). The words are familiar to all Catholics as the opening of the "Hail Mary" prayer. But the Greek text indicated that Mary was greeted simply as "highly favored" (*kecharitōmenē*).[6]

Similarly, the Vulgate reference to marriage as a "sacrament" (*sacramentum*) was called into question when the underlying Greek was seen to be "mystery" (*mystērion*). The Greek text was referring not to a sacramental rite, but to the mystery of salvation revealed in Christ. A third example, and for our purposes the most important, had to do with the words Jesus used when he launched his public ministry. According to the Vulgate, he said, *"Do penance*, for the kingdom of heaven has come near" (Matthew 4:17), and this was interpreted by the Church as a reference to the sacrament of penance. But the original Greek referred not to a sacramental rite of penance, but simply to an inner attitude of repentance.[7] The Protestant Reformers would later make much of these distinctions in their attempt to discredit Catholic teaching on Mary, the sacraments, and the very gospel that Jesus had proclaimed.

Valla's criticism of the Vulgate gained wide circulation thanks to the invention of the printing press. In 1506, Valla's notes on the New Testament were published by Desiderius Erasmus (1469–1536). Perhaps the greatest scholar of the Renaissance, Erasmus also prepared a version of the Greek New Testament for print, and in 1516 it became the first Greek edition ever published. In making available the original text of the New Testament, Erasmus aimed to bring scholars closer to what the biblical authors actually said than had been possible from reading the Vulgate alone.

The Protestant Reformation

One of the most notable admirers of Valla's work was Martin Luther (1483–1546), whom we looked at earlier in Chapter 1. Valla's influence may be seen in the very first of Luther's Ninety-five Theses, which are often taken to mark the beginning of the Protestant Reformation. In his first thesis, Luther proposed that when Jesus called people to repent (Matthew 4:17), "he willed the entire life of believers to be one of repentance."[8] When Luther posted his theses on the cathedral door in Wittenberg on October 31, 1517, he was a Roman Catholic priest, monk, and

Professor of Scripture who was scandalized by the contemporary Church practice of indulgences. This practice led many Catholics to believe that by donating money to the Church they could avoid punishment for their past sins not only in this life but even afterwards in Purgatory.[9]

Luther condemned the practice of indulgences and came to see the entire penitential system of the Church as deviating from the intention of Jesus. At that time, most Catholics regarded the sacrament of penance as working automatically, or, in the language of the Church, *ex opere operato*.[10] But Jesus had called for a change of heart, not a robotic performance of penitential rites. Moreover, Luther was convinced from his own experience that no actions on our part, no "good deeds," could bring salvation. In studying Paul's Letter to the Romans, he had come to the understanding that all we can do is to have faith in God's free gift of salvation in Jesus Christ. Paul says that although we are guilty of having sinned, "God justifies the guilty" (Romans 4:5)—that is, God acquits us through his mercy. All we have to do is accept this gift by faith. The expression "justification by faith alone" would later become one of the leading principles of the Reformation.

Luther's call for the internal reform of the Church was taken by Rome as a challenge to its authority, and he was excommunicated by Pope Leo X in 1520. Nevertheless, with the support of the German nobility, Luther proceeded to launch his own reform of the Church in Germany. (It is important to note that he never regarded himself as having founded a new church.) In Luther's judgment, the papacy and the entire hierarchical system which it symbolized were not only morally degraded but theologically bankrupt. His goal was to return to the purity of the original gospel (literally, "good news") proclaimed by Jesus Christ. The significance of all this is summed up in a statement by Jaroslav

Pelikan: "The Reformation broke out as an appeal from the authority of the institutional church to the authority of the historical Jesus."[11]

Luther believed that to recover the good news in all its purity and splendor it was necessary to return to the one authentic source, the Scriptures. But who, his Catholic critics shot back at him, was competent to interpret the Scriptures? Clearly it was only the teaching office of the hierarchical Church, which God Himself (*sic*) had established. Luther vehemently disagreed.

Pointing to the New Testament's teaching on the priesthood of all believers, he insisted that all Christians—by virtue of the gift of the Holy Spirit received in baptism—had the competence and indeed the duty to interpret the Scriptures for themselves. This principle (sometimes called the principle of private judgment) was directly opposed to the Catholic teaching that in the final analysis it was the Pope who declared what the Scriptures meant.

Luther recognized that for the faithful to become readers and interpreters of the Bible, translations into modern European languages would have to be made, based not on the Latin Vulgate but on the original Hebrew of the Old Testament and the original Greek of the New. Luther himself produced the most famous German translation of the Bible, selecting the most popular German dialect and playing upon it like a virtuoso. Called "the first work of art in German prose,"[12] it was perhaps Luther's most influential instrument in spreading the Reformation, disseminated as it was by "the first of the mass media,"[13] the printing press. So popular was his translation of the New Testament, which he continually revised, that it went through a hundred separate editions in his lifetime.[14] It is a commonplace among scholars that any translation is also an interpretation, and this is demonstrably true in Luther's case. Here is but one example: In Romans 3:28,

Paul wrote that a person is justified "by faith." Luther translates this as "by faith alone" (*alleyn durch den glawben*).[15] But did Paul intend such an emphasis?

Luther assigned different values to different New Testament writings on the basis of two criteria having to do with their theological content. (Scholars call this procedure "content criticism," or *Sachkritik* in German.) One criterion was the degree to which the writing embodied the principle of justification "by faith alone" (and not by good deeds—or "works," as they are called in Paul's Letters). The second criterion was the clarity with which it bore witness to the basic gospel message of God's offer of salvation in Jesus Christ, which Luther regarded as the animating principle of the New Testament.

Luther's dismissal of the Letter of James as "a letter of straw" is a well-known example of his use of these criteria. First of all, the Letter directly contradicted the Lutheran understanding of justification when it stated "a person is justified by works and not by faith alone."[16] Secondly, it failed to proclaim Christ's saving work. The use of the latter criterion illustrates Luther's willingness to "urge Christ against Scripture."[17]

I raise the subject of Luther's "content criticism" because it had momentous consequences in the later development of New Testament interpretation. By distinguishing between the essential gospel of Christ and the various expressions of it by individual biblical authors, Luther unintentionally opened the door to a flood of conflicting interpretations, which has led to the establishment of more than thirty-three thousand different Protestant church bodies or denominations[18] worldwide. Not only that, but some interpreters pushed the distinction even further, ultimately challenging the very idea of the authority of Scripture as a divinely inspired text.[19]

The Enlightenment and the Rise of Deism

"The Bible did not arrive by fax from heaven. . . . The Bible
is a product of *man*, my dear. Not of God. The Bible did not
fall magically from the clouds. Man created it as a historical
record of tumultuous times, and it has evolved through countless translations, additions, and revisions."

Sir Leigh Teabing to Sophie Neveu[20]

The Protestant Reformation sparked conflict throughout Europe:
Catholics fought Protestants and Protestants fought one another.
Purity of doctrine was claimed on every side as justification for going to war. One German prince, a champion of Calvinism, showed
his contempt for the Catholic doctrine of the Eucharist by taking
the host and jeering, "What a fine God you are! You think you are
stronger than I? We shall see! He then tore the host to pieces."[21]

Along with war there were other forms of violence. Protestants as well as Catholics hunted down witches. In one Swiss Can-
ton there were 3,371 persons tried for witchcraft between 1591
and 1680. Every single one was found guilty and executed.[22]

Many were appalled by what they saw and felt that religion
and politics had to be separated for the sake of civil peace. The
English philosopher John Locke (1632–1704) advocated the rel-
egation of religion to the private sphere so that religious disagreements would be less likely to cause upheaval in the State.
He championed religious toleration for all (except atheists and
Roman Catholics, who were by their very nature threats to the
well-being of the State).

In the seventeenth century, progress in science, technology,
commerce, and finance gave Europeans growing confidence in
humanity's potential to gain mastery over every aspect of life.
Human reason was seen as the universal key to progress. Before
this time, reason had been used by different churches to prove
that their particular interpretation of the Bible was the only true

interpretation. But now the question would be whether the Bible itself was true, with reason as the ultimate arbiter.

The exaltation of reason in the latter half of the seventeenth century continued throughout the eighteenth, which came to be called the Age of Enlightenment. The German philosopher Immanuel Kant (1724–1804) famously defined Enlightenment as "humanity's departure from its self-imposed immaturity." He explained, "This immaturity is self-imposed when its cause is not lack of intelligence but failure of courage to think without someone else's guidance. Dare to know! That is the slogan of Enlightenment."[23] The knowledge thus gained would gradually liberate humanity from the chains of ignorance and superstition, the heaviest of which had been placed on it by religious authority.

One manifestation of Enlightenment ideals may be seen in the rise of Deism. Deism asked the rhetorical question, "How could God be just and good if he only revealed himself to one people in one tiny part of the world (ancient Israel) and left all other peoples in darkness?" Deism sought a natural religion available to all peoples everywhere.

Determining precisely what that natural religion consisted in would be the task of reason applied to observation and experience. This in turn implied that past claims, not based on the new method and principles but merely on authority, must be approached with systematic doubt. Thus, in one fell swoop, the trustworthiness of the Christian revelation was undercut. Those who pursued this new line of thought found in the biblical miracles a particularly vulnerable point on which to attack the exclusive claims of Christianity.

First, miracles were outside the realm of ordinary observation and experience, and depended upon the testimony of witnesses. But which was more likely—that a miracle actually occurred or that the testimony was false? But there was a deeper consideration. Why would God have worked miracles in violation of the laws of nature, when those very laws were the supreme witness to God's power and majesty, as Newton himself had said? Thus the Deists used reason to reject claims of miracles.

In their faith in reason the Deists stood in sharp contrast with Luther's view that "reason is a whore," able to be used by any man to serve his dark desires. Yet this faith in reason would triumph in the eighteenth century, as we have seen from our discussions of Voltaire, Benjamin Franklin, and Thomas Jefferson in previous chapters.

But now let's look briefly at the classical expression of the Deist view in *Christianity not Mysterious* (1696) by the Irishman John Toland (1670–1722). He sharply criticized the traditional view that the mysteries of Christianity as proclaimed by the leaders of the early Church must be accepted without question. The truth, he said, is that these Church leaders had often used deception in order to control the masses, twisting Jesus' simple message into unintelligible dogmas, or "mysteries." Toland proclaimed that reason as applied to universal human experience was the only reliable authority. It should be used to interpret the Bible in the same way that it is used to interpret any other book.

According to Toland, beneath all the traditional nonsense put forward by the Church is the plain message that Jesus preached to the poor. Supernatural elements such as the miracles of Jesus were to be rejected as contradicting universal human experience. It follows from all this that the divinity of Jesus as expressed in the Nicene Creed and imposed by the Church as dogma must be rejected also. Upon publication, Toland's book was condemned and consigned to the fires by the Irish Parliament, while Toland himself fled to England to avoid imprisonment.

Another Deist, the Englishman Thomas Woolston (1670–1733), published six *Discourses on the Miracles of our Saviour* between 1727 and 1730. His fundamental thesis was that the miracle stories in the Four Gospels are to be rejected because they are full of "Improbabilities, and Incredibilities, and grossest Absurdities, very dishonorable to the Name of Christ." Woolston's method of discrediting these stories was to hold them up to ridicule. For example, how could one possibly accept the miracle of the fig tree?

According to the story, Jesus, feeling hungry, looked for some fruit on a fig tree. When he found none, he cursed the tree, causing it to wither and die, even though it was not the season for figs. How, Woolston asked, was that any different from a child throwing a chair across the room because his dinner was not ready?

Another miracle he dismissed as absurd was the story in which Jesus cast out demons from a man, causing them to enter a herd of swine, which then stampeded off a cliff and were killed. Woolston observed that if anyone in his day caused a swineherd to lose his entire livelihood in this way he would be convicted of a capital crime and sent to the gallows.

A third miracle was the changing of water into wine at the wedding in Cana of Galilee. Given the amount of wine Jesus is said to have produced, Woolston observed, it would have gotten the entire town drunk. It certainly was not a proof of Jesus' divinity. Indeed, if true, it would bring ridicule upon his person. It must surely be a fabrication by the Evangelist. Woolston also argued that the Virgin Birth and the Resurrection were not to be taken literally but allegorically. For such views, Woolston was convicted of blasphemy and sent to prison, where he later died.

One Deist whose views are of special importance for the purposes of this chapter is the Englishman Thomas Chubb (1679–1747), author of *The True Gospel*. Chubb stated what would become a modern principle in New Testament scholarship. It is that "the Jesus of history" must be distinguished from "the Christ of faith." Chubb rejected the supernatural elements in the Gospels—not only the miracles, but the Virgin Birth and Resurrection as well. Chubb believed that Jesus was a moral teacher, who proclaimed a simple, rational, enlightened message. Jesus was, in short, a Deist before Deism.

Chubb did not think that Jesus intended to found a new religion. The man responsible for that was Paul, who introduced the bizarre notion that Christ's death on the cross was an atoning sacrifice for the forgiveness of sins. Thus Chubb drew the sharpest possible distinction between Christianity and the religion of Jesus. The influence of *The True Gospel* has been momentous, serving as "a template for nearly every subsequent reconstruction of the historical Jesus."[24]

It is not Thomas Chubb, however, who is usually credited with having launched the quest for the historical Jesus, but Hermann Samuel Reimarus (1694–1768), a Lutheran scholar in Hamburg. As a young man, Reimarus was influenced by the ideas of the English Deists, and that influence is present in his revolutionary book, *Apology for the Rational Worshippers of God*. The title implies its true purpose: to defend and promote Deism. But it is remembered mostly for what it says about the Jesus of history. Reimarus knew that his book contained dangerous ideas (most of the English Deists had suffered legal penalties because of their writings), and he dared not publish it. After his death, however, extracts were made by G. E. Lessing and published anonymously as *Fragments of an Unknown Author*, which immediately set off a firestorm in Germany.

Reimarus was the first person to expose in detail the contrasts and contradictions between Jesus as he really was during his ministry and the portrait of him that appears in the Gospels. He argued that the authentic teaching of Jesus as it appears in the Four Gospels is overlaid by later apostolic teaching. Reimarus began by insisting that Jesus must be set in the context of his time and place. He was a Jew preaching to Jews, and his moral message of love of God and neighbor was a repetition of the ethical core of the Old Testament.

The political context must also be considered. For centuries the Jews had longed for a restoration of the Kingdom of Israel as it had existed a thousand years earlier under King David, God's "anointed one"—in Hebrew, *messiah*. Reimarus contended that it was in this sense that Jesus proclaimed himself to be the Messiah and announced the imminent arrival of God's kingdom. The shared hope of Jesus and the Jewish people was that God would deliver them from their Roman oppressors, just as he had delivered them from their Philistine enemies in the time of David and their Egyptian oppressors in the time of Moses.

What all this means is that Jesus never intended to found a new religion, let alone teach such later Church doctrines as his divine nature and the mystery of the Trinity. Such doctrinal distortion was the work of the Apostles. Devastated by the catastrophe of Jesus' death, they reacted by creating a fictitious account of the meaning of Jesus, beginning with the fabricated story of his resurrection from the dead. That the claims that Jesus rose from the dead are false, he argued, is evident from a careful comparison of the resurrection stories of the four Gospels—revealing ten contradictions.

For example, after Jesus' resurrection, Matthew's Gospel indicates that he appeared to his disciples only in Galilee, while Luke's Gospel indicates that he appeared to them only in Jerusalem. How, Reimarus asked, could the Christian religion be based on such a flimsy foundation? Moreover, the return of Jesus in glory to judge the world, which the Apostles used to frighten people into joining their movement, never did take place.

Reimarus marks a watershed in the history of the interpretation of Jesus by raising questions, with clarity and power, that have dominated scholarly study of Jesus ever since: What was his relation to the Jewish teachers of his day? What was his relation to the political aspirations of the Jewish people? To what extent did his view of his mission coincide with the claims made about him by the Apostles after his death? In short, Reimarus brought to the forefront the fundamental question of the relation of the "Jesus of history" to the "Christ of faith."

Reimarus thought of himself as weighing the evidence with scientific objectivity, but in fact his conclusions were largely predetermined by his belief that there can be no supernatural occurrences, and were sharpened by his desire to unmask the impostures of orthodox religion. He clearly aimed at demolishing the claims of Protestant orthodoxy, and few of those who took up the quest after him were so hostile. It is nevertheless fair to say that many Protestant scholars who followed him operated consciously or unconsciously according to similar Enlightenment principles and expected that the quest would recover a portrait of Jesus that more or less conflicted with that presented by the churches—or at least by the Catholic Church.

By questioning the authority of the Bible and encouraging scholars, especially historians, to read it like any other ancient text, Reimarus and Lessing paved the way for the liberal Protestantism which exerted a powerful influence on German religious thought in the nineteenth century. German philosophers and theologians wrote rationalistic lives of Jesus which tended to portray him as a moral teacher of timeless wisdom. Some of these writers tried to salvage Jesus' miracles by proposing rationalistic explanations.

Karl Friedrich Bahrdt (1741–92) explained Jesus' walking on the water by proposing that he had actually been walking on a partially submerged raft, which the apostles were unable to see at night. The raft had been constructed by the Essenes, understood by Bahrdt as a secret society like the Freemasons who collaborated with Jesus behind the scenes in order to promote his ministry. Jesus also did not die on the cross, but had swooned under the influence of medicine supplied to him by Luke the physician, another important collaborator.[25]

Another who argued that Jesus did not die on the cross was J. G. Herder (1744–1803). Like Bahrdt, he rejected Jesus' miraculous cures, arguing instead that what Jesus did was simply tend the sick. Herder is especially remembered for his encapsulation of Jesus' message: "The teaching of Jesus was simple and comprehensible to all: God is your father and you are all brothers one of another."[26] What was needed, Herder said, was a return to the message *of* Jesus, as opposed to the message *about* Jesus.

Historical Research as the Key to Understanding

In the nineteenth century, history as an academic discipline rose to such eminence, especially in German culture, that it was regarded as a key, if not *the* key, to understanding all human activities and endeavors. Without investigating the origins and development of a historical phenomenon, it would remain in some essential way unintelligible. The "quest for the historical Jesus" became a consuming passion for liberal Protestants, who wanted to recover the real Jesus and allow him to speak to their own age. Like Herder, they wanted the religion *of* Jesus—his personal religious views—rather than the religion *about* Jesus that was preserved in mummified form in the creeds and traditions of the churches. An enormous number of "biographies" of Jesus were attempted, some gaining immense popularity.

But of more lasting significance than any of these biographies was the work of the Lutheran scholar Adolf Harnack (1851–1930).

One of the most learned scholars of modern times,[27] while he was still in his thirties he completed a seven-volume[28] *History of Dogma* in which he traced the development of Christian doctrine from its origins to the Reformation. His goal was to demonstrate that Christian dogmas such as those expressed in the Nicene Creed (for example, that Jesus is "the only Son of God, eternally begotten of the Father") were not only unintelligible but a disastrous falling away from the original message of Jesus. By trying to conceptualize who Jesus was in Greek philosophical terms, early Christian theologians had buried the real Jesus beneath an avalanche of alien ideas. Harnack famously summed up his view by saying: "The history of dogma is the dissolution of dogma."

In a series of public lectures entitled "The Essence of Christianity," which after they were published went into fourteen editions, Harnack said that the heart of Jesus' message was the Fatherhood of God and the brotherhood of man. In fact, "The gospel, as Jesus proclaimed it, has to do with the Father only and not with the Son."[29] Jesus' awareness of God as his loving Father is what he wished to share with his followers. Since this inner awareness is unique to each individual, the Christian religion does not require an institutional church. Rather, Christian individuals are called to build a just society.

The Quest Comes to a Halt

At much the same time as Harnack was explaining the essence of Christianity, Albert Schweitzer (1875–1965)—the future medical missionary and winner of the Nobel Peace Prize—stunned the world of Protestant scholarship by publishing a book called *The Quest of the Historical Jesus* (German 1906; English translation 1910). In it he reviewed more than two hundred "lives" of Jesus, from that of Reimarus to those of his own time. In virtually every case, he found that the author had read into the Gospel accounts his own preconceived ideas of who Jesus really was and what he really stood for. In other words, they found precisely what they were looking for, whether it was a reason to follow Jesus or a reason to abandon him or something in between. In truth, he noted, Jesus could not be so easily interpreted in contemporary terms. Instead, Jesus must be seen as "a stranger and an enigma to our time." Entirely embedded in first-century Judaism, Jesus simply cannot be modernized. He had expected that his death would mark the end of history and the beginning of the Kingdom of God. In this expectation he was tragically deluded.

Many responded to Schweitzer by saying that he was just like the scholars he criticized, and that he too had been blind to his own presuppositions. Many others went further and insisted that the Gospels were so saturated with theological beliefs that it was no longer possible to recover the real Jesus of history, deluded or otherwise, no matter how sophisticated and scientific the methods employed were. This in effect closed the door to attempts to reconstruct the life of Jesus for nearly half a century.

For the Lutheran pastor Rudolf Bultmann (1884–1976), perhaps the most influential and certainly the most controversial New Testament scholar of the twentieth century, the quest for the historical Jesus was not only hopeless but perverse. It was hopeless because Jesus and the Apostles viewed the world in a way that is totally unintelligible to us, with individuals possessed by demons, voices coming from heaven, and so on. It was perverse because Christianity never was and never can be a careful weighing of evidence extended indefinitely until rational proof is attained. Christianity, Bultmann asserted, calls for a leap of faith here and now. Thus he turned against the Enlightenment principle of having reason and historical investigation as ultimate arbiters in matters of religion. For him this principle was a false prop that needed to be let go of.

What Bultmann did was to reformulate for the twentieth century Luther's principle that salvation was "by faith alone." The effect that Jesus had on people during his ministry was to challenge them to recognize the reality of God's presence and simultaneously the poverty of their own spiritual resources apart from God. He forced them to make a decision either to rely on God or risk the possibility of total loss. Translated into contemporary language, this means that we must decide between authentic and inauthentic existence.

Jesus spoke of the imminent end of the present age. We too face an imminent end. It is not that of the present age, Bultmann said, but the end of our own lives in death. In the light of this prospect, our decisions here and now determine whether we will live for truth and freedom or for lies and slavery. Thus our decision does indeed entail "judgment," as the Gospels stress. One thing of lasting significance that Bultmann accomplished was to remind preachers and teachers of the urgency of the Christian message. The decision of faith is not something that can be postponed indefinitely to some "more convenient" time.

The Quest Resumes

By the 1950s, the pendulum had begun to swing and Protestant scholars, led largely by Bultmann's former students, began to regain confidence that they could recover at least the authentic sayings of Jesus. It was unwarranted, they said, to assume the faith of the early Christian communities and of the authors of the Gospels simply obliterated all traces of the preaching and teaching of Jesus.

At the same time, growing interest in ancient Judaism, inspired in part by the discovery of the Dead Sea Scrolls in 1947, led scholars to attempt to clarify Jesus' place in the setting of Palestinian Judaism. Most of these scholars have shown greater interest in historical questions than in theological ones. Many have concluded that Jesus is best understood as a prophet who aimed for the renewal of Judaism, not the establishment of a new religion.

In the 1990s, media attention to Jesus was strongly influenced by the Jesus Seminar, founded in 1985 by Robert Funk with John Dominic Crossan as co-chair and made up of some fifty to seventy-five scholars all together. The seminar members debated and then actually voted on the authenticity of sayings and deeds attributed to Jesus in the "Five Gospels" (the four in the New Testament plus *The Gospel of Thomas*) in order to uncover the real Jesus from the rubble of creeds and dogmas under which he has lain buried for nearly two millennia.

The Jesus of the creeds and dogmas is a fiction, said Funk. "What we need is a new fiction . . . a new narrative of Jesus, a new Gospel."[30] To proclaim this new Gospel, the Jesus Seminar has deliberately sought media attention. It also aims to present to the public the fruits of biblical scholarship which otherwise might lie hidden in academic journals or be drowned out by televangelists. The results of the Seminar's work have been, as one member of the Seminar predicted they would be, "startling to most people and deeply offensive to many, not just fundamentalists."[31] One scholar outside the Seminar has criticized it as "a scandalous attack on the foundations of Christianity."[32]

It would appear that fundamentalist teachers, especially the televangelists, are a particular target, but the religious establishment in general is under fire from the Seminar for not making public what Funk considers to be the accepted findings of contemporary scholarship. Among the results of their voting was that only eighteen percent of the sayings attributed to Jesus in the Gospels are authentic. The press intensified the shock value of the Seminar's conclusions, as in this headline from the *Atlanta Constitution*: JESUS NEVER PREDICTED HIS RETURN,

SCHOLARS SAY.[33] By gaining interviews on television news shows, and in magazines, newspapers, and documentaries, members of the Seminar have given the impression that their conclusions represent the mainstream of scholarship, when in fact they have come under severe criticism from some of the most respected scholars in the field.

The picture that emerges from the Seminar's voting on the sayings of Jesus is a portrait in miniature: Jesus is neither a prophet nor a religious reformer; he never claimed he was the Messiah; he did not see himself as having a central role in God's plans for humanity.[34] As for Jesus' crucifixion and resurrection, which dominate the New Testament Gospels, the Seminar voted that after his death Jesus' body simply "rotted in some unknown grave"—the resurrection never occurred. Co-chair John Dominic Crossan has conjectured that Jesus' body was probably thrown into a common grave for criminals, where it would have been eaten by wild dogs. Another member of the Seminar, Gerd Ludemann, has argued that belief in Jesus' resurrection arose from mass hallucination.

Similar views have been expressed by another member of the Jesus Seminar whose books have lifted him, he claims, "onto both a national and international stage,"[35] Episcopal Bishop John Shelby Spong. A former fundamentalist, he says he wants to help others to break free from that mental tyranny, in which people are forced to believe in things which are not possible to believe in any longer. He rejects the idea of the Virgin Birth and interprets the Gospel affirmations of Jesus' Resurrection as poetic expressions of the Apostles' recognition that the ideals Jesus stood for did not die with him on the cross, but live on eternally.

Later Christians erred, says Spong, by taking these stories as literal historical accounts and then going further and concluding that Jesus was divine. Finally, Bishop Spong surmises that Jesus may well have been married to Mary Magdalene and that the story of the wedding at Cana may be a veiled account of Jesus' own wedding.[36] With regard to this last suggestion, it is interesting that Robert Funk has told the media that "more than half the members of the Seminar believe that Jesus probably was not celibate."[37]

Marcus Borg, another member of the Jesus Seminar, has been called today's "most popular liberal voice on Jesus."[38] Raised a conservative Lutheran, he lost his faith but has found it again and is now an Episcopalian. He has written several books on Jesus, and his *Meeting Jesus Again for the First Time* became a bestseller in 1994. He states his purpose with such clarity and charm that I would like to quote him at length:

> We have all met Jesus before. Most of us first met him when we were children. This is most obviously true for those of us raised in the church, but also for anybody who grew up in Western culture. We all received some impression of Jesus, some image of him, however vague or specific.
>
> For many, the childhood image of Jesus remains intact into adulthood. For some, that image is held with deep conviction, sometimes linked with warm personal devotion and sometimes tied to rigid doctrinal positions. For others, both within and outside of the church, the childhood image of Jesus can become a problem, producing perplexity and doubt, often leading to indifference toward or rejection of the religion of their childhood.
>
> Indeed, for many Christians, especially in mainline churches, there came a time when their childhood image of Jesus no longer made a great deal of sense. And for many of them, no persuasive alternative has replaced it. It is for these people especially that this book is written. For them, meeting Jesus again will be—as it

has been for me—like meeting him for the first time. It
will involve a new image of Jesus.[39]

Borg seeks to share with the reader his insight into the significance of Jesus for our time. He regards the traditional image
of Jesus as the divine savior who came down from heaven to save
people from their sins as discredited by modern scholarship and
no longer compelling to many millions of people. Indeed, believing things *about* Jesus necessarily involves being distant from
him. Jesus becomes *an object* of our belief.

Borg wishes to encourage us to follow Jesus not by accepting
second-hand beliefs and doctrines but by experiencing the same
vision and the same Spirit which guided Jesus throughout his
life. Jesus shared with others his own vision of God and invited
others to enter into the same relationship with God as he himself
had. Jesus should therefore be our guide along the way to God.
Borg thinks that many are also led astray by focusing on Jesus as
a moral teacher, because then they become obsessed with meeting requirements and "doing good" and in the process lose site of
the broader context of living in relationship with God.

Borg maintains that the dominant focus of the Christian tradition on sin, guilt, and forgiveness is no longer central to the lives
of many people, who have largely lost the sense of sin. Not that
they do not experience real problems in life, but they do not naturally think of them in such terms. Nor is the corresponding image of God as lawgiver and judge credible to such people. Such an
image can create a feeling of being continually in a state of guilt,
without ever finding peace. In Borg's view, Jesus offered a vision
of God that went far beyond the categories of law, sin, and guilt by
presenting God's compassion as being without limits. All are accepted just as they are. Following Jesus thus becomes a journey
along a path toward ever-increasing compassion and mercy.

How does Borg root his interpretation in what may be known about the historical Jesus? The aspect of the historical Jesus that Borg finds most compelling is his role as a prophet who aimed at the renewal of Judaism. Because Palestine was under Roman occupation at that time, many Jews sought to preserve their national identity by adhering strictly to their laws of holiness, which distinguished them from all other peoples. Among these were laws which required abstaining from pork, ritual cleansing of kitchen utensils, and specific offerings to be made to the Temple. But these laws meant that some Jews were thought of as having higher status (if their wealth enabled them to make greater offerings to the Temple), while others lacked status (if their poverty prevented them from making such gifts). Thus the holiness laws separated Jew from Jew and made many feel inferior and, in a sense, outcast.

Jesus opposed this idea of holiness and instead emphasized God's mercy toward all, regardless of any supposed "merits." All were equal in the sight of God, all were God's children. God's mercy extends to the outcasts of Jewish society and even to the enemies of Israel, the Roman oppressors. For this teaching, Jesus was denounced as the "friend of tax collectors and sinners." According to Borg, followers of Jesus must keep ever present in their minds Jesus' words in Luke's Gospel: "Be merciful, as your heavenly Father is merciful."

Thus the teaching and example of Jesus broke down the walls of separation between Jew and Jew and between Jew and Gentile. Jesus models for his followers a life centered on the experience of a personal relationship with God, which necessarily carries us beyond the limitations of any single tradition, or institution, or set of rules, however helpful these can sometimes be. God must be the God of all peoples.

Another book worth noting because it gathers up a number

of ideas we have encountered thus far is Stephen Mitchell's *The Gospel According to Jesus: A New Translation and Guide to His Essential Teachings for Believers and Unbelievers* (1991). Mitchell claims to be following in the footsteps of Thomas Jefferson, who in his *Life and Morals of Jesus of Nazareth* separated the wheat from the chaff in the Gospels—the wheat being Jesus' "sublime ideas" about morality, the "chaff" being everything else. Mitchell rejects the Virgin Birth, the Resurrection, the divine titles given to Jesus, and the harsh sayings attributed to him.

In doing so, he believes he uncovers a man whose teachings are "in harmony with the supreme teachings of all the great religions." We see a Jesus who has "emptied himself of desires, doctrines, rules—all the mental claptrap and spiritual baggage that separates us from true life—and has been filled with the vital reality of the unnameable." This is the reality that Jesus wished to awaken us to by his message and example: "The love we all long for in our innermost heart is already present, beyond longing." Put another way, Jesus wanted us to share "a feeling, as if we were floating in the womb of the universe, that we are being taken care of every moment."[40]

The Gnostic Jesus[41]

The rapidly growing interest in the Gnostic Gospels is another sign of the desire on the part of many Americans for a more vibrant Jesus, a Jesus who speaks directly to them as individuals, unmediated by any hierarchical institution. In the previous chapter, we looked briefly at *The Gospel of Mary*, *The Gospel of Philip*, and other Gnostic texts. Now we will turn our attention to the most famous of them all, *The Gospel of Thomas*.

Part of an ancient Gnostic library discovered at Nag Hammadi in Egypt in 1945, *The Gospel of Thomas* claims to be a collection of 114 "secret sayings" of Jesus written down by Didymus

Judas Thomas, who was, according to one early tradition, Jesus' own twin. Some of the sayings may have been first set down in writing in AD 50–60, in other words, before the New Testament Gospels were published. But most scholars believe that *The Gospel of Thomas* as a whole is later than those Gospels, perhaps dating from about the year 150.

In 2003, the same year that *The Da Vinci Code* came out, Princeton scholar Elaine Pagels published *Beyond Belief: The Secret Gospel of Thomas*, which quickly became a *New York Times* best seller. Her earlier, award-winning *The Gnostic Gospels* (1979) was acknowledged by Dan Brown himself as having been a source and inspiration for *The Da Vinci Code*.[42] In *Beyond Belief*, Pagels gives a personal account of what *The Gospel of Thomas* has meant to her on her spiritual journey. More than anything else, *The Gospel of Thomas* has inspired her to seek her own spiritual truth, and her ongoing search has brought renewal and healing.

She contrasts this approach with the traditional Christian requirement of belief in the unalterable statements of the Nicene Creed. As she puts it, "Thomas's gospel encourages the hearer not so much to *believe in Jesus* . . . as to *seek to know God* through one's own, divinely given capacity, since all are created in the image of God."[43] The "secret sayings" of Jesus suggested to her that Christianity did not have to be defined in terms of a set of rigid orthodox beliefs. (This is conveyed in the very title *Beyond Belief*.)

The saying she appears to value most, since she quotes it not only here but in many other writings, is this: "Jesus said: 'If you bring forth what is within you, what you bring forth will save you. If you do not bring forth what is within you, what you do not bring forth will destroy you.'" She shares her reaction on first reading it: "The strength of this saying is that it does not tell us what to believe but challenges us to discover what lies hidden within ourselves; and, with a shock of recognition, I realized that this perspective seemed to me self-evidently true."[44]

Yet it was also clear to her why such views would have been suppressed by the ancient Catholic Church, whose insistence on conformity to the faith as officially taught by the Catholic bishops was then fierce. To stray from the one true faith was perilous, the bishops said, because outside the Church there is no salvation (in the ancient Latin formula—*extra ecclesiam nulla salus*). Nevertheless, Pagels contends, "most of us sooner or later find out that, at critical points in our lives, we must strike out on our own to make a path where none exists."[45] Otherwise we may find that "unquestioning acceptance of religious authority" leads to spiritual starvation and death.

One reviewer of *Beyond Belief* made this prediction: "Pagels's conclusion will resonate with those American Catholics who feel betrayed by the official church."[46] Pagels's book is just one of many on *The Gospel of Thomas* to be found in all the big-chain bookstores, suggesting that the appeal of *The Gospel of Thomas* goes well beyond disaffected Catholics. Perhaps it is tapping something deep in the American psyche. In this regard, Harold Bloom's remark is worth noting. He says, "There is little in the Gospel of Thomas that would not have been accepted by Emerson."[47] And for Bloom, as he has stated many times and in many places, Emerson is the founder of "the American religion."[48]

Scholar and author Bart Ehrman, a friend of Pagels, has also reflected on the marginalization and suppression of other forms of early Christianity that resulted from the historical victory of orthodox Christianity. In his *Lost Scriptures: Books that Did Not Make It into the New Testament* (2003), he includes writings that were once considered sacred by some Christian groups but came to be labeled heretical after the formation of the New Testament.

These "Scriptures" became lost partly because:

> only one set of early Christian beliefs emerged as vic-
> torious in the heated disputes over what to believe and
> how to live that were raging in the early centuries of the
> Christian movement. These beliefs, and the group who
> promoted them, came to be thought of as "orthodox"
> (literally meaning, "the right belief"), and alternative
> views . . . came to be labeled "heresy" (false belief) and
> were then ruled out of court. Moreover, the victors in
> the struggles to establish Christian orthodoxy not only
> won their theological battles, they also rewrote the his-
> tory of the conflict.[49]

Thus, he argues, history was written by the winners, so that for
centuries afterward these other forms of Christianity were simply thought of as heretical—if they were considered at all. This,
he says, entailed incalculable losses to Christianity.

The rediscovery of so many ancient texts in our time provides an opportunity for religious seekers and others:

> The broader interest in and heightened appreciation for
> diverse manifestations of religious experience, belief,
> and practice today has contributed to a greater fascina-
> tion with the diverse expressions of Christianity in vari-
> ous periods of its history, perhaps especially in its ear-
> liest period. This fascination is not simply a matter of
> antiquarian interest. There is instead a sense that alter-
> native understandings of Christianity from the past can
> be cherished yet today, that they can provide insights
> even now for those of us who are concerned about the
> world and our place in it.[50]

Like Pagels, Ehrman is a respected scholar, so it is interesting that some of the ideas he expresses, such as the idea that

history is written by the winners, are also central claims in *The Da Vinci Code*,[51] suggesting that not all Dan Brown's claims are merely his own private eccentricities.

Concluding Reflections

We have looked at examples of how Jesus has been sought through historical study and through alternative scriptures. These examples have sometimes led to understandings of Jesus very different from the official teachings of the Catholic Church and of the mainline Protestant churches.

Let me state plainly that I have deliberately chosen examples that many would regard as radical, because these are the sort that have been most publicized by the media. Not only that, but ordinary professors in universities across America are often tempted to shock students out of their slumber by quoting a radical point of view. And this temptation is made harder to resist by the fact that professors' livelihoods depend on their being rated "exciting" on their student evaluations.

For such reasons, radical views of Jesus are just about everywhere, not just in the supermarket tabloids (although in my own view the most entertaining of these are to be found there—things like Jesus' own recipe for chocolate-chip brownies). The problem the general public faces is the difficulty of evaluating the many claims about Jesus that are presented. The success of *The Da Vinci Code* has emboldened publishers to flood bookstores with every imaginable interpretation of Jesus, many claiming to offer "astonishing revelations," so that even avid readers are likely to be getting, at best, a very mixed education.

Surely Jesus' message was nothing if not challenging. Unfortunately, part of the appeal of many of these books, in addition to their sensational claims, is their transformation of Jesus' message into one that caters to our wishes, rather than challenging us. Let me give you an example. In his book *Honest to Jesus: Jesus for the New Millennium*, Robert Funk argues that the Catholic Church took the notion that Jesus was born of a virgin literally, when it ought to have taken it figuratively as a symbol of his divinely inspired mission. It then used its interpretation that Jesus was born asexually to promote the idea that "abstinence is godly and sex is dirty," except when married couples use sex for the sole purpose of procreation (although even then it is suspect). Funk goes on to recommend leaving all that behind and practicing "responsible, protected recreational sex between consenting adults."[52] But it is not obvious why anyone should accept Funk as a "sex expert" as well as a biblical scholar, and certainly his recommendation does not follow logically from his critique of Catholic teaching.

Funk's recommendation, which I offer merely as an example, may be contrasted with the bracing words of the Danish philosopher Søren Kierkegaard (1813–1855):

> The matter is quite simple. The Bible is very easy to understand. But we Christians are a bunch of scheming swindlers. We pretend to be unable to understand it because we know very well that the minute we understand we are obliged to act accordingly. My God, you will say, if I do that my whole life will be ruined. How would I ever get on in the world?
>
> Herein lies the real place of Christian scholarship. Christian scholarship is the Church's prodigious invention to defend itself against the Bible, to ensure that we can continue to be good Christians without the Bible coming too close. Dreadful it is to fall into the hands of the living God. Yes, it is even dreadful to be alone with the New Testament.[53]

To all, including myself, who have done scholarly work on the Bible, these are sobering words. On the other hand,

Kierkegaard's comment that "the Bible is very easy to understand" needs to carry a warning label of its own, since verses of the Bible taken out of context have been used time and again to justify acts of unimaginable savagery and cruelty.

But let's return to the quest for the historical Jesus, the real Jesus that people would have met during his ministry. The main point I wish to emphasize is that the quest cannot bring anyone to the fullness of faith in the risen Lord. This failure necessarily follows from the nature of the principal method the quest for this Jesus uses, the historical-critical method. This has been expressed in an exceptionally clear and evenhanded way by Pope Benedict XVI:

> [I]t is important . . . to recognize the limits of the historical-critical method. For someone who considers himself directly addressed by the Bible today, the method's first limit is that by its very nature it has to leave the biblical word in the past. It is a *historical* method, and that means that it investigates the then-current context of events in which the texts originated. It attempts to identify and to understand the past—as it was in itself—with the greatest possible precision, in order then to find out what the author could have said and intended to say in the context of the mentality and events of the time. To the extent that it remains true to itself, the historical method not only has to investigate the biblical word as a thing of the past, but also has to let it remain in the past.[54]

Yet that method does not preclude others. Indeed, some of the questions it raises (but cannot answer) suggest the need for alternative approaches. One such question is this: What was it that led to the New Testament claims that Jesus was divine? The evidence points above all to the belief that God had raised

Jesus from the dead and elevated his status to that of Lord. To his followers, calling Jesus "Lord" meant that he was now "in the position of God towards them."[55] Historians encounter immense difficulties when they try to interpret Jesus' resurrection as a historical event, since the New Testament implies that his resurrection transcends the normal categories of space and time. And yet as one of the greatest modern historians, Jaroslav Pelikan, remarked shortly before his death in 2006: "If Christ is risen, nothing else matters. And if Christ is not risen—nothing else matters."[56]

Historians as historians also lack any way of confirming the Apostles' claim that Jesus is Lord. As St. Paul himself says, "No one can say 'Jesus is Lord' except by the Holy Spirit."[57] What historians *can* do is to acknowledge that the Apostles' belief in Jesus' resurrection and his elevation to Lordship was so absolute that they were willing to suffer and die for it. If their belief had been overshadowed by doubts and fears, then not long after Jesus' crucifixion Peter and the other disciples would probably have repented for having followed a false teacher—*and* sought reconciliation with the Jewish authorities who had denounced him.

Such, at any rate, are some basic points Church leaders would make in response to the limited conclusions about the historical Jesus reached using the historical-critical method. At its best, the historical-critical method has important things to say, but its scope and power are limited, and for that reason it cannot have the last word.

Epilogue

As soon as it was published, *The Da Vinci Code* took the world of popular literature by storm, going on to become one of the best-selling novels of all time. It also generated a fierce negative response which included a barrage of books and articles written to demolish its claims about the Bible and the history of Christianity.

What fascinated me most, however, was that a novel whose entire plot was based on scandalous charges against the Catholic Church could be so phenomenally successful. What did this say about the reputation of the Catholic Church—the largest Christian denomination in America and in the world? I decided to explore how the Catholic Church came to be viewed with such skepticism and suspicion, even with regard to its most fundamental teachings about Jesus.

But it was not just the negative view of the Catholic Church and indeed traditional Christianity in general that intrigued me. I also wanted to explore the spiritual hunger that made some of Dan Brown's claims so appealing. Time and again readers I met spoke of how the novel had kindled in them a yearning for "a more human Jesus."

This book is the result of my exploration. It is not an exhaustive study, as you have seen, but I have tried to bring to light at least some of the important causes of the huge chasm that exists between the Catholic Church and so much of American culture. I hope this book will spark conversation, both about how the Catholic Church can become more responsive to the signs of the times without compromising the truth of the Gospel, and about what Christianity means in the new millennium. What is at stake, I believe, is nothing less than the future of Christianity itself.

The topics presented in this book are controversial, even explosive, but we have no choice but to handle them with courage and honesty. For the Church's part, it must continue to respond to its ongoing need for renewal and reform. Christians must acknowledge that they have contributed to the alienation many feel toward the Christian faith. As the Second Vatican Council said of believers in God in general, "To the extent that they neglect their own training in the faith, or teach erroneous doctrine, or are deficient in their religious, moral or social life, they must be said to conceal rather than reveal the authentic face of God and religion."[1]

I hope this book will serve as a starting point on the road to genuine dialogue. And to promote that, I would like to recommend discussing it in small groups. From my own experience as a teacher, I have come to believe that discussion in small groups can be enormously helpful in bringing people to a clearer understanding of what is being presented and of what their true feelings about it are. I also believe that dialogue can be an avenue for change. When we have established mutual trust and respect by listening, then we are ready, in St. Paul's words, to "speak the truth with love," challenging one another to grow "to maturity, to the measure of the full stature of Christ."[2]

I hope you have enjoyed reading this book. But more importantly, I hope you will talk about it with others who believe that the issues it raises really do matter.

Acknowledgments

I could not have written this book without the generous help of many people, and I would like to express, however inadequately, my gratitude to them all. I would like to thank first the wonderful group of students at the University of Scranton who worked, without pay, researching various topics or commenting on drafts of different chapters of this book: Brad Burke, Jillian Camarote, Claire Goyette, Justine McGuire, Eileen Patterson, Tiffany Rogers, Peter Ruane, and Amanda Szewczyk. Of these, my special thanks go to Eileen Patterson and Peter Ruane who made themselves available from the beginning of this project to very near the end.

In the Introduction I mentioned two other students, Katie German and Jenna Brown, and I want to mention them again here, with gratitude. They started the ball rolling by coming to me separately one week in January 2005 and asking me serious questions about *The Da Vinci Code* at a time when I wasn't even planning to read it.

My colleagues in the University's Department of Theology and Religious Studies read and discussed one long chapter with me. Even though I ultimately decided not to include that chapter in the book, I learned a great deal from our discussion and was able to apply some of their recommendations to other chapters. I am particularly indebted to Mary Anne Foley and Charlie Pinches for assistance on two other chapters.

Outside my own Department, Roy Domenico and Lee Penyak of the Department of History each read a chapter and offered useful suggestions. Josephine Dunn, also of the Department of

History, saved me from making a fool of myself on the subject of Leonardo. Outside my university, Carl Richard, Professor of History at the University of Louisiana at Lafayette, graciously answered a question I had about Thomas Jefferson and the other Founders.

Friends read various chapters with an eagle eye and suggested ways of improving them: Chuck and Anne Emerson, Shirley Isaac, and Julia O'Sullivan. My sister Madeleine and my brother Chris did the same.

I must also thank two readers for the Press: John Hunckler, for his painstaking work as copy editor, and the anonymous reviewer for the Press, whose words I have excerpted for the back cover.

Virtually everyone who read any part of the book made valuable suggestions. In fact, there was such an abundance of them that I was not able to incorporate them all. For that reason, none of the shortcomings of this book can be blamed on them; they are entirely my own.

There were two other people who out of sheer generosity made time to read this book and write blurbs for the back cover: Adela Yarbro Collins of Yale Divinity School, and Luke Timothy Johnson of the Candler School of Theology, Emory University. As a professor, I know how difficult it is to find the time to take on additional academic work, especially in the middle of a semester, and I want to express my deepest appreciation to each of them for doing so.

The book as a whole has been guided through the long and arduous process of publication by Jeff Gainey, Director of the University of Scranton Press, and Patty Mecadon, the production manager. I am deeply indebted to them both. I might add that it was during a casual conversation with Jeff about *The Da Vinci Code* that he suggested I put my ideas in a book. If not for that conversation and Jeff's enthusiasm for the project, I am sure I would never have undertaken it. I would also like to pay tribute to Charles Kratz, Dean of the Weinberg Memorial Library of the University of Scranton, and to his wonderful staff for going far beyond the call of duty to obtain books and information for me.

The stunning cover photograph of St. Patrick's Cathedral in New York City is by Christopher Coleman (www.flickr.com/photos/iceman9294), and I am deeply grateful to him for allowing me to reproduce it.

I would like to thank Jack Finnerty and his staff at the Albright Memorial Library in Scranton and Leah Rudoph and her staff at the Abington Community Library in Clarks Summit. Many of the books I used came from their New Acquisitions shelves.

Finally, I would like to acknowledge the many people not named here who shared their thoughts on *The Da Vinci Code* with me. They include other colleagues, other students, and the people who attended my PowerPoint presentations and seminars. Their thoughts inspired me to take the journey that has resulted in this book.

To all, my sincerest thanks and appreciation.

Notes

Introduction

[1] All page references are to the original hardback edition of Dan Brown's *The Da Vinci Code* published by Doubleday.

[2] Olson and Miesel, *The Da Vinci Hoax*, 284.

[3] Read the entire interview at http://www.sojo.net/index.cfm?action=sojomail.display&issue=060509

[4] Marshall, "The Da Vinci Opportunity."

Chapter 1
People and Events in the History of Anti-Catholicism

[1] In his Foreword to Olson and Miesel, *The Da Vinci Hoax*, 11.

[2] Olson and Miesel, *The Da Vinci Hoax*, 295.

[3] Sheler, "Debating 'Da Vinci.'"

[4] Canto XIX 103–17; Revelation 17.

[5] Quoted in Duffy, *Saints and Sinners*, 137.

[6] This is my adaptation of a comment allegedly made by Henry Sidgwick about Sir Richard Jebb, as reported in Bertrand Russell, *Portraits from Memory*, 64.

[7] For Hanno see Bedini, *The Pope's Elephant, passim.* The reference to Luther appears on p. 211.

[8] Coulton, "Reformation," 35.

[9] McGinn, *Antichrist*, 334, n. 6.

[10] Cf. Berlin, *The Age of Enlightenment*, 113.

[11] Garraty and Gay (eds.), *The Columbia History of the World*, 565.

[12] Quoted in Bald, *Banned Books*, 185.

[13] Quoted in Zagorin, *How the Idea of Religious Toleration Came to the West*, 295.

[14] Quoted ibid., 297.

[15] Quoted ibid., 298.

[16] Durant and Durant, *The Age of Voltaire*, 737.

[17] Quoted by Peter Gay, Introduction to Voltaire, *Philosophical Dictionary*, 17.

[18] Voltaire, *Philosophical Dictionary*, 492.

[19] Pearson, *Voltaire Almighty*, 407.

[20] Berlin, *The Age of Enlightenment*, 29.

[21] Pelikan, *The Christian Tradition*, vol. 5, 208. The words "all have sinned" are quoted from Romans 3:23.

[22] Greeley, "An Ugly Little Secret Revisited," 163–65.

[23] Mill, *On Liberty*, as quoted in Morris, *American Catholic*, 68.

[24] Himmelfarb, "Editor's Introduction," in Mill, *On Liberty*, 49.

[25] For this entire paragraph I am indebted to Ebenstein, *Great Political Thinkers*, 542–44.

[26] Morris, *American Catholic*, 69.

[27] De Rosa, *Vicars of Christ*, 246.

[28] Ibid.

[29] Ibid., 247.

[30] Chadwick, *The Secularization of the European Mind in the Nineteenth Century*, 111–12.

[31] Acton, *Selected Writings of Lord Acton*, vol. 3, 340.

[32] Hunter, *Culture Wars*, 69.

[33] Ibid., 36.

[34] McGreevy, *Catholicism and American Freedom*, 12.

[35] Jenkins, *The New Anti-Catholicism*, 45.

[36] Quoted ibid., 41–42.

[37] Manchester, *One Brief Shining Moment*, 101–4.

[38]. Error 77 in Pius IX, *Syllabus of Errors*.

[39] Greeley, *The Catholic Revolution*, 56–57.

[40] Quoted in Olson and Miesel, *The Da Vinci Hoax*, 40.

Chapter 2
The Controversy in the Catholic Church over Contraception

[1] Noonan, *Contraception*, 202.

[2] The historical references to the nineteenth century were taken

on June 22, 2006 from http://www.pbs.org/wgbh/amex/pill/time-line/index.html.

[3] Quoted in Noonan, *Contraception*, 409.

[4] Augustine, *The Morals of the Manichees*, 18.65, quoted in Noonan, *Contraception*, 120.

[5] http://www.pbs.org/wgbh/amex/pill/timeline/index.html.

[6] Carey, *The Roman Catholics*, 136.

[7] This and the following quotation are taken from Kaiser, *The Politics of Sex and Religion*, 93.

[8] *Pastoral Constitution of the Church in the Modern World, 49.*

[9] All quotations are taken from the new, revised translation of *Humanae Vitae* published by Ignatius Press, San Francisco, in 1998. The numbers given refer to the sections of this encyclical.

[10] Allitt, *Religion in America Since 1945*, 109.

[11] Häring, "The Encyclical Crisis," 588.

[12] Weigel, *The Courage to be Catholic*, 68, 72.

[13] Greeley, *The American Catholic*, 156.

[14] McClory, *Turning Point*, 149–50.

[15] See Ford and Grisez, "Contraception and the Infallibility of the Ordinary Magisterium," 258–312 (esp. 312).

[16] John Paul II, *Familiaris Consortio*, 32.

[17] *L'Osservatore Romano*, English edition, no 27 (6 July, 1987), 12–13.

[18] Dulles, "'Humanae Vitae' and the Crisis of Dissent," 774–77.

[19] Quoted in Peter Steinfels, *A People Adrift*, 259.

[20] Ferguson, "Eurabia?" quoted in Weigel, *The Cube and the Cathedral*, 21.

Chapter 3
The Catholic Church and the Sex Abuse Scandals

The principal source for this chapter was *Betrayal: The Crisis in the Catholic Church*, by The Investigative Staff of *The Boston Globe*. For the most important quotations, I have given page numbers in these notes. Other quotations and references may be located fairly easily by means of *Betrayal*'s Index. *Betrayal* also contains extensive notes on its own sources, as well as photocopies of original letters and other documents. My other sources for quotations and references are indicated in the notes.

[1] As translated by J. B. Phillips, *The New Testament in Modern English*.

[2] Brown, *The Da Vinci Code*, 233 (ellipsis points in the original).

[3] Ibid., 234.

[4] Ibid., 235, 249.

[5] Conducted by the Scripps Survey Research Center at Ohio University and reported in the Scripps Howard News Service on December 21, 2006 by Thomas Hargrove.

[6] See for example Olson and Miesel, *The Da Vinci Hoax*, pp. 40 and 294–95. The idea that anti-Catholicism is "the last acceptable prejudice" is explored in Philip Jenkins's *The New Anti-Catholicism* and in the books by Mark Massa and Margaret O'Brien Steinfels. For references to anti-Catholicism elsewhere in this book, see the Index under "anti-Catholicism."

[7] Quoted in Robinson and Rezendes, "Abuse scandal far deeper than disclosed, report says" (italics added).

[8] *Betrayal*, 18.

[9] Ibid., 14.

[10] "On July 24 Maryetta Dussourd": BishopAccountability.org 2004, accessed at http://www.bishop-accountability.org/assign/Geoghan-John-J-History.htm

[11] Ephesians 4:15.

[12] The entire handwritten letter is photocopied in *Betrayal*, 222–25, followed by a typed version on pp. 226–27.

[13] The story of Father Gauthé is presented in detail in Berry, *Lead Us Not Into Temptation*.

[14] See Berry and Renner, *Vows of Silence*, 51–52.

[15] Quoted in MacQuarrie, "Vocal critic of abuse by clergy found dead."

[16] MacQuarrie, "McSorley's death."

[17] Quoted in MacQuarrie, "Vocal critic of abuse by clergy found dead."

[18] France, *Our Fathers*, 589.

[19] BishopAccountability.org 2004, accessed at http://www.bishop-accountability.org/assign/Geoghan-John-J-History.htm

[20] Law's entire letter is photocopied on p. 240 of *Betrayal*.

[21] Quoted ibid., 130.

[22] Bonavoglia, *Good Catholic Girls*, 62.

[23] Berry and Renner, *Vows of Silence*, 289.

[24] *Time* magazine, May 6, 2002, p.31.

[25] Ibid.

[26] Bonavoglia, *Good Catholic Girls*, 322.

[27] Ibid., 44–45.

[28] The source for this entire paragraph is the article by Paulson.

[29] The source for this entire paragraph is the article by Paulson.

[30] Ferro, *Sexual Misconduct and the Clergy*, 3.

[31] Michalski, "The Costs of Child Sexual Abuse Litigation Threaten the Catholic Church," 76.

[32] Steinfels, *A People Adrift*, 40.

[33] Ibid., 63.

[34] Quoted on the first, unnumbered page of blurbs inside the front cover of the paperback edition of *Betrayal*.

[35] Berry and Renner, *Vows of Silence*, 277.

Chapter 4
The Controversy in the Catholic Church over Homosexuality

[1] Brown, *The Da Vinci Code*, Chapter 32.

[2] For the preceding history, I am dependent upon Crompton, *Homosexuality and Civilization*.

[3] Keefe, "Homosexuality," 69.

[4] Hamer and Copeland, *The Science of Desire*, 134.

[5] *The Digital Decade*, 82.

[6] Allitt, *Religion in America Since 1945*, 232.

[7] Schüklenk and Riley, "Homosexuality," 599.

[8] Quoted in Meacham, *American Gospel*, 234–35.

[9] Leviticus 20:13. See also 18:22.

[10] Noonan, *Contraception*, 240, quoting the *Summa Theologica* 2–1.94.2.

[11] *Catechism of the Catholic Church*, Section 2357. For the connection with Aquinas, see Moore, *A Question of Truth*, 183.

[12] Section 7.

[13] Genesis 19:8 (New American Bible).

[14] Hays, *Moral Vision*, 381.

[15] Milgrom, *Leviticus 17–22*, 1568, 1750, 1785–90.

[16] Bagemihl, *Biological Exuberance*, 78.

[17] Barton, "Can Animals be Gay?"

[18] Bagemihl, *Biological Exuberance*, 657–59 and 737–42.

[19] Ibid., 78.

[20] Ibid., 270.

[21] Ibid., 64.

[22] Dinitia Smith, "Love That Dare Not Squeak Its Name," 3.

[23] Nussbaum, in Finnis and Nussbaum, "Is Homosexual Conduct Wrong?" 101.

[24] Schüklenk and Riley, "Homosexuality," 602–3.

[25] Matthew 19:4–5; cf. Mark 10:2–9.

[26] Matthew 19:26 (New American Bible) and parallels.

Chapter 5
Opus Dei and Conspiracy

[1] Scripps Survey Research Center at Ohio University. (See Chapter 3, note 1 above.)

[2] Posner, *Case Closed*, 404.

[3] Kurtz, *The Crime of the Century*, 169.

[4] Posner, *Case Closed,* 457.

[5] Ibid., ix.

[6] Jennings, *ABC News Presents The Kennedy Assassination*.

[7] Ibid.

[8] Domina, "Kennedy Assassination," 12.

[9] For refutations see Posner, *Case Closed*, and Jennings, *ABC News Presents The Kennedy Assassination*, and above all Bugliosi, *Reclaiming History*.

[10] ABC News poll reported in Jennings, *ABC News Presents The Kennedy Assassination*.

[11] Brown, *The Da Vinci Code*, 34.

[12] Except where indicated otherwise in the notes, I am following

the account given in Wise, *Spy*, which is generally regarded as the best book on the Hanssen case. Wise's book contains an excellent index which will enable readers to find almost any name or subject with ease.

[13] Vise, *Bureau*, inside front jacket.

[14] McGeary, "The FBI Spy."

[15] Shannon and Blackman, *The Spy Next Door*, inside front jacket.

[16] Vise, *The Bureau and the Mole*, 41.

[17] Except where indicated otherwise, the source of my description of Opus Dei is Allen, *Opus Dei*.

[18] Baumann, "Let There Be Light: A look inside the hidden world of Opus Dei."

[19] Brown, *The Da Vinci Code*, 12.

[20] Ibid., 14.

[21] "Sue Is a numerary": Havil, *The Spy Who Stayed Out in the Cold*, 153. "wears cilice": Shannon and Blackman, *The Spy Next Door*, 59.

[22] Quoted in Havill, *The Spy Who Stayed Out in the Cold*, 42.

[23] Baumann, "Let There Be Light: A look inside the hidden world of Opus Dei."

[24] Ibid. For "1998" see Havill, *The Spy Who Stayed Out in the Cold*, 97.

[25] Shannon and Blackman, *The Spy Next Door*, 83.

[26] The words are those of Bonnie Hanssen as related by her lawyer, Plato Cacheris (quoted in Wise, *Spy*, 26).

[27] Shannon and Blackman, *The Spy Next Door*, 83–85.

[28] Thomas, "A Spy's Secret World."

[29] Shannon and Blackman, *The Spy Next Door*, 14.

Chapter 6
Classic Voices in American Religion:
Thomas Jefferson, Ralph Waldo Emerson, and William James

[1] Quoted in Bernstein, *Thomas Jefferson*, 234.

[2] For discussion, see ibid., 230–35.

[3] Meacham, *American Gospel*, 22–23.

[4] Quoted in Gaustad, *Sworn on the Altar of God*, 209.

[5] Ibid., 181–82

[6] Richard, *The Founders and the Classics*, 191.

[7] Quoted in Gaustad, *Sworn on the Altar of God*, 69.

[8] Quoted in Meacham, *American Gospel*, 85.

[9] Lepore, "Party Time," 96.

[10] Quoted in Appleby, *Thomas Jefferson*, 60.

[11] Quoted ibid., 58.

[12] Quoted in Holmes, *The Faiths of the Founding Fathers*, 85.

[13] Bernstein, *Thomas Jefferson*, 8, 208

[14] Quoted in Meacham, *American Gospel*, 29.

[15] Quoted in Holmes, *The Faiths of the Founding Fathers*, 88.

[16] Brown, *The Da Vinci Code*, 233.

[17] Quoted in Richard, *The Battle for the American Mind*, 99.

[18] Brown, *The Da Vinci Code*, 341–42.

[19] Quoted in Pelikan, *Jesus Through the Centuries*, 190.

[20] Quoted in Holmes, *The Faiths of the Founding Fathers*, 85.

[21] Quoted ibid., 83. (I have modified the punctuation.)

[22] Quoted in Meacham, *American Gospel*, 4.

[23] Holmes, *The Faiths of the Founding Fathers*, 87.

[24] Richard, *The Battle for the American Mind*, 94.

[25] Gaustad, *Sworn on the Altar of God*, 37, 188.

[26] Quoted ibid., 134.

[27] Meacham, *American Gospel*, 4.

[28] Richard, *The Battle for the American Mind*, 102.

[29] Quoted in Pelikan, *Jesus Through the Centuries*, 193.

[30] Bloom, *Genius*, 337.

[31] Bloom, *The American Religion*, 43.

[32] Quoted in Ahlstrom, *A Religious History of the American People*, 605.

[33] Pelikan, *The Melody of Theology*, 69.

[34] Quoted in Ahlstrom, *A Religious History of the American People*, 602.

[35] Emerson, *The Spiritual Emerson*, 103 (from "Self-Reliance").

[36] Ibid., 23 (from *Nature*).

[37] Ibid., 1 (editor's Introduction).

[38] Quoted in Bloom, *The American Religion*, 259.

[39] Emerson, *The Spiritual Emerson*, 96 (from "Self-Reliance").

[40] Quoted ibid., 7 (editor's Introduction).

[41] Quoted ibid., 13 (editor's Introduction).

[42] Ibid., 70 (from "The Divinity School Address").

[43] Ibid., 78 (from "The Divinity School Address").

[44] Ibid., 70 (from "The Divinity School Address"). (I have omitted one comma for the sake of clarity.)

[45] Ibid., 71 (from "The Divinity School Address").

[46] Ibid., 72 (from "The Divinity School Address").

[47] Ibid., 10 (editor's Introduction).

[48] Quoted in McGreevy, "Anti-Catholicism in the United States," 157.

[49] Quoted in McGreevy, *Catholicism and American Freedom*, 88.

[50] Conkin, *Puritans and Pragmatists*, 165.

[51] Emerson, *Collected Works*, vol. 2, 77–78 ("Spiritual Laws").

[52] Brown, *The Da Vinci Code*, 125–26.

[53] Francis Cardinal George, Archbishop of Chicago, referring to Olson and Miesel, *The Da Vinci Hoax*, in his Foreword to the book (p. 11).

[54] Olson and Miesel, *The Da Vinci Hoax*, 41.

[55] Quoted in Alister McGrath, *The Twilight of Atheism*, 59.

[56] Oliver Wendell Holmes, *Ralph Waldo Emerson* 420–21.

[57] Menand, *The Metaphysical Club*, 82–83.

[58] James, *Writings, 1902–1910*, 1122.

[59] Ralph Gabriel, quoted in McGreevy, *Catholicism and American Freedom*, 177.

[60] Quoted in Perry, *The Thought and Character of William James*, 121.

[61] James, *Writings, 1902–1910*, 522.

[62] Ibid., 506.

[63] James, "The Will to Believe," 26.

[64] James, *Writings, 1902–1910*, 534.

[65] James, *The Varieties of Religious Experience*, 31.

[66] James, *Writings, 1902–1910*, 770–71.

[67] James, *The Varieties of Religious Experience*, 525.

[68] Ibid., 334–37.

[69] Quoted in Perry, *The Thought and Character of William James*, 270.

[70] Quoted in McGreevy, *Catholicism and American Freedom*, 141, from a letter to Mrs. Henry Whitman dated July 24, 1890.

[71] Quoted in Perry, *The Thought and Character of William James*, 269–70.

[72] Brown, *The Da Vinci Code*, 231.

[73]. Quoted in Jones, *The Life and Work of Sigmund Freud*, vol. 2, p. 57.

[74]. Peale, *The Power of Positive Thinking*, 220. See also 116.

[75]. By psychiatrist M. Scott Peck.

[76]. Lord Acton, *Essays*, vol. 2, p. 383.

Chapter 7
The Rise of Modern Science
as a Challenge to the Catholic Church

[1] Pascal, *Pensées*, sect. 2, no. 206.

[2] Blackwell, "Galileo Galilei," 107 and 109.

[3] Quoted in Gingerich, "The Copernican Revolution,"102.

[4] Blackwell, "Galileo Galilei," 108.

[5] Coyne, "The Church in Dialogue with Science," 104. Other authorities give different years.

[6] Weigel, *Witness to Hope*, 629–31.

[7] O'Grady, "The Perils of Penance," 7.

[8] Coyne, "The Church in Dialogue with Science," 103.

[9] The title of this work in English is *Mathematical Principles of Natural Philosophy*.

[10] Sir Isaiah Berlin, Introduction to Berlin, ed., *The Age of Enlightenment*, 15.

[11] Weinberg, *Facing Up*, 197, quoted in Gleick, *Isaac Newton*, 238, n. 29.

[12] Gleick, *Isaac Newton*, 111.

[13] Westfall, "Isaac Newton," 160. Cf. Gleick, *Isaac Newton*, 113.

[14] Westfall, "Isaac Newton," 161.

[15] Barrett et al., *World Christian Encyclopedia*, vol. 1, 16.

[16] He borrowed the term from the English philosopher Herbert Spencer, although Darwin regarded Spencer as having quite misunderstood his theory.

[17] Jones, *Darwin's Ghost*, 9.

[18] Bunch and Hellemans, *The History of Science and Technology*, 473.

[19] Zimmer, *Evolution: The Triumph of an Idea*, 135.

[20] Ibid., 135–41.

[21] Jones, *Darwin's Ghost*, 17.

[22] Moore, *A Question of Truth: Christianity and Homosexuality*, 213.

[23] The opinion is that of Richard Dawkins, though I'm afraid I cannot recall which of his books it appears in.

[24] Darwin, *Autobiography*, 87.

[25] *Dogmatic Constitution on the Church*, 16.

[26] Bowlby, *Charles Darwin: A New Life*, 297.

[27] Scott, *Evolution vs. Creationism*, 109.

[28] Goodstein, "Judge Rejects Teaching Intelligent Design."

[29] Ibid.

[30] *Humani Generis*, sections 36–37.

[31] The Pope cites Genesis 1:27–29.

[32] John Paul II, Pope, "Address to the Pontifical Academy of Sciences (October 3, 1981)," 279.

[33] Ayala, "Evolution, Theory of," 858.

[34] See Furcht and Hoffman, *The Stem Cell Dilemma*, pp. xxiii, 2–4.

[35] http://archives.cnn.com/2001/HEALTH/08/10/nash.stem.cells.cnna/

[36] *Catechism of the Catholic Church*, section 2274.

[37] Ibid., section 2377.

[38] Furcht and Hoffman, *The Stem Cell Dilemma*, 92.

[39] http://archives.cnn.com/2001/HEALTH/08/10/nash.stem.cells.cnna/

[40] Furcht and Hoffman, *The Stem Cell Dilemma*, 4.

[41] Ibid., 102.

Chapter 8
The Rise of Modern Psychology as a Challenge to the Catholic Church

[1] Edward Erwin in Erwin, *The Freud Encyclopedia*, xiv.

[2] Auden, "In Memory of Sigmund Freud" [1939], stanza 17.

[3] "Freud, the Greatest Modern Writer," *New York Times Book Review*, 23 March 1986.

[4] Erwin, *The Freud Encyclopedia*, xiii.

[5] Edward Erwin in Erwin, *The Freud Encyclopedia*, xiv, citing Friman et al. (This comparison does not include biblical authors.)

[6] Grünbaum, "Critique of Psychoanalysis," 118.

[7] Freud, *Studies on Hysteria*, 88.

[8] Freud, *A Short Account of Psychoanalysis*, quoted in Grünbaum, "Critique of Psychoanalysis," 117.

[9] Gay, *Freud*, 293.

[10] Freud, *The Interpretation of Dreams*, SE 5, p. 608.

[11] Griffin, *Pornography and Silence*, 163.

[12] Ibid., 160.

[13] Freud, "Psychoanalysis," *Encyclopædia Britannica*, 671.

[14] Freud, *Three Essays on Sexuality*, 173.

[15] Ibid., 173, 188.

[16] Excerpted from Maddi, *Personality Theories: A Comparative Analysis*, 47–48. (The order of the sentences has been changed for the sake of clarity.)

[17] Gatterer *et al.*, *Educating to Purity*, 264.

[18] Ranke-Heinemann, *Eunuchs for the Kingdom of Heaven*, 318.

[19] Gay, *Freud*, 610 and n.

[20] Storr, *Freud*, 8.

[21] Ibid., 104.

[22] Ibid., 111.

[23] Quoted in Bettelheim, *Freud and the Soul*, v.

[24] Storr, *Freud*, 1.

[25] Lucy Dawidowicz, quoted in Griffin, *Pornography*, 176.

[26] Watson, *The Modern Mind*, 12

[27] Jones, *Sigmund Freud*, vol. 3, p. 376.

[28] E.g., "A Religious Experience" (1928), in SE 21, p. 170.

[29] Quoted in Storr, *Freud*, 86.

[30] Freud, *Introductory Lectures on Psychoanalysis*, in SE 16, 284–85.

[31] Newman, *Grammar*, 76, quoted in Kenny, *The Unknown God: Agnostic Essays*, 148–49, and commented upon at 154.

[32] We have already quoted Ernest Jones's statement that Freud "went through his life from beginning to end as a natural atheist" (*Sigmund Freud*, vol. 3, p. 376). As for Newman, he himself remarked that the existence of God "is as certain to me as the certainty of my own existence" (*Apologia*, 216).

[33] Gay, *Freud*, 207.

[34] Freud, *Five Lectures on Psychoanalysis*, SE 2, 9–55.

[35] From the online catalogue of the Albright Memorial Library, Scranton, PA.

[36] Gay, *Freud*, 453–54.

[37] Hunt, *The Story of Psychology*, 566.

[38] Bettelheim, *Freud and the Soul*, 4.

[39] Gilgen, *American Psychology Since World War II*, 66–67, cited in Hunt, *The Story of Psychology*, 566, n. 20.

[40] Hale, *The Rise and Crisis of Psychoanalysis in the United States*, 288.

[41] Fagan, *Has Sin Changed?* 94.

[42] Ibid., 98.

[43] Shakespeare, *Antony and Cleopatra*, I.iii.11.

[44] This formulation of St. Alphonsus' view is given in Gatterer *et al.*, *Educating to Purity*, 13, n. 1.

[45] Farraher and Friedrichsen, "Masturbation," 316.

[46] On masturbation, see *Catechism of the Catholic Church*, section 2352; on hell, see section 1035.

Chapter 9
Mary Magdalene, the Place of Women in the Catholic Church, and the Sexuality of Jesus

[1] Dante, *Inferno* 7.46–48.

[2] http://www.msnbc.msn.com/id/7205300/

[3] *The Economist*, March 18, 2006, p. 40.

[4] Brown, *The Da Vinci Code*, 244 and 245.

[5] Quoted in Olson and Miesel, *The Da Vinci Hoax*, 89.

[6] Luke 8:4.

[7] Witherington, *The Gospel Code*, 71–73.

[8] Matthew 27:56; Mark 15:40; John 19:25.

[9] Matthew 27:61; Mark 15:47.

[10] Matthew 28:1–10; Mark 16:1–8; Luke 24:10.

[11] The accuracy of this term is currently being debated in scholarly circles, but its familiarity makes its use convenient in a book like this for general readers.

[12] Brown, *The Da Vinci Code*, 247.

[13] Brown, *The Da Vinci Code*, 246.

[14] The most celebrated collection of Gnostic documents we have, as well as the oldest leather-bound books in existence (dating from about 350), the Nag Hammadi Library takes its name from the Egyptian town in whose vicinity it was discovered in 1945.

[15] Compare Saying 108 of the Gospel of Thomas, where Jesus says: "He who will drink from my mouth will become like me. . . . [A]nd the things that are hidden will be revealed to him." (Regarding the Gospel of Thomas, see Chapter 10.)

[16] See for example John 20:8.

[17] Pagels, *The Gnostic Gospels*, 15–16, 70–79.

[18] Pagels, *The Gnostic Gospels*, 71.

[19] Vermès, *The Changing Faces of Jesus*, 272–73.

[20] Homily 33, translated from Patrologia Latina 76, column 1239, in Susan Haskins, *Mary Magdalen: Myth and Metaphor.* I have changed *unguent* to *ointment.*

[21] Luke 8:1–2.

[22] Surtz, *The Works and Days of John Fisher*, 5–7.

[23] Calvin also ridiculed the fact that three different places claimed to have the Magdalene's remains.

[24] Change noted in Olson and Miesel, *The Da Vinci Hoax*, 84. But as David Tresemer and Laura-Lea Cannon remarked, this change was the equivalent of "a small erratum buried in the back pages of a newspaper" (quoted in Picknett, *Mary Magdalene*, 47).

[25] 1 Timothy 1:15.

[26] Tertullian, *The Apparel of Women*, 118 (italics added).

[27] 1 Tim 2:12–15

[28] Jerome, Letter 22.7.

[29] Jerome, *On the Priesthood*, VI, 8.

[30] Augustine, *The Soliloquies* I, x, 17.

[31] Revelation 14:4.

[32] Aquinas, *Summa Theologiae*, 2–2.70.3.

[33] Ibid., 2–2.165.2 ad 1; and 2–2.163.4; (ad = response to)

[34] Aquinas, *In Omnes S. Pauli Apostoli Epistolas Commentaria*, 2:197, cited in Johnson, *The first and second letters to Timothy*, 35.

[35] Aquinas, *Summa Theologiae*, 2–2.149.4.

[36] Noonan, *Contraception*, 238–39, citing Thomas Aquinas, *Commentary on the Sentences of Peter Lombard*, 4.31, "Exposition of Text"; *ST* 2–2.154.11.

[37] *Quaestiones super de animalibus* XV q. 11, cited in Ranke-Heinemann, *Eunuchs for the Kingdom of Heaven*, 178–79.

[38]. *The Da Vinci Code*, 125.

[39] Heinrich and Sprenger, *The Malleus Maleficarum*, Part I. Question 2. p. 21

[40] Ibid., ix.

[41] Declared a dogma of the Church in AD 649.

[42] http://www.brainyquote.com/quotes/quotes/p/patroberts141339.html

[43] Warner, *Alone of All Her Sex: The Myth and the Cult of the Virgin Mary*, says, "Blue is the colour of the Virgin, 'the sapphire,' as Dante wrote, who turns all of heaven blue."

[44] Luke 20:34–35 (Today's English Version).

[45] John 1:14.

[46] Hebrews 4:15 NRSV, where *tempted* is given as an alternative translation.

[47] *Declaration on Certain Questions Concerning Sexuality* (1975).

[48] Greeley, *Jesus*, 60.

[49] Ibid., 61.

[50] John 20:11–18.

[51] Greeley, *Jesus*, 76.

[52] See John 4:27.

[53] Dorr, *Time for a Change*, 125.

Chapter 10
The Quest for the Historical Jesus

[1] Brown, *The Da Vinci Code*, 235.

[2] Ibid., 253.

[3] See www.danbrown.com.

[4] Gratian (twelfth century), quoted in Duffy, *Saints and Sinners*, 137.

[5] Pelikan, *Jesus Through the Centuries*, 152–53.

[6] Ephesians 5:32 is where the Vulgate has *sacramentum* and the

Greek has *mystērion*. Luke 1:28 is where the Vulgate has *gratia plena* ("full of grace") and the Greek has *kecharitōmenē*. Both illustrations are given in Pelikan, *Jesus Through the Centuries*, 153.

[7] Matthew 4:17. This illustration is given in Pelikan, *Jesus Through the Centuries*, 153.

[8] Quoted in Pelikan, *Jesus Through the Centuries*, 157.

[9] Martos, *Doors to the Sacred*, 81.

[10] Ibid., 81.

[11] Pelikan, *Jesus Through the Centuries*, 157.

[12] Hans Volz, "Continental Versions to c. 1600," 103.

[13] Barzun, *From Dawn to Decadence*, 4.

[14] Pelikan, *Jesus Through the Centuries*, 159.

[15] McGrath, "Luther," 416.

[16] James 2: 24.

[17] Quoted in Morgan, "*Sachkritik*," 605.

[18] Barrett et al., *World Christian Encyclopedia*, vol. 1, 16.

[19] The idea of this paragraph derives from Johnson, *The Real Jesus*, 69.

[20] Brown, *The Da Vinci Code*, 231.

[21] Harrisville and Sundberg, *The Bible in Modern Culture*, 31, quoting Elector Frederick III of the Palatinate (1515–76).

[22] Ibid., 32.

[23] Quoted in Barzun, *From Dawn to Decadence*, 441.

[24] Allen, *The Human Christ*, 109.

[25] Ibid., 134–35.

[26] Quoted in Kümmel, *The New Testament: The History of the Investigation of its Problems*, 83.

[27] John Macquarrie, *Twentieth-Century Religious Thought*, 88.

[28] In the English translation.

[29] Quoted in Kümmel, *The New Testament: The History of the Investigation of its Problems*, 183.

[30] Quoted in Johnson, *The Real Jesus*, 8.

[31] R. Fortna, quoted in Johnson, *The Real Jesus*, 15.

[32] Johnson, *The Real Jesus*, 10.

[33] Ibid., 20.

[34] Witherington, *The Jesus Quest*, 56.

[35] Spong, *Resurrection: Myth or Reality?*, p. xii, quoted in Johnson, *The Real Jesus*, 35.

[36] Johnson, *The Real Jesus*, 32–34.

[37] Quoted in Johnson, *The Real Jesus*, 13.

[38] Borg and Wright, *The Meaning of Jesus*, inside front cover.

[39] Borg, *Meeting Jesus Again for the First Time*, 1.

[40] The quotations from Mitchell, *The Gospel According to Jesus*, 9, 13, 10 and 12, are presented (in that order) in Johnson, *The Real Jesus*, 37–39.

[41] The accuracy of the label "Gnostic" has been heavily criticized by some leading scholars, but I agree with Bart Ehrman that it still has its usefulness.

[42] Altmann, "Book on religious roots."

[43] Pagels, *Beyond Belief*, 34.

[44] Ibid., 32, where the saying (number 70) from the Gospel of Thomas also appears.

[45] Ibid., *Beyond Belief*, 184–85.

[46] Perkins, "Getting Past Orthodox Doctrine," 24.

[47] Bloom, *Where Shall Wisdom Be Found?* 260.

[48] See Chapter 6.

[49] Ehrman, *Lost Scriptures*, 1–2.

[50] Ehrman, *Lost Christianities*, 257.

[51] In Brown, *The Da Vinci Code*, Sir Leigh Teabing states that "history is always written by the winners" (p. 256).

[52] Funk, *Honest to Jesus*, 313–14.

[53] Quoted in McLaren, *The Secret Message of Jesus*, 216.

[54] Benedict XVI, *Jesus of Nazareth*, xvi.

[55] Evans, "Resurrection," 587.

[56] Quoted in Marty, "Professor Pelikan," 47.

[57] 1 Corinthians 12:3.

Bibliography

Note: Where two dates are given, the one in brackets indicates the first printing.

Acton, John Emerich Edward Dalberg-Acton, Baron, *Selected Writings of Lord Acton*, 3 vols., ed. J. Rufus Fears (Indianapolis, IN: LibertyClassics, 1985–88).

Ahlstrom, Sydney E., *A Religious History of the American People* (New Haven, CT: Yale University Press, 1972).

Allen, Charlotte, *The Human Christ: The Search for the Historical Jesus* (New York: The Free Press, 1998).

Allen, John L., Jr., *Opus Dei: An Objective Look Behind the Myths and Reality of the Most Controversial Force in the Catholic Church* (New York: Doubleday, 2005).

Allitt, Patrick, *Religion in America Since 1945: A History* (New York: Columbia University Press, 2003).

Alsan, Marcella, "The Church & AIDS in Africa: Condoms and the Culture of Life," *Commonweal* (April 21, 2006), 17 –19.

Altmann, Jennifer Greenstein, "Book on religious roots resonates with lay readers," *Princeton Weekly Bulletin*, February 9, 2004, www.princeton. edu/pr/pwb/04/0209/1b.shtml

Appleby, Joyce, *Thomas Jefferson* (New York: Times Books, 2003).

Aquinas, Saint Thomas, *Summa theologiae*, Latin text and English translation, introductions, notes, appendices, and glossaries (New York: McGraw-Hill, 1964–).

Auden, W. H., "In Memory of Sigmund Freud," in Ellmann, Richard, and Robert O'Clair (eds.), *The Norton Anthology of Modern Poetry*, 2nd ed. (New York: W. W. Norton, 1988), 744–46.

Augustine, *The Soliloquies*, in *Augustine: Earlier Writings*, translated by John H. S. Burleigh (Philadelphia: Westminster, 1953), 23–63.

Ayala, Francisco Jose, "Evolution, Theory of," *The New Encyclopædia Britannica*, 15th ed. (Chicago: Encyclopædia Britannica, 2002), vol. 18, 855–83.

Bagemihl, Bruce, *Biological Exuberance: Animal Homosexuality and Natural Diversity* (New York: St. Martin's, 1999).

Bald, Margaret, *Banned Books: Literature Suppressed on Religious Grounds*, revised ed. (New York: Facts on File, 2006).

Barbour, Ian G., *When Science Meets Religion* (San Francisco: HarperSanFrancisco, 2000).

Barrett, David B., George T. Kurian, and Todd M. Johnson, *World Christian Encyclopedia: A Comparative Survey of Churches and Religions in the Modern World*, 2nd ed. (Oxford: Oxford University Press, 2001).

Barton, Laura, "Can Animals be Gay?", *The Guardian*, 23 May 2007. Accessed at http://www.guardian.co.uk/environment/2007/may/23/g2.conse rvationandendangeredspecies

Baumann, Paul, "Let There Be Light: A look inside the hidden world of Opus Dei," washingtonmonthly.com, October/November 2005. Accessed at http://www.washingtonmonthly.com/features/2005/0510.baumann. html

Barzun, Jacques, *From Dawn to Decadence: 500 Years of Western Cultural Life—1500 to the Present* (New York: HarperCollins, 2000).

Bedini, Silvio A., *The Pope's Elephant* (Nashville, TN: J. S. Sanders, 1998).

Benedict XVI, Pope (Joseph Ratzinger), *Jesus of Nazareth: From the Baptism in the Jordan to the Transfiguration*, trans. Adrian J. Walker (New York: Doubleday, 2007).

Berlin, Isaiah (ed.), *The Age of Enlightenment: The 18th Century Philosophers* (New York: New American Library, 1956).

Berlinski, David, *Newton's Gift: How Sir Isaac Newton Unlocked the System of the World* (New York: The Free Press, 2000).

Bernstein, Richard B., *Thomas Jefferson and the Revolution of Ideas* (Oxford: Oxford University Press, 2003).

Berry, Jason, *Lead Us Not Into Temptation: Catholic Priests and the Sexual Abuse of Children* (New York: Doubleday, 1992).

———, and Gerald Renner, *Vows of Silence: The Abuse of Power in the Papacy of John Paul II* (New York: The Free Press, 2004).

Betrayal: The Crisis in the Catholic Church, by the Investigative Staff of *The Boston Globe* (Boston: Little, Brown, 2003).

Bettelheim, Bruno, *Freud and the Soul* (New York: A. A. Knopf: Distributed by Random House, 1983 [1982]).

Blackwell, Richard J., "Galileo Galilei," in Gary B. Ferngren (ed.), 105–16.

Bloom, Harold, *The American Religion: The Emergence of the Post-Christian Nation* (New York: Simon & Schuster, 1992).

———, "Emerson: The American Religion," in Harold Bloom (ed.), *Ralph Waldo Emerson: Modern Critical Views* (New York: Chelsea House, 1985), 97–121.

——— ———, "Freud, the Greatest Modern Writer," *New York Times Book Review*, March 23, 1986.

———, *Genius: A Mosaic of One Hundred Exemplary Creative Minds* (New York: Warner Books, 2002).

———, *Jesus and Yahweh: The Names Divine* (New York: Riverhead Books, 2005).

———, *Where Shall Wisdom Be Found?* (New York: Riverhead Books, 2004).

Bonavoglia, Angela, *Good Catholic Girls* (New York: HarperCollins, 2005).

Borg, Marcus J., *The God We Never Knew: Beyond Dogmatic Religion to a More Authentic Contemporary Faith* (San Francisco: HarperSanFrancisco, 1997).

———, *Meeting Jesus Again for the First Time: The Historical Jesus and the Heart of Contemporary Faith* (San Francisco: HarperSanFrancisco, 1994).

———, and N. T. Wright, *The Meaning of Jesus: Two Visions* (San Francisco: HarperSanFrancisco, 1999).

Bowlby, John, *Charles Darwin: A New Life* (New York: W. W. Norton, 1991).

Breuer, Josef, and Sigmund Freud, *Studies on Hysteria*, in *The Standard Edition of the Complete Psychological Works of Sigmund Freud*, ed. J. Strachey (London: Hogarth, 1953–74), volume 2, pages 1–306.

Brown, Dan, *The Da Vinci Code* (original hardback edition) (New York: Doubleday, 2003).

Browne, Sylvia, *The Mystical Life of Jesus* (New York: Dutton, 2006).

Bugliosi, Vincent, *Reclaiming History: The Assassination of President John F. Kennedy* (New York: W. W. Norton, 2007).

Bunch, Bryan, and Alexander Hellemans, *The History of Science and Technology* (New York: Houghton Mifflin, 2004).

Carey, Patrick W., *The Roman Catholics* (Westport, CT: Greenwood, 1993).

Catechism of the Catholic Church (San Francisco: Ignatius, 1994).

Chadwick, Owen, *A History of the Popes 1830–1914* (Oxford: Clarendon, 1998).

———, *The Secularization of the European Mind in the Nineteenth Century* (Cambridge: Cambridge University Press, 1975).

Coggins, R. J., and J. L. Houlden (eds.), *A Dictionary of Biblical Interpretation* (London: SCM Press, 1990).

Conkin, Paul K., *Puritans and Pragmatists: Eight Eminent American Thinkers* (New York: Dodd, Mead & Company, 1968).

Coulton, George Gordon, "Reformation," *Encyclopædia Britannica* (Chicago: Encyclopædia Britannica, 1963), vol. 19, 32–43.

Coyne, George V., S.J., "The Church in Dialogue with Science," *The New Catholic Encyclopedia Jubilee Volume: The Wojtyla Years* (Washington, DC: The Catholic University of America, 2001), 101–107.

Crompton, Louis, *Homosexuality and Civilization* (Cambridge, MA: Belknap Press of Harvard University Press, 2003).

Dangerfield, Whitney, "Darwin's Tortoise?" in *National Geographic*, May 2006, 20.

Darwin, Charles, *The Autobiography of Charles Darwin, 1809 –1882*, edited by Nora Barlow (New York: W. W. Norton, 1993 [1958]).

———, *The Origin of Species* and *The Descent of Man*, Modern Library edition (New York: Random House, n.d.).

Dawkins, Richard (presenter), "The Blind Watchmaker: The Evolutionary Ideas of Richard Dawkins," from the BBC series "Horizon" (1987), distributed by Films for the Humanities & Sciences (Princeton, NJ, 1998).

———, *The God Delusion* (Boston: Houghton Mifflin, 2008 [2006]).

Declaration on Certain Questions Concerning Sexual Ethics (Persona Humana). Accessed at http://www.vatican.va/roman_curia/congregations/cfaith/documents/rc_con_cfaith_doc_19751229_persona-humana_en.html

De Rosa, Peter, *Vicars of Christ* (New York: Crown, 1988)

Diamond, Jared, *The Third Chimpanzee: The Evolution and Future of the Human Animal* (New York: HarperCollins, 1992).

Digital Decade (The): The 90s, Editors of Time-Life Books (Alexandria, VA: Time-Life Books, 2000).

Dogmatic Constitution on the Church (Lumen Gentium). Accessed at http://www.vatican.va/archive/

Domina, Thurston, "Kennedy Assassination," in *St. James Encyclopedia of Popular Culture*, edited by Tom Pendergast and Sara Pendergast (Detroit: St. James, 2000), vol. 3, 16–17.

Dorr, Donal, *Time for a Change: A Fresh Look at Spirituality, Sexuality, Globalisation and the Church* (Dublin: Columba, 2005 [2004]).

Duffy, Eamon, *Saints and Sinners: A History of the Popes* (New Haven, CT: Yale University Press, 1997).

Dulles, Avery, "'*Humanae Vitae*' and the Crisis of Dissent," *Origins*, April 22, 1993, 774–77.

Durant, Will, and Ariel Durant, *The Age of Voltaire* (New York: Simon & Schuster, 1965).

Ebenstein, William, *Great Political Thinkers: Plato to the Present*, 4th ed. (New York: Holt, Rinehart and Winston, 1969).

Ehrlich, Paul R., and Anne H. Ehrlich, *One with Nineveh: Politics, Consumption, and the Human Future* (Washington, DC: Island Press, 2004).

Ehrman, Bart D., *Lost Christianities: The Battles for Scripture and the Faiths We Never Knew* (New York: Oxford University Press, 2005 [2003]).

———, *Lost Scriptures: Books That Did Not Make It into the New Testament* (New York: Oxford University Press, 2005 [2003]).

Emerson, Ralph Waldo, *The Collected Works of Ralph Waldo Emerson, Volume II: Essays, First Series* (Cambridge, MA: Harvard University Press, 1979).

———, *The Spiritual Emerson: Essential Writings*, ed. David M. Robinson (Boston: Beacon Press, 2003).

Erwin, Edward (ed.), *The Freud Encyclopedia: Theory, Therapy, and Culture* (New York: Routledge, 2002).

Evans, C. F., "Resurrection," in *A Dictionary of Biblical Interpretation*, edited by R. J. Coggins and J. L. Houlden (Nashville, TN: Abingdon, 1998) 586–89.

Fagan, Seán, *Has Sin Changed?* (Wilmington, DE: Michael Glazier, 1977).

Farraher, J. J., and T. A. Friedrichsen, "Masturbation," in *The New Catholic Encyclopedia*, 2nd ed., (Detroit, MI: Thomson/Gale, in association with the Catholic University of America, 2003), vol. 9, 315–17.

Ferguson, Niall, "Eurabia?" in *New York Times Magazine*, April 4, 2004.

Ferngren, Gary B. (ed.), *Science and Religion: A Historical Introduction* (Baltimore, MD: The Johns Hopkins University Press, 2002).

Ferro, Jeffrey, *Sexual Misconduct and the Clergy* (New York: Facts on File, 2005).

Finnis, John, and Martha C. Nussbaum, "Is Homosexual Conduct Wrong? A Philosophical Exchange," in Alan Soble (ed.), *The Philosophy of Sex: Contemporary Readings*, 4th ed., 97–102.

Fitzmyer, Joseph A., *The Biblical Commission's Document "The Interpretation of the Bible in the Church": Text and Commentary* (Rome: Editrice Pontificio Istituto Biblico, 1995).

Ford, John C., and G. Grisez, "Contraception and the Infallibility of the Ordinary Magisterium," *Theological Studies* 39 (1978), 258–312.

France, David, *Our Fathers: The Secret Life of the Catholic Church in an Age of Scandal* (New York: Broadway Books, 2004).

Freud, Sigmund, *Five Lectures on Psychoanalysis,* in *The Standard Edition of the Complete Psychological Works of Sigmund Freud*, ed. J. Strachey (London: Hogarth, 1953–74), volume 2, pages 9–55 (abbreviated as *SE* 2, 9–55).

———, *The Interpretation of Dreams*, in *SE* 4 and 5, 1–621.

———, *Introductory Lectures on Psychoanalysis*, in *SE* 15–16, 9–496.

———, "Psychoanalysis," in *Encyclopædia Britannica* (Chicago: Encyclopædia Britannica, 1963), vol. 18, 670–72.

———, "A Religious Experience," in *SE* 21, 167–72.

———, *A Short Account of Psychoanalysis*, in *SE* 19, 191–209.

———, *Studies on Hysteria*, see under Breuer, Josef.

———, *Three Essays on the Theory of Sexuality*, in *SE* 7, 130–243.

Friman, P., K. Allen, M. Kerwin, and R. Larzelere, "Changes in Modern Psychology," *American Psychologist* 48 (1993), 658–64.

Fukuyama, Francis, *Our Posthuman Future: Consequences of the Biotechnology Revolution* (New York: Farrar, Straus and Giroux, 2002).

———, "Women and the Evolution of World Politics," *Foreign Affairs* 77, no. 5 (September/October 1998), 24–40.

Funk, Robert W., *Honest to Jesus: Jesus for a New Millennium* (San Francisco: HarperSanFrancisco, 1996).

Furcht, Leo, and William Hoffman, *The Stem Cell Dilemma: Beacons of Hope or Harbingers of Doom* (New York: Arcade, 2008).

Garraty, John A., and Peter Gay (eds.), *The Columbia History of the World* (New York: Harper & Row, 1972).

Gatterer, Michael, et al., *Educating to Purity: Thoughts on Sexual Teaching and Education Proposed to Clergymen, Parents and Other Educators*, authorized translation from the 3rd German ed., adapted and supplemented with an extensive appendix by Rev. C. Van der Donckt (Ratisbon, NY: F. Pustet, 1912).

Gaudium et Spes: See *Pastoral Constitution on the Church in the Modern World*.

Gaustad, Edwin S., *Sworn on the Altar of God: A Religious Biography of Thomas Jefferson* (Grand Rapids, MI: W. B. Eerdmans, 1996).

Gay, Peter, *Freud: A Life for Our Time* (New York: W. W. Norton, 1988).

Gilgen, Albert R., *American Psychology Since World War II: A Profile of the Discipline* (Westport, CT: Greenwood, 1982).

Gingerich, Owen, "The Copernican Revolution," in Gary B. Ferngren (ed.), 95 –104.

Gjertsen, Derek, *The Newton Handbook* (New York: Routledge & Kegan Paul, 1986).

Gleick, James, *Isaac Newton* (New York: Pantheon, 2003).

Goodstein, Laurie, "Judge Rejects Teaching Intelligent Design," in *The New York Times*, December 21, 2005, www.nytimes.com/2005/12/21/ education/21evolution.html

Greeley, Andrew, *The American Catholic: A Social Portrait* (New York: Basic Books, 1977).

———, *The Catholic Revolution: New Wine, Old Wineskins, and the Second Vatican Council* (Berkeley: University of California Press, 2005).

———, *Jesus. A Meditation on His Stories and His Relationships with Women* (New York: Tom Doherty, 2007).

———, "An Ugly Little Secret Revisited: A Pretest on Anti-Catholicism in America," in *American Catholics, American Culture: Tradition and Resistance*, edited by Margaret O'Brien Steinfels (Lanham, MD: Rowman & Littlefield, 2004), 162–68.

Green, Michael, *The Books the Church Suppressed: Fiction and Truth in* The Da Vinci Code (Oxford: Monarch Books, 2005).

Griffin, Susan, *Pornography and Silence: Culture's Revenge Against Nature* (London: The Women's Press, 1988 [1981]).

Grünbaum, Adolf, "Critique of Psychoanalysis," in *The Freud Encyclopedia: Theory, Therapy, and Culture*, edited by Edwin Erwin, 117–36.

Hale, Nathan G., Jr., *The Rise and Crisis of Psychoanalysis in the United States: Freud and the Americans, 1917–1985* (New York: Oxford University Press, 1995).

Hamer, Dean, and Peter Copeland, *The Science of Desire: The Search for the Gay Gene and the Biology of Behavior* (New York: Simon and Schuster, 1994).

Häring, Bernard, "The Encyclical Crisis," in *Commonweal* (September 8, 1968).

Harrisville, Roy A., and Walter Sundberg, *The Bible in Modern Culture: Baruch Spinoza to Brevard Childs*, 2nd ed. (Grand Rapids, MI: William B. Eerdmans, 2002).

Haskins, Susan, *Mary Magdalen: Myth and Metaphor* (New York: Harcourt Brace, 1993).

Havill, Adrian, *The Spy Who Stayed Out in the Cold: The Secret Life of FBI Double Agent Robert Hanssen* (New York: St. Martin's, 2001).

Hays, Richard B., *The Moral Vision of the New Testament: A Contemporary Introduction to New Testament Ethics* (San Francisco: HarperSanFrancisco, 1996).

Hitchcock, James, "Introduction," in Olson, Carl E., and Sandra Miesel, 13–16.

Holmes, David L., *The Faiths of the Founding Fathers* (Oxford: Oxford University Press, 2006).

Holmes, Oliver Wendell, *Ralph Waldo Emerson* (Boston: Houghton Mifflin, 1885).

Hunt, Morton M., *The Story of Psychology* (New York: Doubleday, 1993).

Hunter, James Davison, *Culture Wars: The Struggle to Define America* (New York: Basic Books, 1991).

Investigative Staff of *The Boston Globe*: see *Betrayal*.

James, William, *The Varieties of Religious Experience*, edited with an introduction by Martin E. Marty (New York: Penguin, 1985).

———, "The Will to Believe," in *The Will to Believe, and Other Essays in Popular Philosophy, and Human Immortality: Two Supposed Objections to the Doctrine* (New York: Dover, 1960).

———, *Writings, 1902–1910* (New York: Viking, 1987).

Jenkins, Philip, *Hidden Gospels: How the Search for Jesus Lost Its Way* (New York: Oxford University Press, 2001).

———, *The New Anti-Catholicism: The Last Acceptable Prejudice* (New York: Oxford University Press, 2003).

Jennings, Peter (presenter), *ABC News Presents The Kennedy Assassination: Beyond Conspiracy* (DVD: 2004 [2003]).

Jerome, Letter 22. Accessed at http://www.newadvent.org/fathers/3001022.htm

John Chrysostom, *On the Priesthood*. Accessed at http://www.newadvent.org/fathers/1922.htm

"John Courtney Murray: American Theologian" (Sparkill, NY: Hallel Videos, 1996).

John Paul II, Pope, "Address to the Pontifical Academy of Sciences (October 3, 1981)," *Origins* 11, no. 18 (October 15, 1981), 277–80.

———, *Familiaris Consortio* (1981). Accessed at http://www.vatican.va/holy_father/john_paul_ii/apost_exhortations/documents/hf_jp-ii_exh_19811122_familiaris-consortio_en.html

————, "Message to Pontifical Academy of Sciences on Evolution," revised translation, *Origins* 26, no. 25 (December 5, 1996), 414–16.

Johnson, Luke Timothy, *The First and Second Letters to Timothy: A New Translation with Introduction and Commentary*. The Anchor Bible, vol. 35A (New York: Doubleday, 2001).

————, *The Real Jesus: The Misguided Quest for the Historical Jesus and the Truth of the Traditional Gospels* (San Francisco: HarperSanFrancisco, 1997 [1996]).

Jones, Ernest, *The Life and Work of Sigmund Freud*, 3 vols. (New York: Basic Books, 1953–57).

Jones, Steve, *Darwin's Ghost: The Origin of Species Updated* (New York: Random House, 2000).

Kaiser, Robert Blair, *The Politics of Sex and Religion: A Case History in the Development of Doctrine, 1962–1984* (Kansas City, MO: Leaven, 1985).

Keefe, Jeffrey, O.F.M., "Homosexuality," in *The New Catholic Encyclopedia*, 2nd ed., (Detroit, MI: Thomson/Gale, in association with the Catholic University of America, 2003), vol. 7, 66–71.

Kenny, Anthony, *The Unknown God: Agnostic Essays* (London: Continuum, 2005).

Krämer, Heinrich, and James Sprenger, *The Malleus Maleficarum*, translated with an introduction, bibliography, and notes by Montague Summers (New York: Dover, 1971).

Kümmel, Werner Georg, *The New Testament: The History of the Investigation of its Problems* (Nashville, TN: Abingdon, 1972).

Kurtz, Michael L., *The Crime of the Century: The Kennedy Assassination from a Historian's Perspective*, 2nd ed. (Knoxville, TN: The University of Tennessee Press, 1993).

Lepore, Jill, "Party Time: Smear Tactics, Skulduggery and the Debut of American Democracy," in *The New Yorker*, September 17, 2007. Accessed at http://www.newyorker.com/arts/critics/books/2007/09/17/070917crbo_books_lepore

MacQuarrie, Brian, "McSorley's death recalls a life long lost," *The Boston Globe*, June 13, 2004, http://www.boston.com/news/local/articles/2004/06/13/mcsorleys_death_recalls_a_life_l...

————, "Vocal Critic of Abuse by Clergy Found Dead," *The Boston Globe*, February 24, 2004, http://www.boston.com/globe/spotlight/abuse/print5/022404_mcsorley.htm

Macquarrie, John, *Twentieth-Century Religious Thought*, 4th edition (London: SCM Press, 1988).

Maddi, Salvatore R., *Personality Theories: A Comparative Analysis* (Pacific Grove, CA: Brooks/Cole, 1996).

Manchester, William, *One Brief Shining Moment: Remembering Kennedy* (Boston: Little, Brown, 1983).

Manuel, Frank E., *A Portrait of Isaac Newton* (Cambridge, MA: Belknap Press of Harvard University Press, 1968).

———, *The Religion of Isaac Newton* (Oxford: Clarendon, 1974).

Marshall, Bishop Paul V., "The Da Vinci Opportunity," May 17, 2006. Accessed at http://www.diobeth.org

Martos, Joseph, *Doors to the Sacred: A Historical Introduction to Sacraments in the Catholic Church*, revised ed. (Liguori, MO: Liguori/Triumph, 2001).

Marty, Martin E., "Professor Pelikan," in *The Christian Century*, June 13, 2006, 47.

Massa, Mark, *Anti-Catholicism in America: The Last Acceptable Prejudice* (New York: Crossroad, 2003).

McClory, Robert, *Turning Point: The Inside Story of the Papal Birth Control Commission, and How* Humanae Vitae *Changed the Life of Patty Crowley and the Future of the Church* (New York: Crossroad, 1995).

McGeary, Johanna, et al., "The FBI Spy," in *Time*, March 5, 2001. Accessed at http://www.time.com/time/magazine/article/0,9171,999348,00.html

McGinn, Bernard, *Antichrist: Two Thousand Years of the Human Fascination with Evil* (San Francisco: HarperSanFrancisco, 1994).

McGrath, Alister, "Luther," in R. J. Coggins and J. L. Houlden (eds.), *A Dictionary of Biblical Interpretation*, 414–16.

———, *The Twilight of Atheism: The Rise and Fall of Disbelief in the Modern World* (New York: Doubleday, 2004).

McGreevy, John T., "Anti-Catholicism in the United States: The View from History," in *American Catholics, American Culture: Tradition and Resistance*, edited by Margaret O'Brien Steinfels (Lanham, MD: Rowman & Littlefield, 2004), 155–61.

———, *Catholicism and American Freedom: A History* (New York: W. W. Norton, 2003).

McLaren, Brian D., "Brian McLaren on *The Da Vinci Code*," an interview by Lisa Ann Cockrel published in *Sojourners*, May 9, 2006.

Accessed at http://www.sojo.net/index.cfm?action=sojomail.
displc&issue=060509

———, *The Secret Message of Jesus: Uncovering the Truth that Could Change Everything* (Nashville: W Publishing Group, 2006).

Meacham, Jon, *American Gospel: God, the Founding Fathers, and the Making of a Nation* (New York: Random House, 2006).

Menand, Louis, *The Metaphysical Club: A Story of Ideas in America* (New York: Farrar, Straus and Giroux, 2001).

Michalski, Dan, "The Costs of Child Sexual Abuse Litigation Threaten the Catholic Church," in Louise I. Gerdes (ed.), *Child Sexual Abuse in the Catholic Church* (San Diego: Greenhaven, 2003), 75–83.

Miesel, Sandra: see under Olson, Carl E.

Milgrom, Jacob, *Leviticus 17–22: A New Translation with Introduction and Commentary.* The Anchor Bible, vol. 3A (New York: Doubleday, 2000).

Mill, John Stuart, *On Liberty*, ed. with an introduction by Gertrude Himmelfarb (Harmondsworth, Middlesex, England: Pelican, 1979).

Mitchell, Stephen, *The Gospel According to Jesus: A New Translation and Guide to His Essential Teachings for Believers and Unbelievers* (New York: HarperCollins, 1991.)

Moore, Gareth, *A Question of Truth: Christianity and Homosexuality* (London: Continuum, 2003).

Moore, James, "Charles Darwin," in Ferngren, Gary B. (ed.), 208–18.

Morgan, Robert, "*Sachkritik*," in *A Dictionary of Biblical Interpretation*, edited by R. J. Coggins and J. L. Houlden, 604–05.

Morris, Charles R., *American Catholic: The Saints and Sinners Who Built America's Most Powerful Church* (New York: Times Books, 1997).

Moyers, Bill, *A World of Ideas: Conversations with Thoughtful Men and Women about American Life Today and the Ideas Shaping Our Future*, ed. Betty Sue Flowers (New York: Doubleday, 1989).

Newman, John Henry, *An Essay in Aid of a Grammar of Assent*, edited, with an introduction and notes, by I. T. Ker (Oxford: Clarendon, 1985).

———, *Apologia pro Vita Sua: Being a History of His Religious Opinions*, ed., with an introduction and notes, by Martin J. Svaglic (Oxford: Clarendon Press, 1967).

Niebuhr, Reinhold, *The Nature and Destiny of Man*, Vol. 1: *Human Nature* (New York: Scribner's, 1964).

Noonan, John T., Jr., *Contraception: A History of Its Treatment by the Catholic Theologians and Canonists*, Enlarged Edition (Cambridge, MA: Harvard University Press, 1986).

———, *The Lustre of Our Country: The American Experience of Religious Freedom* (Berkeley: University of California Press, 1998).

O'Grady, Desmond, "The Perils of Penance," *Commonweal* 121, no. 18 (October 21, 1994), 7.

Olson, Carl E., and Sandra Miesel, *The Da Vinci Hoax: Exposing the Errors in The Da Vinci Code* (San Francisco: Ignatius, 2004).

Pagels, Elaine, *Beyond Belief: The Secret Gospel of Thomas* (New York: Random House, 2003).

———, *The Gnostic Gospels* (New York: Random House, 1979).

Pascal, Blaise, *The Pensées*, translated with an introduction by J. M. Cohen (Baltimore, MD: Penguin, 1961).

Pastoral Constitution on the Church in the Modern World (Gaudium et Spes). Accessed at http://www.vatican.va/archive/

Paul VI, Pope, *Humanae Vitae* (San Francisco: Ignatius, 1988).

Paulson, Michael, "A long crisis in church returns to the forefront," *The Boston Globe*, July 24, 2003, http://www.boston.com/globe/spotlight/abuse/print4/072403_analysis.htm

Peale, Norman Vincent, *The Power of Positive Thinking* (Kingswood, U.K.: World's Work Ltd., 1980 [1953]).

Pearson, Roger, *Voltaire Almighty: A Life in Pursuit of Freedom* (New York and London: Bloomsbury, 2005).

Pelikan, Jaroslav, *The Christian Tradition*, Vol. 5: *Christian Doctrine and Modern Culture (since 1700)* (Chicago: University of Chicago Press, 1989).

———, *Jesus Through the Centuries: His Place in the History of Culture* (New Haven, CT: Yale University Press, 1985).

———, *Mary Through the Centuries: Her Place in the History of Culture* (New Haven, CT: Yale University Press, 1996).

———, *The Melody of Theology: A Philosophical Dictionary* (Cambridge, MA: Harvard University Press, 1988).

———, *The Riddle of Roman Catholicism* (New York: Abingdon, 1959).

Perkins, Pheme, "Getting Past Orthodox Doctrine," in *America* 189, no. 1 (July 7 –July 14, 2003), 24.

Perry, Ralph Barton, *The Thought and Character of William James* (Cambridge, MA: Harvard University Press, 1948).

Phillips, J.B., trans., *The New Testament in Modern English* (New York: Macmillan, 1962).

Picknett, Lynn, *Mary Magdalene* (New York: Carroll & Graf, 2003).

Pius IX, Pope, *Syllabus of Errors*. Accessed at http://www.papalencyclicals. net/Pius09/p9syll.htm

Pius XI, Pope, *Casti Connubii*. Accessed at http://www.vatican.va/holy_father/pius_xi/encyclicals/documents/hf_p-xi_enc_31121930_casticonnubii_en.html

Posner, Gerald, *Case Closed: Lee Harvey Oswald and the Assassination of JFK* (New York: Random House, 2003).

Ranke-Heinemann, Uta, *Eunuchs for the Kingdom of Heaven: Women, Sexuality and the Catholic Church*, translated by Peter Heinegg (New York: Penguin, 1990).

Richard, Carl J., *The Battle for the American Mind: A Brief History of a Nation's Thought* (Lanham, MD: Rowman & Littlefield, 2004).

———, *The Founders and the Classics: Greece, Rome, and the American Enlightenment*, (Cambridge, MA: Harvard University Press, 1994).

Rieff, Philip, *The Triumph of the Therapeutic: Uses of Faith After Freud* (Chicago: University of Chicago Press, 1987 [1966]).

Robinson, Walter V. and Michael Rezendes, "Abuse scandal far deeper than disclosed, report says," *The Boston Globe*, July 24, 2003, http://www.boston.com/globe/spotlight/abuse/stories4/072403_report.htm

Rowland, Tracey, *Ratzinger's Faith: The Theology of Pope Benedict XVI* (Oxford: Oxford University Press, 2008).

Russell, Bertrand, *Portraits from Memory, and Other Essays* (New York: Simon and Schuster, 1956).

Scott, Eugenie C., *Evolution vs. Creationism: An Introduction* (Westport, CT: Greenwood, 2004).

Schüklenk, Udo, and Tony Riley, "Homosexuality, Societal Attitudes Toward," in *Encyclopedia of Applied Ethics*, edited by Ruth Chadwick (San Diego, CA: Academic Press, 1998) vol. 3, 597–608.

Shannon, Elaine, and Ann Blackman, *The Spy Next Door: The Extraordinary Secret Life of Robert Philip Hanssen, the Most Damaging FBI Agent in U.S. History* (Boston: Little, Brown, 2002).

Sheler, Jeffrey L., "Debating 'Da Vinci,'" USNews.com, posted 5/14/06. Accessed at http://www.usnews.com/usnews/news/articles/060522/22davinci.htm

Smith, Dinitia, "Love That Dare Not Squeak Its Name," in *The New York Times*, February 7, 2004. Accessed at http://query.nytimes.com/gst/fullpage.html?res=9506EFD9113BF934A35751C0A9629C8B63

Smith, Janet E., Humanae Vitae*: A Generation Later* (Washington, DC: The Catholic University of America Press, 1991).

Soble, Alan (ed.), *The Philosophy of Sex: Contemporary Readings*, 4th ed. (Lanham, MD: Rowman & Littlefield, 2002).

Spong, John Shelby, *Resurrection: Myth or Reality?* (New York: HarperCollins, 1994).

Steinfels, Margaret O'Brien (ed.), *American Catholics, American Culture: Tradition and Resistance* (Lanham, MD: Rowman & Littlefield, 2004).

Steinfels, Peter, *A People Adrift: The Crisis of the Roman Catholic Church in America* (New York: Simon & Schuster, 2003).

Storr, Anthony, *Freud* (Oxford: Oxford University Press, 1989).

Surtz, Edward, S.J., *The Works and Days of John Fisher* (Cambridge, MA: Harvard University Press, 1967).

Tarnas, Richard, *The Passion of the Western Mind: Understanding the Ideas That Have Shaped Our World View* (New York: Ballantine, 1991).

Tattersall, Ian, and Jeffrey H. Schwartz, *Extinct Humans* (Boulder, CO: Westview, 2000).

Tertullian, *The Apparel of Women* (*De cultu feminarum*), translated by Edwin A. Quain, S.J., in *Tertullian: Disciplinary, Moral and Ascetical Works*, translated by Rudolph Arbesmann, O.S.A., et al. (New York: Fathers of the Church, 1959).

Thomas, Evan, "A Spy's Secret World," in *Newsweek*, March 5, 2001. Accessed at http://www.newsweek.com

Tolle, Eckhart, *A New Earth: Awakening to Your Life's Purpose* (New York: Penguin, 2006 [2005]).

Vermès, Géza, *The Changing Faces of Jesus* (New York: Viking Compass, 2001).

Vise, David A., *The Bureau and the Mole: The Unmasking of Robert Philip Hanssen, The Most Dangerous Double Agent in FBI History* (New York: Atlantic Monthly Press, 2002).

Voltaire, *Philosophical Dictionary*, Translated, with an Introduction and Glossary by Peter Gay (New York: Basic Books, 1962).

Volz, Hans, "Continental Versions to c. 1600," in *The Cambridge History of the Bible*, vol. 3: *The West, from the Reformation to the Present Day*, ed. S. L. Greenslade (Cambridge: Cambridge University Press, 1963), 94–110.

Ward, Keith, *Religion and Human Nature* (New York: Oxford University Press, 1998).

Warner, Marina, *Alone of All Her Sex: The Myth and the Cult of the Virgin Mary* (New York: Vintage, 1983 [1976]).

Watson, Peter, *The Modern Mind: An Intellectual History of the 20th Century* (New York: HarperCollins, 2001).

Weigel, George, *The Courage to be Catholic: Crisis, Reform, and the Future of the Church* (New York: Basic Books, 2002).

——, *The Cube and the Cathedral: Europe, America, and Politics Without God* (New York: Basic Books, 2005).

——, *Witness to Hope: The Biography of Pope John Paul II* (New York: Cliff Street Books, 1999).

Weinberg, Steven, *Facing Up: Science and Its Cultural Adversaries* (Cambridge, MA: Harvard University Press, 2001).

Westfall, Richard S., "Isaac Newton," in Ferngren, Gary B. (ed.), 153–62.

Wise, David, *Spy: The Inside Story of How the FBI's Robert Hanssen Betrayed America* (New York: Random House, 2002).

Witherington, Ben, III, *The Gospel Code* (Downers Grove, IL: InterVarsity, 2004).

——, *The Jesus Quest: The Third Search for the Jew of Nazareth* (Downers Grove, IL: InterVarsity, 1995).

Zagorin, Perez, *How the Idea of Religious Toleration Came to the West* (Princeton, NJ: Princeton University Press, 2003).

Zimmer, Carl, *Evolution: The Triumph of an Idea* (New York: HarperCollins, 2001).

Index

About the Author

Dr. Plumer is a popular speaker and seminar leader at universities and many other venues. Contact him at DaVinciDialogue@ aol.com.